# Sisters

ALSO BY CHARLES HIGHAM

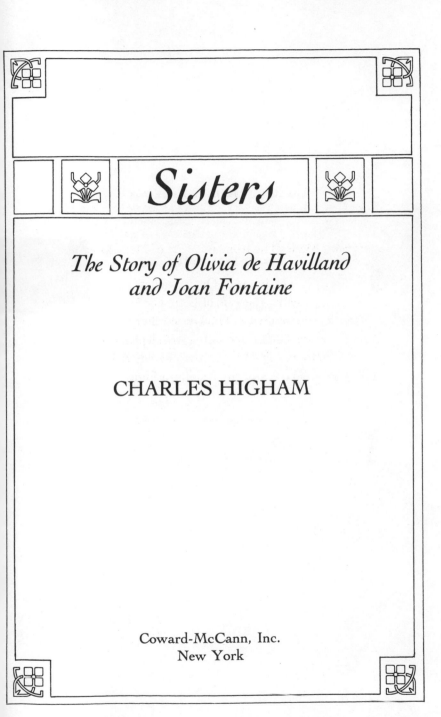

# Sisters

## The Story of Olivia de Havilland and Joan Fontaine

### CHARLES HIGHAM

Coward-McCann, Inc.
New York

Designed by Richard Oriolo

Library of Congress Cataloging in Publication Data

Higham, Charles, date.
Sisters, the story of Olivia de Havilland and Joan Fontaine.

1. De Havilland, Olivia.   2. Fontaine, Joan,
1917-    .  3. Moving-picture actors and actresses—
United States—Biography.  I. Title.
PN2287.D36H53      1984      791.43′028′0922   [B]   83-23153
ISBN 0-698-11268-7

Printed in the United States of America

*Second Impression*

*For Frances Mercer*

# Sisters

 # Prologue

 It is a Gothic storm, right out of *Psycho*. I walk up a path surrounded by rank growths of cryptomeria, fern, and stinging nettles to a house to match: high-eaved, dun brown, covered by a dead Virginia creeper and ivy, in strands grown black with time; the windows blinded by heavy brown wooden shutters, the porch made of green collapsing clapboard, flanked by tossing shrubs. As the rain beats down heavier, I ring a doorbell that makes a faint sepulchral chime deep inside. When there is no response, I obstinately ring it again.

At last, a wizened Filipino houseman in a white hospital coat opens the suitably creaking door. I ask if I can come in. I am there to see the owner, Hazel Bargas, who is still alive at ninety-three, just sixty-three years from the day that dumpy, snobbish, ambitious Lilian Rusé de Havilland arrived from Japan at the same front door with her two young children—animated, spunky, outgoing Olivia, and sullen, miserable, cantankerous Joan. Hazel Bargas had been their landlady all those many years ago; and neighbors had told me that she still lived on, fifty years after closing the door to paying guests, seldom going out, trapped in a time warp.

The houseman shows me in and I walk into a funnellike hallway that leads me directly into the past. Virtually nothing has changed from the day those *Jane Eyre* children trailed behind their mother in 1918. The hall is a gloomy reminiscence of the Brown Decade, flanked by large, somber, hand-tinted prints of paintings of receptions in sixteenth-century Swedish courts; a faded aspidistra wilts in a brown bowl on a small, rickety bamboo table. Through an open door to the left is the dining room, with basket chairs, round cedar table, lazy Susan, and dishes, mostly Swedish to go with Hazel's family, laid out regularly on high shelves near the ceiling. There are landscapes of Swedish and Scottish lowlands, complete with gamboling sheep and shepherds with crooks against fleecy skies that mirror the coats of their flock. To the right is a proper front parlor, the upright piano still carrying the group-sing book propped behind metal holders, the mantel shelf with oval family photographs, brown now in silver baroque frames. A Grand Rapids desk and bookshelves hold the same books that Olivia and Joan read as children: turn-of-the-century editions of *Little Women*, *The Water Babies*, *The Forest Lovers*, and *Alice Through the Looking Glass*. A stairway leads upward to a white door that severely cuts off the whole upper part of the house, including the rooms where the boarders, among them the de Havillands, lived, and the attic where some of their childhood clothes remain, rotting with age and damp in old steamer trunks.

The Filipino houseman ushers me into the kitchen with its imposing Franklin stove. Mrs. Bargas is seated in a wheelchair, but there is much vitality in the face under the black polished, almost Japanese wig. The features are bonily carved, and striking. The eyes are dark brown, twinkling with surprising sharpness behind antique spectacles, an infectious smile creasing her face. This tough woman laughs often, and shows no self-pity as she tells how she is the last of her clan to have survived. Her wedding ring has bitten so deeply into her bony finger that it would take a saw to remove it.

She tells me that she has remained in the house almost consistently for half a century, seldom venturing even down leafy Oak Street to the sprawling suburban stretch of the Sunnyvale–Saratoga Road. Presidents and kings have come and gone; America has survived the Depression, World War II, the Cold War, the assassination of the Kennedys, and Watergate; and Hazel Bargas has concerned herself only with surviving in her tiny, fragile world.

I ask her about her illustrious boarders of 1918 to 1924, questioning her directly on the basis of Joan's memoirs, *No Bed of Roses*, in which a cruel, monstrous Olivia is shown making Joan's life a perfect hell. "No, no!" the old lady exclaims, her eyes sharpening with a distaste and anger over Joan that haven't shriveled in five decades. To the loud, irritable clashing of dishes in the sink—the houseman seems to symbolize her feelings audibly as he attacks the washing-up—she goes on in the loud, emphatic tones of the very deaf. "It was Olivia who was so sweet, so kind. She couldn't do enough for me or my parents, Mr. and Mrs. Lundblad, or we enough for her. She was always full of life and laughter and we loved to watch the dear little thing dancing and twirling about with her little dollies. She would get up on my knee and kiss me. I was like an auntie to her. It's hard to believe even then I was over thirty years old!

"But *Joan!* We all hated her! She would always be sick on purpose and she would lie in bed all day and she wasn't really sick at all, she was just hungry for attention. And she was so rude! She was insulting to everyone! I never heard her say a kind thing about her sister or anyone else!" The Filipino houseman adds, through a particularly loud clash of dishes, "There was bad jealousy in the house. Joan was jealous!"

I realize with a shock that he, too, has not left the establishment since he joined circa 1920.

Hazel Bargas goes on: "We had so little to do with Joan and her tantrums—we refused to feed her and she had to go out for meals to anyone who was softhearted enough to put up with her squalling. Oh, how I disliked her! She used to walk about with round shoulders, all hunched over, while Olivia was upright and sparkling and loved life. Mother loved everyone, but she could find only a little love for Joan. Mrs. de Havilland was a nice woman, but I didn't like either of her husbands. Walter de Havilland was here one time: He was haughty and rude and had no charm at all. As for the second husband, George Fontaine—the less said, the better. He had a son of his own, the girls' half brother, who was weak and sickly and lived upstairs. We had to give the boy patent medicine all the time."

How much truth was there in Hazel Bargas's picture of the two most famous sisters and rival siblings in show business history? An hour before, I had been in the Saratoga school, once called the Saratoga Grammar School, where the genial head teacher has told me much about Olivia's time there, showing me excerpts from the old school magazines, with Olivia's poems, maxims, and short stories. But there was no mention in the magazines of Joan's existence, except in one slighting reference by Olivia herself, and it was subtly clear from the head teacher's flow of speech that only Olivia counts in Saratoga today. She is often present on the scene, revisiting her childhood country like one who has never gone away. It is as though Joan had never even inhabited that lush and leafy suburb on the outskirts of ugly San Jose, a region that today is defaced by gas stations, sprawling condos, its roll of low hills punctured by the telephone poles that ruin most of the American landscape, but which sixty years ago was rustic, innocent, and sweet with birdsong. Why, I ask myself, has Joan been so completely eliminated from Saratoga? What is the essence of the conflict between the sisters that resulted in this?

Meeting the de Havilland sisters—Olivia in 1965, Joan in 1977—was very instructive. Olivia, dignified, matronly, proper, correct, yet sentimental and romantic underneath, was the opposite of Joan, who was relaxed, supersophisticated, brittle, unromantic, and pagan. Of course, Olivia was the bigger star, the greater actress; but Joan in effect created their lifelong rivalry—a rivalry fanned by their mother, Lilian—through a series of "firsts" that broke all the rules of sister-hood: She was the first to lose her virginity; the first to marry; the first to win a large contract that kept her time free while Olivia was re-duced to a grueling schedule at Warner Brothers; she was the first to win an Academy Award—for *Rebecca*, a part Olivia was up for; and the first to give birth; she was certainly the first to find a degree of happiness in life.

In the first eighteen months of her life, Olivia enjoyed her mother's undivided attention. Her father, as we shall see, had little or no interest in her as a child. When Joan was born, Olivia had to undergo the traditional ordeal of an older child: seeing her domain eroded, having to endure a rival for mother's attention. Her crying fits, as they would be in pictures, were heroic; she already acted up a storm to preclude anyone noticing the baby. Her technique, then and later, was to ignore Joan whenever possible, a fact that Joan resented from the beginning. Much to Olivia's fury, Joan would lash back by exer-cising a junior sister's prerogative in imitating her elder sibling: A wispy shadow, she would trail around behind her, mimicking her.

Many elder sisters act as surrogate nursemaids, or sergeants; Olivia did not. When their mother, in a typically Victorian gesture, ran off with them from Japan where they were born and resettled in Califor-nia, Lilian's second husband, George Fontaine, snatched Olivia's au-thority in the matter of taking care of her younger sister. Thus deprived of her natural sibling power, Olivia chose simply to eclipse rather than discipline Joan. She set out successfully to be pretty, sexy, the belle of school proms and weekend picnic outings; it was not until

*WRONG!*

*For She won in 1941 Suspicion*

later that, pressured by her mother and stepfather, she tried to push Joan around. Joan, of course, savagely resented Olivia's driving her.

Olivia was typical of older sisters in being excessively responsibility-conscious, dictatorial, a demanding perfectionist in her youth. She wanted so much of herself and others that it made it hard for her to relax, enjoy sensual pleasure, and take joy in being alive. Whenever she had feelings of fear, insecurity, and weakness, a need for help—feelings that elder sisters are not supposed to have—she would find that the people she had chosen as mates, friends, or acquaintances were as weak as matchsticks to lean on. She had been afraid of the strong because they could have competed with her; she had turned to the weak and they could not support her strength.

Olivia was always proud of being in charge of herself and her destiny. But much of her suffering could have been alleviated if early on she had been more tender to Joan, as capable of listening, of accepting kindness, concern, and advice, as she is today.

At first, Joan leaned on Olivia, wanted her authority, and resented her indifference. It was natural for a younger sister to imitate an elder, but she felt it was unnatural for the elder sister to resent the imitation. As Joan grew, she had to fight like all younger siblings to assert herself. She tried a variety of sicknesses that had a melodramatic consistency and were designed to ensure that she would be the center of attention. However, this attempt to excite sympathy inevitably backfired since nothing is more boring to parents or children than a sickly, neurotic, and self-pitying little girl.

Having failed to achieve her theatrical purpose, Joan turned to tantrums; these also failed to make a mark. She then abandoned discipline and religious or moral considerations and adopted a life-style of high individuality, never attaching herself deeply to anyone. She enjoyed being alone, preferring relationships that did not bind.

It was the typical approach of a younger sister. And by doing the exact opposite of Olivia, she attracted as much attention. Yet she had one thing in common with her elder sibling—she could not resist a chance to exercise power. She would gather friends to her and then deliver some barb, and people would disappear, frightened, correctly, that Joan would not only see through them but tell them what she saw.

In a moment of rare self-revelation, Olivia once said to Joan's husband, William Dozier, "Can you imagine what it's like to be an elder sister and have your younger one do everything first?" It was when she married Marcus Goodrich that Olivia wanted to say to Joan, "I, too, can be married." But Joan was not impressed; after all, Joan had married a star, Brian Aherne, and a famous producer, Dozier, and Olivia had married only a little-known novelist. "What a pity Marcus Goodrich has had four wives and written only one book!" Joan said, thus undermining her relationship with Olivia for many years. Indeed, it was this remark that caused Olivia to turn her back on Joan, when Joan made a theatrical gesture of congratulation to Olivia, at the 1946 Academy Awards.

Beaten to the punch and the altar, an elder sister most desperately needs her younger sister's support when she finally does marry. Joan's comment about Goodrich was unquestionably the most savage blow that Olivia had received.

Joan triumphed in another way, too. When the Bel Air fire of 1960 destroyed her home and earned her the basis in insurance money of her first fortune, Joan financially eclipsed Olivia. And Olivia had to face humiliation by coming to Joan and asking her for money. When their father died in 1968, they shared in the ritual of scattering the ashes, and when their mother died seven years later they also shared the remains. But both these occasions drove them farther apart. The ashes were symbols of their own burnt-out relationship.

Above all, the sisters disliked each other not so much because of their differences as because of their similarities. Few actresses admire themselves; they become actresses to conceal their true identities and overcome their insecurities. That is why they need constant flattery and reassurance. The de Havilland girls, however, could not escape themselves, because each could see herself in mirror of the other. There was not only the accumulation of mutual humiliation, of one career outpacing the other, then vice versa; there was the pain of seeing the ego, the drive for money and power and dominance, in the mirror image, and the unhappiness that a desire for conquest will bring. Today, Olivia has sought to take over from Joan by befriending Joan's daughters, her ex-husband Bill Dozier, her close friends Abby and Connie Wolf; she has sought to re-create her own childhood by constantly traveling to the California town where the sisters grew up, sewing up a network of support in that pretty backwater, while Joan is forgotten there; she does not go back.

And Joan, of course, does not care. Whereas Joan has shaken off her childhood, Olivia inhabits it. Though Olivia is far more famous now, Joan, the younger, the put-upon, the crushed, today seems the victor in this lifelong struggle.

**One**

 Close to a thousand years ago, a fine gray fortress stood proudly above the sluggish blue-green estuary of the river Saire, south of Barfleur on the northwestern coast of the fair land of Normandy in France. Its name was Haverland Castle. Today, only crumbling bricks remind travelers of its noble keep; but in the days of chivalry, the edifice housed the fierce and impetuous knights who gave the castle its name. The Haverlands were Normans, gallant predators, of powerful sinew and bone. They owned much land, land that stretched as far as a man could ride in a day, and the possession of that land gave them the right to the title *baron* that they most zealously preserved.

In the year 1061, sixteen months before the Norman invasion of England, the Haverlands were leaders in the first colonization of the beautiful island of Guernsey in the Channel Isles, and they built abbeys and castle strongholds along with the duke of Normandy and the lords of Saint Sauveur, the hereditary vicomtes of the Cotentin. When a body of pirates, black-visaged and equipped with scimitars, landed in their proud dark ships and scourged the subtropical isle, Duke William, soon to be known as William the Conqueror, dispatched the Haverland heir to drive the marauders out. He succeeded, thus earning the gratitude of his seigneur.

The Lord of Haverland accompanied William in his invasion of England in the famous year of 1066, and stood before the conqueror's throne, raising his fine sword in homage. It was the beginning of a golden heritage. The Haverlands were present during the Crusades, serving with gallantry at Jerusalem; they were involved in conquest and triumph in all parts of the world. They became known as Guernsey tenants of the kings, and retained intimate connections with successive generations of the royal family. Thomas, Sieur de Havilland (as the name became), fought with courage at the siege of Mont Orgeuil Castle in Jersey, a bloody battle that lasted seventeen weeks. With Thomas, the family divided into two bloodlines: the Guernsey line, through Thomas's elder son of the same name; and the Dorsetshire and Somerset line from his younger son, James.

By the sixteenth century, the Havilland coat of arms was established: a silver shield, denoting grandeur, magnificence, dignity, and fame, nourished by abstinence and chastity; Haverland Castle appeared on the shield, blackened by fires of battles long ago, shown dully reflected in the waters of the Saire. The Havilland motto was *Dominus fortissima turris* (8 Proverbs, 10).

Traditionally vassals of the king, the de Havillands deserted the royal cause in the civil war of Charles I against Oliver Cromwell and supported Cromwell. In Guernsey, the handsome and dashing James de Havilland and his cousin Peter de Beauvoir led the Roundheads. Appointed parliamentary commissioners for Guernsey, they sought to confront and apprehend King Charles's lieutenant governor, Sir Peter Osborne, and seize his fortress, Castle Cornet. Osborne locked himself up with his garrison force in the castle and sent a message out by white-flagged courier inviting James de Havilland and his cousin to a meeting with his officers aboard the royal vessel *George* in the harbor of St. Peter Port to discuss terms of surrender.

When James and Peter went aboard the vessel, they were seized by Osborne's men and clapped in irons as insurrectionaries. Thrown into a dungeon of Castle Cornet, they languished miserably in rat-ridden, damp, dark conditions without enough food for several weeks. But they were young and sturdy and possessed of great resolution. With much enterprise, they managed to secure a transfer to a higher cell, which they knew was located above a storage room. They spent weeks cutting a hole in the wooden floor with the knives they used for food, and at last, lowering a hook through the hole, brought up some cotton twine. They twisted the cotton into three strands and lowered themselves into the storeroom, escaping down a wall to rocks at low tide.

Pursued by gunfire, they reached St. Peter Port on a Sunday, with church bells pealing through the tall cobbled streets; and with a stroke of theatricality, they marched joyfully down the aisle in the middle of a service, to be greeted with a standing ovation by the entire congregation. In order to avoid a local revolution, Sir Peter Osborne was compelled to issue them a pardon; thus the Havillands were woven into the very tapestry of British history.

Another colorful figure of the dynasty was James Havilland of Somerset, who figured in a well-known incident. During the French Revolution, a French man-of-war captain seized his yacht and took him prisoner to Brest. In an argument over a game of cards with one of his prison warders, James challenged the guard, who threatened to run him through with a sword. But James snatched a poker from the fire and ran it through the Frenchman's mouth and out of one cheek, "with a peculiar hissing sound [a contemporary chronicler reported] that is usual when iron enters hot water." Thus, James was able to escape.

Still another of the clan, John Havilland, became the leading architect for President Monroe. He built the Tombs, the infamous New York prison, on loose sand, its walls based on Egyptian prototypes and designed to last for all time. In Europe he devised horseshoe auditoriums for theaters for the first time, and in England he erected the prison known as Pentonville Jail. His talent in many fields of architectural construction earned him the highest of honors.

Several of the dynasty were clergymen, the best known being the Reverend Charles Richard de Havilland, a graduate in arts of Oriol College, Oxford, a scholar and vicar of Cobo, Guernsey, and garrison chaplain there. He married two members of the Molesworth family: the first, Agnes Maria, daughter of Major General Arthur Molesworth. It was typical of the parson's obstinacy before fate that when Agnes died in 1862, he should propose at once to her cousin, the Honorable Margaret Letitia, whom he married three and a half years later; and that when his firstborn son, Sausmarez, died at the age of three months, he immediately sired another of the same name.

The Reverend Charles Richard was busy between sermons and tithe-gathering, for he had ten children in all. By the second marriage, Charles sired Lionel John, who, like his firstborn, died in childhood; George Maitland, who died a bachelor; and, youngest and strangest of the breed, Walter Augustus, who became the father of Olivia and Joan.

The Reverend Charles, grandfather of Olivia and Joan, was eccentric to an umpteenth degree. He was severe, and the Sabbath was observed with propriety; the children were forbidden to play games or read anything except the Bible, forbidden to converse, and had to carry candles until the hot wax burned their fingers.

The half brothers and sisters all exhibited bizarre traits, and Olivia's and Joan's father, Walter Augustus, born on August 31, 1872, was no exception. Much of Walter's childhood was spent away from his father and his eccentric half brother, Charles, at Havilland Hall at St. Peter Port, a run-down, once handsome edifice in the Georgian style with a portico and drafty, high-ceilinged rooms. It stood at the head of a valley, and a stream passed by it marking the boundary of the city. Walter developed strong legs by walking up the steep streets of the port. He grew up to be tall and bony, handsome and scholarly, with a fine, delicately carved face under rich brown hair. He walked with the quick, nervous stride of a racehorse. Gifted with the robust constitution of his Havilland forebears, he was also flawed by the inbreeding of his family and was afflicted by an ungovernable temper, along with a fretful, edgy, difficult nature. His brilliance was not accompanied by easy charm, and those who were drawn to him because of his vivid eyes and obvious intellect were repelled because he could not tolerate fools gladly and had no patience with mediocrity. His father and half brother wanted him to become a churchman, but his finicky concern over authenticity in the translations of the Scripture, and his desire for worldwide adventure, overcame his better principles. Also, it was clear from the beginning that the sex drive traditional in the Havillands would not be satisfied by marriage and a large family. Walter was looking for wider fields to conquer.

Impervious to criticism and inspired in the field of literature and law, Walter made his mark in the gray corridors of Cambridge, and his muscular arms earned him plaudits on the Varsity rowing team. But his popularity was always undermined by his sharp tongue as he criticized the standard version of the Bible, the administration of the Church of England, and the threat of the working classes.

Armed with a law degree, but with no liking for the idea of a conventional career at the British bar, Walter, like his uncles and half brothers, felt a compulsion to get as far away as possible from the dour and sober constraints of the British Isles.

He settled on Japan, a shrewd choice—unless one accepts Joan Fontaine's account of Walter's decision-making process. According to Joan, he rested a finger on a rapidly spinning globe that came to a halt at the island of Hokkaido. But this may have been a legend that he or Joan's mother fostered, since Walter was not a man prone to taking random chances. Japan in that year of 1893 was urgently in need of British lawyers. Embroiled in disputes with neighboring countries, emerging as an industrial force in the Meiji era, and conducting an uneasy relationship with the English-speaking countries, Japan was beginning its long era of economic conquest and acquisitiveness in which the expropriation of foreign patents became notorious. Walter must have had the foresight to realize that a lawyer would be an ideal adjunct or assistant to government in that process of acquisition.

The six-week journey on the Peninsula and Orient Line to Yokohama, via the Suez Canal, India, and Hongkong, for a total fare in those days of seventy pounds, first-class, was monotonous and suffocating. Walter traveled directly from Yokohama to the northern island province of Hokkaido, where he had to work as a teacher of English until he could secure his Japanese law degree. Hokkaido was an impressive place. The capital, Hakodate, stood against a background of stark and treeless mountain peaks, volcanoes spitting red ashes, ranges of hills thinly covered in scrub, temples in the foothills, and belts of cryptomeria. The houses, mostly made of wood, were one-story, brown, and cramped; the suburbs were impermanent, poor and straggling. So fierce were the winds that boulders had to be placed on the grass-and-wood roofs to keep them from blowing away. In the spring, the streets were alive with cherry blossoms; but when the rains came, the streets turned to mud, giving birth to a multitude of frogs. Kite and balloon sellers were jostled by salesmen of rat poison, who did a thriving trade because of the city's rodent population. Indeed, there were salesmen everywhere, thrusting wares of every conceivable sort at the new arrival. There were blind masseurs; medicine salesmen; bird catchers who trapped sparrows in fine nets; and fortune-tellers with mirrors, sandboxes, and divining sticks.

Walter de Havilland was a cold and authoritarian teacher; but his students, raised in the rigid traditions of Japan, did not resent him. In fact, he earned great respect as he moved to posts at successive universities. In the process, he built up so great a knowledge of patent law that by the turn of the century he was the most trusted Western expert on the subject in Japan. When China ceded to the Meiji emperor the Pescadores, Formosa, and the Liantung Peninsula, later ceded to China again when Japan revised treaties with foreign nations and signed the Anglo-Japanese alliance in 1902, the importance of his position strengthened. During the Russo-Japanese War of 1904–1905,

Korea became a protectorate of Japan, and in 1908 Walter published a definitive book on Korean patents that proved to be a bible for the Japanese Imperialist business figures in charge of that tragic and beleaguered country. After the Treaty of Portsmouth, when Japan again assumed the lease of the Liantung Peninsula, and the Franco-Japanese Treaty guaranteeing the integrity of China, the question of patents again became crucial and paramount.

Book after book from his pen showed Walter de Havilland's command of Japanese and the respect in which he was held by the Japanese government. He was a prominent professor of law at the Waseda University in Tokyo. Much of the law he taught, as well as his feeling about life, he drew from German sources. He sympathized with German principles of pure Aryanism and he was captivated by Japanese ideas of imperial power. With the contradictoriness of very right-wing people, he managed to square his feelings of racism with his love of Japan. He was, in addition, deeply anti-Semitic.

In 1912, shortly after he became famous in Japan for his publications on patent law, and also for a book that became the standard work on the traditional Japanese game known as *go*, Walter Augustus met a brown-haired, thirty-two-year-old, tiny, snobbish, but attractive and charming girl called, by odd coincidence, Lilian Augusta Ruse, whose brother taught at Waseda University. Although Lilian claimed to be of high birth, her birth certificate (she was born in Reading, England, on June 11, 1880) makes clear that she was in fact the daughter of a humble ironmonger's assistant. Her father must have scrimped and scraped his way up in the ironmongery business in order to give her and her brother a decent education. Lilian always kept her family background a mystery, so much so that Joan Fontaine, in her memoirs, seems to know nothing of it. Lilian would have been mortified if anyone had discovered her father's education and occupation, and it is significant that her children literally know nothing of their maternal grandparents.

Eager and ambitious, a good singer, Lilian had managed to obtain a scholarship to the Royal Academy of Dramatic Arts, in London, where she received a sound grounding in acting principles, although she displayed little talent, a fact that no doubt later drove her to a vicarious interest in her daughters' careers. She worked as an assistant to the distinguished actor-manager Sir Herbert Beerbohm Tree, whose extraordinary talent inspired her, but to whose brilliant company she could not hope to aspire. She was held back by a streak of puritanism and dullness that came from her provincial background, and that she never broke free from.

At Waseda, where her brother taught music, she sang in a choir and appeared in semiprofessional theatricals put on by the British community in Tokyo. Just passable as an actress, she made up for her deficiencies to some extent with her soft, warm nature and her big eyes that inevitably captivated men. It was her quality of womanliness and her almost Victorian air of discipline, correctness, and propriety that made Walter Augustus feel that Lilian Augusta would be a suitable mate. It is doubtful that "love" entered into the picture, although, given Walter's consuming sex drive, there was probably a strong physical attraction. Lilian was something of a tease, and led him on maddeningly.

Like his elder daughter, Olivia, Walter had a compulsion that would brook no obstacles. He pursued Lilian all the way to England and, on board ship, proposed to her with the toss of a coin. She finally married him in New York City on November 30, 1914. Returning to Tokyo, they lived in a large house where Lilian, who had a pretty singing voice, would entertain at evening musicals. But, for all her gay, theatrical, and slightly self-important ways, Lilian was nervous and insecure in her marriage. Walter, seemingly in contradiction to his impeccable public image, had assumed the role of a Japanese gentleman in conducting an elaborate secondary existence in which he spent night after night not with his wife but with the girls of the red-light district.

The brothel district of Tokyo was a labyrinth of tiny, narrow streets, twisting like earthworms, with balconied buildings three stories high. The streets were lit by candles in globes even as late as 1914. Many of the buildings had bamboo bars on the windows, earning them the name "cages"; and large women, some of them lesbians, would stand outside, along with the ever-present pimps, advising passersby of the beauties within. Inside the houses Walter frequented, the girls, always very young, would sit in brightly colored kimonos, like wax dolls. Usually introduced to the brothels at the age of six, they had been taught never to smile, but they would offer cigarettes (taboo to most Japanese women) and tiny cups of saké, and sometimes they would play the samisen and dance. For the special customers, distinguished figures like Walter de Havilland, there was often the privilege of deflowering a young virgin. It was customary for the girl to prostrate herself on the floor before the ritual of defloration, to show that she was of the earth, while the man was of heaven. Fifty percent of her income went to the brothelkeeper.

It was difficult for the tiny, upright Lilian, a typical British provincial girl with her Berkshire accent and prim, purse-lipped ways, to tolerate Walter's behavior, uncommon—at least on the surface—to British husbands. Perhaps she hoped that her pregnancy in late 1915 would encourage her husband to be more faithful; but when Olivia was born on July 1, 1916, followed by Joan on October 22 of the following year, there was no indication that Walter de Havilland was about to change his habits.

The girls were born into a city of violent contrasts, moving belatedly and painfully into the full-scale industrial force of the twentieth century. In those years, before the earthquake of 1923 that was to change the city beyond recognition, Tokyo was a gray and featureless maze of single-story dwellings and low, gloomy office buildings unrelieved by a single feature of consequence save the imposing Imperial Palace and its murky moat and Frank Lloyd Wright's Aztec puzzle of an Imperial Hotel. Although a city of two million souls, Tokyo was made almost entirely of wood and was swept by fires day and night, most of them caused by arsonists, who proliferated everywhere. Only the most luxurious quarters—which included the de Havilland home—were lit by electricity; the rest of the city was illuminated by gas so that anyone looking at it from a distant vantage point would have thought it was inhabited by a million glowworms. There was no sewage system to speak of, nor paving in the streets, and in rainy periods the streets flowed with human excrement. Thousands of people lived in tiny rooms like those in train sleepers, without doors, placed back to back, housed as tight as herrings in a barrel.

An early sound heard by the two girls was that of the electric tramcar that clanged through the writhing streets that had risen higgledy-piggledy from the holocaust of 1889. The streets, strange to foreigners because not a single word was in Roman letters, were mysterious, dangerous, and seemingly endless; you could ride miles on a ricksha and never come to the end of the wilderness of hovels and huts. The journey on a tramcar was especially unpleasant since the Japanese, so careful and meticulous at home, had no respect for public transportation and scattered newspaper, banana and orange peels, and wrappings from rice or noodles all over the floors. When the de Havilland children went on a trip, it was via the old Ueno Station, a depressing construction in those days, with an iron roof leaning insecurely on frail wooden posts that snapped like matchsticks in the frequent tremors that shook the city on its ocean of mud. Another dominant sound of those times was the clacking of hundreds of wooden clogs on the uneven wooden platforms.

They were tormented times for a child to grow up in. Cold and impervious, Walter de Havilland was indifferent to the plight of the people; but the rice riots that came at the end of World War I were appalling to Lilian, and the outbreaks of violence, savagely quelled by the police, filled her provincial British heart with terror.

In addition to Lilian's other tribulations, she suffered from the fact that Walter was a monster to her. It was one thing to indulge himself in the brothel district while neglecting her sexually and reducing her to the role of a glorified housekeeper in charge of Japanese servants. But he committed the unforgivable sin—he took a dainty, tiny maid, Yoki-san, as his mistress within the house itself—and Lilian decided she had no alternative but to leave at once. She chose California, evidently hoping the United States would offer a more complete escape for her than Britain. She sailed in 1919, and for a time lived in San Francisco with her two children, then three and two.

Both Joan and Olivia had exceptionally high IQ's; at the age of three, Joan scored 160 on an infant intelligence test. She also showed an early theatrical bent: She was commonly seen sitting in a graveyard, leaning against a tombstone and reading romantic verse. One of Lilian's friends said later, "This melancholy pursuit seemed suitable since Joan was a wasted-looking creature and to all intents and purposes had one foot planted in the area."

Both girls were sickly. Olivia had pneumonia, and Joan, perhaps in competition, German measles. Already at that early age, there were indications of the deadly sibling rivalry that would seriously affect both girls' lives. It is clear that Olivia, devastatingly pretty with chestnut hair and enormous brown eyes, was closer to her mother than the pallid and fragile Joan. Moreover, Olivia's fighting instinct was visible, already asserting itself in her refusal to even go near Joan's crib, or to allow Joan in hers. Lilian had her head in the clouds, dreaming already of her daughters' theatrical or musical future, dedicating herself to combing and brushing Olivia's hair, and trying to appease the constantly crying Joan, who was vocally indicating an imaginary or actual neglect.

Because of the girls' frail health, especially Joan's, in 1920 Lilian took them to live in San Jose, at the rambling old Vendome Hotel. There, they confused the guests by talking a babyish version of Japanese more often than English. It was at the run-down hotel that Olivia took a liking to a tall, sober, upright, bespectacled guest named George Fontaine, a department-store manager who in many ways resembled Walter de Havilland in terms of character. Olivia decided that he was to be their father, despite the fact that (as her infant mind of course did not comprehend) Walter and Lilian were still married.

George Fontaine had lost his parents in an epidemic when he was a small child, and at the age of twelve he had to support five sisters and two brothers. His father had run a trading post in the wilds of northern Minnesota; now in the severe winters and harsh summers of that beautiful but difficult state of the Union, George would rise each morning to milk the cows; then he would open up the store, sweep it and dust it, unpack all the crates, and serve at the counter. In order to conserve his time and energy, he had to lay out each day in hours and proportions of hours. The children's food, too, was weighed and measured meticulously lest any child feel left out or be less than satisfactorily nourished. His philosophy was "I work: therefore I am," and he was puritanical and severe to a degree. He married late, and both his wife and his daughter died in an epidemic, like his parents.

In 1920, following a short time in San Jose, the de Havilland family traveled to the small town of Saratoga, California, where they moved into the Lundblad boardinghouse, run by Mr. and Mrs. Lundblad, a cheerful couple from Sweden, and their bustling daughter, Hazel, who was married to Joseph Bargas. Although Joan's memoirs indicate a happy family atmosphere with Joseph Bargas playing Santa Claus at Christmas and being warm and kind to the children, Hazel Bargas remembers only her parents' hatred of Joan and their exclusion of her from any family meals. Hazel speaks of Joan's tantrums and refusal to get out of bed for long periods at a time; her rudeness to everyone; and her irritating, allegedly imaginary headaches and fits of vomiting. Actually, Olivia, though pretty, well cared for, and full of life, also continued to suffer from imperfect health.

Lilian traveled to Japan to arrange a divorce from Walter de Havilland in 1924.* Later she made her living at a milliner's store in San Jose, traveling there by horsedrawn bus even after automobiles were in general use. She augmented her income by the many free dinners, lunches, motoring expeditions, and concerts paid for by George Fontaine, whom she married in 1925. Finally, she managed to find enough money to move into a sad little green-painted wooden cottage that stood just up the road opposite the Lundblad boardinghouse; for good measure, she snapped up the house's neighboring dwelling, and made them into one residence. Every effort to make Walter de Havilland send money failed. That cold man had little or no interest in his

---

*The grounds were desertion; Walter de Havilland was the plaintiff and no alimony was asked for.

children; such emotional life as he had was divided between his mistress (the former maid) and prostitutes; soon, he married the maid.

George Fontaine, meanwhile, raised his stepchildren like orphans in a Victorian novel. When Joan started biting her nails, he dug a grave in the garden and showed it to her; as she screamed with fear, he told her that he would throw her into it if she continued. Restrained from this action only by Lilian's entreaties when Joan persisted, Fontaine put the child's wrists in handcuffs and shackled her to a post, where the local children mocked her.

The cottages were heated by large iron Franklin stoves, one in the middle of each living room. The stoves exuded noxious odors and always threatened, via strange rattling noises, to explode. At one time, Lilian, in a fit of unaccustomed cruelty, threw Joan's Felix the Cat doll into a stove, provoking a fit of total hysteria.

The rain constantly dripped through the ceiling or splashed off the rusted gutters. The children seldom had enough to eat, and George Fontaine scarcely improved matters by having the children catch flies on the windowpanes and deposit them in boxes while he timed them with a stopwatch. If the slightest harm came to the flies, the children were punished.

The sheets on their beds had to be khaki, and the girls had to do military exercises every morning. They were drilled rigorously at all times. Olivia flatly refused to learn to sew; every time Fontaine or Lilian forced a torn coat or shirt into her hands to repair with needle and thread, she would instantly prick her finger with the needle and scream very loudly at the sight of blood. When asked to wash dishes, she would quietly let one slip through her fingers with the words "It has a will of its own." When Olivia passed her hand-me-downs on to Joan, Olivia always made deliberate tears in them so that Joan would have to sew them.

George Fontaine showed a perverted streak, not only subjecting the girls to even stricter discipline but interfering with their genitals in the bathtub, so terrifying them that they dared not mention it to the neighbors.

They attended Saratoga Grammar School, and Fontaine would spy on them behind bushes to see that they arrived at school and church on time. Once when they played hookey, he asked Olivia if she had done so; she lied that she had not. When Joan told the truth, he beat Joan. When he forbade the girls to wear silk stockings and high heels to school, they hid the forbidden footwear, wore Oxfords and short socks, and then changed halfway up the street. If he caught them, he beat them.

To test if they had cleaned the house, Fontaine always put a length of string in a different place; if it was not found and thrown away, then he could prove the girls had not cleaned everything. Often, when they were waiting for the school bus for an outing, he would loom up, announcing they could not go because they hadn't found the string. He used to encourage Olivia to read the Gospel to Joan, and Olivia took special pleasure in reading the Crucifixion, emphasizing gruesome details in additional material.

The girls responded differently to Fontaine's pressure. One day, he told Olivia and Joan to fetch sticks from the yard, with which he would beat them. Olivia came back with a twig. Joan meekly fetched a long switch. Fontaine beat her with it and Olivia ran out, returning laughing with a two-by-four. Then she disappeared again.

When there was a difference of opinion, Fontaine took extraordinary measures. Returning from Japan, her divorce absolute, Lilian gave Joan a book of Andersen fairy tales. Joan said she would prefer a mirror. After endless discussion, George Fontaine drew up a contract on a school pad: Joan would be forced to read the fairy tales, and Olivia must gaze in the mirror in front of Joan for an indefinite period of time.

The children were put to work doing the laundry, polishing shoes, weeding, and dusting. At one stage Joan decided, quite methodically after Olivia had been hitting her with alarming frequency, that she would murder her sister. She would pick up George Fontaine's revolver and shoot Olivia between the eyes. Already a precocious addict of newspapers, she looked forward to a world-famous trial. Olivia must have sensed Joan's intent, because she hit her only once that day. George Fontaine sent Joan to a convent school to mend her manners. Joan hated it there and finally was sent home. The moment she returned, Olivia was sent to the same convent, also for a short time. Neither sister was convent material.

While Joan wilted and wailed, Olivia joined a gang in Saratoga known as the Fearless Five. She and the four other girls spent most of their time cutting up in the neighborhood. One particular target of their hatred was a neighborhood scold, an old woman who refused to allow the children to play near her house. There were two turns made of stone that surmounted the pillars on either side of the woman's gate. Olivia dubbed them "soup tureens." The Fearless Five drew straws to decide who would be the first to climb up a gatepost and sit in an urn. Olivia drew the straw, and with great nimbleness she climbed the gate. The old woman emerged, carrying a two-by-four. The Fearless Four turned out to be not so fearless, and fled. Olivia was brought down from her perch by the infuriated woman and had to run like the wind to escape her.

When asked what she thought of Joan, Olivia would say, with icy sweetness, "Joan is most beautiful in repose." She had a recurring nightmare that has stayed with her all of her life. She dreamed that she was standing on a cliff with the waves beating on the sand and Joan lying unconscious below. A tidal wave approached from the horizon. She wasn't sure whether she should run down the cliff path and rescue Joan, or, if she did, whether both would be lost. After a great deal of consideration, she did nothing and she woke as Joan was swept away. When Joan was asked how she expected to die, she said, "In *Peter Pan*—when Olivia cuts the wire!"

Olivia and Joan called themselves the Two Musketeers and allied against George Fontaine, whom they dubbed the Iron Duke; but Joan proved to be so wishy-washy a musketeer that Olivia dismissed her and called herself the Lone Musketeer. Sometimes, Olivia would get into trouble, and at one stage she had to write a hundred times "I will in the future be modest and I will not again display my bloomers during basketball." She liked to wear bloomers because she could hide salt in them to kill snails at the Grotto of Mary, Mother of Christ, to be absolved for the sin of boasting.

Not every aspect of the girls' lives was depressing. Lilian was devoted to the notion that the two girls would fulfill the longings of her own life and would benefit from her training at the Royal Academy of Dramatic Arts. Thus, she trained the children in deportment, with books on their heads and perfect speech, and had them act out scenes from favorite plays. During these sessions, life was not quite so painful and difficult, and even George Fontaine relented slightly. Lilian was a follower of the Delsarte School of Drama, a major influence on the styles of silent screen actresses. This mode of histrionics emphasized gesture to express emotion and called for a degree of "centering" in which the performer mobilized all of his energy into his expression and posture. It was not a realistic mode, and the girls used to irritate the neighbors with their emphatic recitals and almost Kabukiesque whirlings about. But the training worked to an extent on Olivia, who once again moved ahead of Joan.

Despite a tendency to suffer from stage fright, Olivia emerged in school plays. In the eighth grade, she was determined to appear as either Hansel or Gretel—she would have played both if she could—in a very amateurish "operetta" version of the Grimm's fairy tale. When the teacher producing the show informed her coolly that she would not be acceptable for either part, Olivia announced that she had memorized the roles of Mother, Second Angel and Head Witch. With lightning changes of costume, begged from bits and pieces of neighbors' clothes, she proceeded to provide such striking impressions of all three that the teacher dissolved in laughter and awarded them to her.

Her most serious attack of stage fright occurred at the age of nine when she appeared in a pageant called *Cinderella of the Redwoods* staged at Stanford University. She was cast as Daisy, a fairy who ran out of the redwood trees to comb Cinderella's hair. Before she could utter her first line, she burst into tears. A hand thrust her onto the stage, and with supreme control she pulled herself together and gave a perfect performance.

Both girls loved silent movies, and on rare occasions wrung permission from their formidable stepfather to attend them. But Olivia always insisted on playing out the starring role, with Joan as a supporting actress. When Olivia triumphed in *Hansel and Gretel*, Joan was reduced to being a ghost in a cardboard cloud. When Olivia starred in hockey and school debates, and won a silver cup in recognition of her public speaking, Joan took a back seat.

But for all the tensions and strains, the crying jags and fights of sibling rivalry, the behavior of George Fontaine and the weakness of Lilian, life in Saratoga had its compensations. There were chicken-pie-and-ice-cream socials, joyous, noisy events when even the sternest let their hair down. There were lovesick young boys who asked the two girls for flowers or locks of their hair in lockets they would wear over their hearts. There were walks to Congress Springs, trout angling, running after rabbit or quail, looking for the wild strawberries that grew in the woods, putting blackberries in wicker panniers until the juice ran through the bottom, and returning home to help mother make blackberry pies and shortcake.

In the spring, Oak Street and the surrounding hills were a blaze of wildflowers, dominated by the golden poppies known as the *copas de oro*, or pots of gold, and there were lilac, lupins, and violets everywhere in a shimmering sea of color. The live oaks shaded the rich green gardens and front yards of the old and gracious homes of the district; and picnics, with everyone in white, seated under the trees, made a pretty sight. There were bicycling expeditions and maidenhair-fern expeditions; the catching of bullfrogs; skinny-dipping in creeks, always forbidden and joyously clandestine; and the pleasure of going to Mr. Cloud's General Store with its smells of coffee beans, spices, and shoe leather, and its huge glass bottles in the window, apothecary jars with brightly colored mysterious fluids in them that no one actually seemed to drink.

A great favorite of the de Havilland girls was Mrs. Ida Barnett, who specialized in making the school cafeteria a paradise of wholesome food. She cooked casseroles, stews, and chicken pot pies at home and then conveyed them to the cafeteria, where they were heated up on the kerosene stove. There was a flat charge of fifteen cents for each dish.

In 1930, Olivia became associate editor of *Aero Vista*, the school magazine of Saratoga Grammar. She was listed in the "Record of Achievement in School Activities" as speedball captain, basketball and baseball star, prominent figure in the girls' glee club, chairman of the "White Elephant Booth" (a kind of glorified garage sale), and chief performer at the Washington Minuet. Not surprisingly, *Aero Vista* was abrim with Olivia's contributions and clearly advertised her prowess in every field. Joan's absence from the pages is also not surprising. On the editorial page of the June 1930 edition, Olivia appeared at the top of the masthead announcing the founding of the school newspaper "due to the assistance of Miss Bambauer . . . our English teacher [who] has taken the responsibility of organizing the various departments and establishing a Press Club." Olivia's editorial announcement continued self-importantly: "The object of our paper is to inform the Saratoga Public of the activities and accomplishments of the school, and thereby stimulate its interest in us. We also wish to keep the student body informed of all the activities of the school. We sincerely hope that this school paper which we have originated, will be a success, will be educational, amusing, and informative, and worthy of our school."

Olivia contributed a short story to her magazine about a boy called Tiger, with unbrushed hair and a red jersey, who played football. She also published a lyrical poem of her own composition, *Autumn*, that was carefully rhymed and scanned. Interestingly, Olivia was a self-appointed reporter on film events, and wrote in 1930: "Once a month, a film play is presented which takes up the topic being studied in the 7th Grade, the most recent of which was entitled *The Eve of the Revolution*, depicting the tumult preceding the War of Independence, and showing many historical incidents." The members of the class of 1930 entered into the final page of one issue of the magazine their last wills and testaments. Olivia's will was characteristic. It read, "To my sister Joan, I, Olivia de Havilland, will my ability to capture boys' hearts in order to keep it in the family."

The big event of 1930 was the arrival of the gracious, sweet-natured, and inspired actress and teacher Dorothea Johnston. She came to Saratoga with her mother, who bought the charming Saratoga Inn. Johnston had a strong influence on Olivia. She also held classes in dancing in which the two girls learned to pirouette to waltzes and gavottes, graduating to a level at which they could appear at the annual Saratoga Prune Festival.

The girls moved on to the Los Gatos Union High School. Ill most of the time, Joan could attend for only a few hours a day, but once again Olivia flourished, rapidly becoming the editor of the school magazine, *The Wildcat*, her face smiling from the masthead. She was outstanding in the Peninsula Debate League championship, helping to win the contest on the issue that Germany should be released from the arms restrictions placed on her by the Treaty of Versailles. Neither Olivia nor her fellow debater, James Gibb, realized what the consequences of such a release would involve.

Olivia became secretary of the Student Officers' body and carried out her duties with enthusiasm. She starred in *Alice in Wonderland*, *Pride and Prejudice*, and in a version of *Quality Street* by J. M. Barrie, as Phoebe Throssel, a part later played in the film version (in which Joan was to appear) by Katharine Hepburn. Olivia was also active in the Dramatic Club. In the summary of the class of 1932 published in *The Wildcat*, she was described in its brochure as "charming"; her besetting sin, "gray matter"; her ambition, to be "another Katharine Cornell"; and her certain fate, to be "a circus queen." Again, there was no reference to Joan anywhere in the school magazine.

Miserable after a further stay at the Lundblads', where she had to serve in the kitchen washing dishes, fighting constantly with Hazel Bargas, Joan finally reached the end of her tether when Olivia hurled her to the floor in an argument and jumped on her so violently that she broke her collarbone. Baby-sitting at the time, Joan was in so much pain from the injury that she dropped the child to the floor and almost killed it. In desperation, lying in a hospital recuperating, she wrote to her long-lost father and begged him to rescue her.

Reluctantly, that difficult man arrived to bring his younger daughter home. As though he wanted to slight Olivia by making Joan seem more "advanced" and sophisticated, he bought her a grown-up wardrobe; and when they sailed by Japanese ship from San Francisco harbor, Joan looked like a miniature socialite. But she hated the outfit and did not like the fact that she was supposed to be "grown-up," almost as though she were her father's sister. Nerves and the nausea of her second sea voyage made her ill for days and nights, but she at last recovered and had her first serious date, with the washing-machine heir Fred Maytag, a handsome twenty-two-year-old. The steamer, *Tatsuta Maru*, was cramped and airless, and the tropical heat and typhoons during the crossing were exhausting; but Maytag buoyed up Joan's spirits, and for the first time in her life she felt she was a woman.

The real problems arose when she reached Tokyo. She hated her father's new wife, Yoki-san, who was garishly dressed in European clothes and flourished a cigarette holder. This vulgar display was totally out of order for a Japanese lady of distinction; it was typical of Walter de Havilland and his eccentricity that he should choose such a woman for his wife.

Nonetheless, Joan soon learned why Walter enjoyed being married to a Japanese woman and living in a Japanese household. For all of her Western airs, Yoki-san, the former downstairs maid, existed entirely for the sake of her husband. She subordinated her personal wishes and ideas to him; she waited on him as though she were still his maid. When he returned home after a day in his patent office, she arranged his clothing and his bath, supervised the food that was brought to him, and picked up whatever he had thrown on the floor. The servants were under orders to obey his slightest whim. When he had an outburst of temper, she would not respond but would instead, in geisha fashion, soothe his brow or simply disappear if instinct told her that he wanted to be left alone. So total was her slavery that if Walter so much as blinked, she knew whether the gesture indicated pleasure or displeasure. The house was active or silent, filled with guests or empty, cluttered or swept clean, according to Walter de Havilland's restless, mercurial, and ever-changing whims.

In the history of siblings, we are told that the father is often drawn sexually to his younger daughter, but normally the father represses the feelings aroused by the young girl's budding attractiveness. However, Walter de Havilland was so spoiled, self-indulgent, and domineering that he would scarcely deny himself any chosen expression, and he often let his incestuous feelings for Joan be known. Still a virgin and very insecure about sexual matters, Joan was certainly not ready for incest. Whatever knowledge she had was gleaned from hurried and surreptitious reading of manuals—and from the fact that the shoji screens of the de Havilland residence did not block out the noisy lovemaking of her passionate father and his wife.

Joan became a pupil at the American School, which was in every way an excellent establishment. She was far ahead of her fellow pupils in sophistication; her nearest competitor in that regard was the attractive Eleanor Child, who recalled recently that Joan, far removed from the shy wren who had left California, was the belle of the school and had no end of boyfriends. She remembered the young Joan as frivolous, antic, and full of charm; freed from her sister's influence, she was falling in "love" every other day and, despite sinus problems caused by the fumes of a thousand factories and the odor of the Tokyo gutters, she managed to have a good time. The city around her was still being rebuilt ten years after the earthquake of 1923, and the rattle of drills, the blasting of excavation sites, made the noise more nerve-racking than that of New York.

For contrast and relief, there were the glories of the Japanese countryside: the cool, grave temples, sober in their setting of pine and cryptomeria: the pebbled paths and ornamental lakes that made rural Japan a work of art in which each human inhabitant served a purpose. Joan learned her love of beauty, harmony, and order in Japan; later she would bring an Oriental precision and balance to her successive homes.

Finally, she realized that the situation with her father was going to be impossible. On one occasion, when his wife was sick, he even suggested that Joan go to bed with him. This was a severe shock; and when he told her, following her angry refusal, that she would not be allowed to continue her education but would be reduced to the status of a servant, she decided to go home. De Havilland gave her a ticket then, but he cut off both her and Olivia's allowance from that moment on.

# *Two*

 While Joan was on the high seas, bound for San Francisco, whirling from one handsome beau to another in the ship's Saloon, Olivia was hard at work on her Shakespeare debut. Max Reinhardt's production of *The Dream* was staged by Dorothea Johnston in the open-air auditorium of the Saratoga School, set among the oaks and pines and bushes and banks of flowers, as Shakespeare surely would have wished it to be. Olivia, already burning with the ambition that would soon consume her, begged for and won the crucial part of Puck. Despite the fact that she was already blossoming as a young woman, she was sufficiently tomboyish, athletic, and filled with buoyant energy, humor, and impish charm to be ideal for the part. At the same time, while Lilian primly and puritanically forbade her to wear makeup, even lipstick, or to bob her hair, she still exuded a powerful sexual appeal. The resulting ambiguity of her presence added piquancy to the asexual role of Puck.

Despite her provincial background and location, Dorothea Johnston kept in close touch with current theatrical events. She had gotten wind of the fact that the great Max Reinhardt was going to arrive from Germany in the immediate future to present a national tour of *The Dream*, beginning at Hollywood Bowl, with a presentation at the University of California at Berkeley, in connection with the California

Festival of Arts. Reinhardt was the leading theatrical producer of Europe. His genius had revitalized the German theater from the beginning of the century. Electric, magnetic, with a shock of graying hair, blazing eyes, and a rugged physique, he had an aura of greatness about him that impressed everyone he met. Although his productions were theatrical in the best sense—huge, elaborate, heroically carried off—they also had an all-consuming realism. Indeed, he loved to introduce nature itself to the stage, using real trees, water, simulations of weather from snow to fine rain, and the sounds of birdsong, wind, and water. He had a surging confidence in his own genius, but now, in 1934, with Hitler in power in Germany, he had at last to face defeat. His Jewish origins were sufficient to ensure his ruin under the Wehrmacht. His palace of Leopoldskron near Salzburg was taken from him and given to the honorary Aryan princess and secret agent Stefanie Hohenlohe, who contemptuously sent Reinhardt's books to America, saying that they cluttered up the place, but retained all of his priceless furniture and paintings.

*The Dream*, to be produced in September 1934, at the Bowl after the summer music season was over, was financed under the auspices of several public figures, including Harry Chandler of the *Los Angeles Times*, John G. Bullock of the department store of the same name, and the real-estate promoter William May Garland. Reinhardt had cabled his son Gottfried to secure a cast of fabled fame and excellence: Chaplin as Bottom, John Barrymore as Oberon, Greta Garbo as Titania, Fred Astaire as Puck, Joan Crawford as Hermia, Clark Gable as Demetrius, and Gary Cooper as Lysander. Needless to say, Gottfried, as he recalls today, was quite nonplussed and succeeded in interesting none of these people.

Felix Weissberger, Reinhardt's skillful, English-speaking assistant director, and Catherine Sibley, Reinhardt's assistant, traveled to Berkeley to check out the Greek Theater that was situated in the green fields of the university campus. Dorothea Johnston heard of this and invited him to see her own production in Saratoga. Reinhardt's scouts, in the place of honor in the outdoor orchestra seats, watched as the attractive teen-age players darted about through the trees with antic, merry laughter and sprightly, athletic prancings. To their surprise, they were enchanted; surely Shakespeare would have loved the freshness and beauty of these young people speaking his verse so naturally in a setting of unspoiled countryside.

And they liked Olivia the best of the whole cast. Her Puck was youth personified: sweetness and mocking naughtiness combined in a richly irresistible whole, each line spoken as though it had been thought for the first time, not a word "recited" as though from a book. The scouts saw at once the raw but unmistakable talent before them.

After the performance, Olivia boldly went to Weissberger* and asked for a chance to read for the same part in the Bowl production, saying, "I'd be happy to be a tree." He smiled and said she could certainly come and watch the rehearsals as one of a group of students brought from all over the country for the great occasion. For the time being, Olivia had to be content with this, but she instinctively felt that Weissberger was keeping an eye on her. Despite the reluctance of George Fontaine, Olivia scraped up enough money from her parents to go to Hollywood. She was nervous, but ambition overcame everything. When she arrived in Hollywood, however, she was shocked to learn that the very young Mickey Rooney had been cast as Puck. Swallowing her disappointment, she went to the rehearsal hall to watch Weissberger in the early run-throughs of the cast. She was impressed by the beautiful young Gloria Stuart as Hermia, and dazzled by the good looks of John Davis Lodge (of the famous political family) as Theseus. These were the first two players to be cast by Reinhardt when he arrived in Los Angeles.

For Olivia, the experience of watching Reinhardt, with his thick, wavy hair, his fierce driving gestures, coaxing remarkable performances from the players along with Weissberger and Catherine Sibley was most exciting. She saw the casting director, Fred Niblo, who had made the silent epic *Ben Hur*, selecting the players at auditions and asked him for a chance, but the best he could offer her was understudy to the actress Jean Rouveral, who was herself understudy to Gloria Stuart as Hermia. She watched every move Gloria made, aching for her part. She studied not only her own potential role but those of the others as well. She observed how Reinhardt, despite his lack of English, conveyed through Weissberger every inflection, every rhythm, every tempo of the speeches. She marveled at his fluid movements that belied his heavy body, his sudden appearances in the orchestra, conducting the Los Angeles Philharmonic and chorus as the great day of opening approached. She heard him discuss his plans to incorporate the hills and forests surrounding the Hollywood Bowl into the production itself.

She was fascinated to see how he, through Weissberger, made the players use their whole bodies as they said the lines, expressing the

*By some accounts, she saw Catherine Sibley; even her own published accounts have differed.

emotion in full. Reinhardt brought out the nervous energies of his players as no one else could, arranging them in a semicircle around him, drawing from his director's "Bible," into which he had poured a lifetime of theatrical magicianship. As the dress rehearsal approached, he took each actor aside and, with intense humor and brilliance, conveyed his approval to them. It was painful to Olivia to be excluded as a mere understudy.

At the same time that the rehearsals continued through twelve hours a day, Reinhardt was busy converting the Hollywood Bowl to meet his extraordinary specifications. Teams blasted aside the earth and dumped in tons of fresh soil, trees, and glades to give an impression of a fairy forest in place of the stage. The music shell was taken down and moved to one side, a bridge was built from the canyon to the northern hills, and wires were strung in the trees for Puck to swing on.

By the time the dress rehearsal came along, the Bowl had been transformed by Reinhardt's theater magic, so that the audience of 20,000 could see a hundred oak, elm, and aspen trees that had been imported from northern California and set up to form the fairy wood. Reinhardt wandered through the hills, pondering how to achieve the transitions from forest to palace without the possibility of scene changes. Ultimately, he designed a series of banners and movements of courtiers and court ladies to overcome the problem.

Then, at the last minute, Olivia had a fantastic stroke of luck. Jean Rouveral, Gloria Stuart's understudy, was rushed into a motion picture, and then, wonder of wonders, Gloria Stuart was as well! The news was devastating for Miss Stuart, who recalls that when she heard she was going to have to appear in a wretched production called *Maybe It's Love*, instead of the most prestigious theatrical attraction in Los Angeles history, she burst into tears and became almost hysterical. Completely rehearsed, as ready as though she had been playing the part herself, Olivia rushed into the breach. Miss Stuart's contractual obligation to First National Pictures was Olivia's salvation. Gloria Stuart says that she went backstage on the first night at the Bowl to congratulate Olivia, who, to her shock and dismay, turned her back on her. This story is hard to believe; it is more likely that the young girl was totally embarrassed and petrified by Miss Stuart's appearance and, not knowing what to do or say, turned aside to conceal her feelings. But it was twenty years before Gloria Stuart spoke to her again.

Up to that moment, Reinhardt had hardly been aware of Olivia; but now he focused his attention on the nervous, ambitious, ravishingly pretty girl who stood so awkwardly in the wings, waiting for her chance. As soon as she spoke some of the lines, he recognized in her the fire, the insolence, the temperament that displayed to him a blazing young actress. From 10:00 A.M. until midnight, for the last few days before the dress rehearsal, he plunged her into the process that would result in a paring away of her weaknesses and a gradual but definite exposure of the steely, innate strength of her personality as an actress.

Olivia opened herself to Reinhardt's guidance. Until now she had been a pretty but amateurish beginner; he discovered in this virgin girl a temperament and style she did not know she could muster. Lilian stayed with her overprotectively around the clock, trying to make her eat, rest, go home between rehearsals, but she would not leave for an instant in case she should suddenly be called for. It is clear she wanted to give her whole personality over to Reinhardt, who taught her how to walk, how to smile, how to perfect emotion, how to use stillness and repose to great effect, and how to break up the line of Shakespeare's pentameters in a meaningful and powerful way.

Olivia had to fight to overcome stage fright on the opening night at the Bowl, which took place on Monday, September 17, 1934. She was not quite eighteen years old. The audience was studded with stars and the leading society figures of the Los Angeles Establishment. Arc lights, some fifty of them, formed a canopy above the Bowl, augmented by 4,000 special studio spotlights that, the *Los Angeles Times* reported, made "a Cubist pattern against the curtain of the night."

As actor John Boles announced the arrival of the galaxy of stars, cordons of police had to control the crowd. Boxes were sold at $5 each, a large sum for those days, and greetings were called out from tier to tier as Joan Crawford, Gary Cooper, Clark Gable, Norma Shearer, Louis B. Mayer, Jack Warner, and all the other major figures of the industry recognized each other. The spectacle was extraordinary. When the Mendelssohn music struck up, the hills were punctured by one tiny brilliant light after another until it seemed that they were covered with fireflies. The wedding procession of Oberon and Titania emerged, crossing the great bridge, 350 feet long, the cast dressed in gold, rose, and yellow, giving the effect of sun flashing on water. As the action moved to the kingdom, the firefly lights suddenly were extinguished and replaced with theatrical mists, lit from below, in which the creatures of the elfin world moved in shadow and silhouette. Puck, laughing happily, swung from wires down the bridge itself, as though suspended in air; and when a dancer performed, only her hands were illuminated, fluttering like butterfly wings in the night.

The fairies and their companions constantly seemed to be jumping from trees or hurtling up through holes in the forest floor, or they suddenly would be seen decked in leaves or moss. Oberon, played by Philip Arnhold in purple costume and silver mask, and Titania, acted by Julie Haydon in diaphanous chiffon and silver stars, made a grand royal couple of Fairyland. At the dress rehearsal, a procession of courtiers had become lost in the underbrush; but now the movements of all concerned had been choreographed to perfection, and there were no hitches on that night of all nights in Los Angeles history. The only problem was that the fire department had to crawl through the bushes alongside the procession at the wedding to make sure the sagebrush didn't catch fire from the torches. This meant that the wedding march had to be played over and over again, as it took ages for the procession to complete its journey.

Olivia was a triumph as Hermia. Seizing her chance with both hands, she played with an all-out nervous energy, a teasing, mocking, vibrant style that can still be appreciated in the motion-picture version of *The Dream*. She would be forever grateful to Reinhardt for having given her this opportunity.

One of those attending the first night was the Warner Brothers producer Hal Wallis, who was so taken with Olivia that he agreed with Reinhardt at once that she would be perfect for the movie production, which he had already discussed in meetings with Reinhardt the previous year at Leopoldskron. He telephoned Jack Warner in New York and told him to fly out at once, since the production was on a limited five-night run. Jack Warner characteristically replied that it was one hell of a flight for a blind date, that he assumed Mrs. Wallis (Louise Fazenda) was out of town, and that in any case no one could pronounce Olivia de Havilland. But Wallis was filled with quiet determination and wouldn't take no for an answer.

Grumblingly, Warner flew back across the continent and turned up at the last night's performance. Despite his influence, he could get a seat only at the back of the auditorium, but even through binoculars he knew Wallis was right. The next day, Wallis brought Olivia in to see him, and he was captivated by her extreme prettiness—her shining chestnut hair, big brown eyes, Cupid's bow lips, and dainty figure. He also sensed the resolution behind the almost babyish front and knew right away, with his showman's instinct for talent, that this diminutive, seemingly modest girl had the makings of a star. He wrote in his memoirs, *My First Two Thousand Years in Hollywood*, "She had a fresh young beauty that would soon stir a lot of tired old muscles around the film town. She had a voice that was music to the ears, like a cello, low and vibrant, and the Hollywood wolves would be milling around in the woods, hoping she could be had."

Unbeknownst to Olivia, Bette Davis had already been selected to play Hermia in the movie, but she was having one of her fights with the studio and to her fury Warner overruled her and decided to take Olivia instead. The problem was that Olivia had signed with the California Arts Association to undertake the national tour, and the association was being obstinately insistent that she not leave the tour early to prepare for the film, which would have to be held up. Olivia set off with her mother on the tour, which led her first to the San Francisco Opera House, where the company was again a triumph; then to Berkeley; and to Chicago.

Each of these productions was striking in its own right. The opera house was redesigned with a set made up of irregular steps and labyrinthine walks; lighting glowed through a glass floor center stage and green flowery gauze formed an illusion of a forest, trees changing into columns, and columns into trees.

At Berkeley, the faculty glade with oak trees became the fairy wood surrounding the big outdoor amphitheater. As the audience walked up the hill to take its seats, torchbearers stood around the walls holding torches high. The wedding scene took place in otherwise pitch-darkness, until gradually the moon, artificially augmented by silver-blue lights, broke through and shone on the scene.

While Olivia was appearing at Berkeley in *The Dream*, Joan arrived from Japan, scarcely recognizable from the young girl who had shyly embarked two years earlier. She was very pretty, almost as pretty as Olivia; she'd had her hair dyed blond on board the *President Hoover* and for a time kept it that way. Typically, Walter de Havilland had failed to advise Lilian or George Fontaine of the date of her arrival and there was no one at the dock to greet her. She had to call a family friend to rescue her, and she stayed with another friend, Mrs. O. A. Hale, widow of the owner of the local department store where George Fontaine was the manager.

Lilian, now teaching drama at Stanford University and still living with Fontaine in the house on La Paloma in Saratoga, seemed disinterested in having Joan live with her. Olivia, however, resumed her bossy elder sister's ways and laid down the law concerning Joan's future. She would certainly not allow Joan to go to college under any circumstances; Olivia had given up Mills College to do *The Dream* and there was no way that Joan would be better educated. Olivia's money would be turned over to George Fontaine, who would in turn give Joan a tiny allowance. This was on condition that Joan obediently "danced classical ballet and obtained a mastery of French." Lilian sided with Olivia, further provoking the intense rivalry between the sisters. Indeed, when Joan innocently seized the hand of one of Olivia's male fellow cast members at a Sunday musicale, Lilian turned on her and accused her of being a whore and of trying to steal Olivia's boyfriend.

Joan was desperate. Lilian's constant prodding of her, and Olivia's contempt, combined with her father's rejection of her when she had refused his sexual advances, left her very much alone in life. She was depressed, realizing, as she would realize often during her life, that her mother would side with her sister whenever possible.

Meanwhile, Olivia playing in *The Dream* in Chicago, could thrill to the thought that she had left Joan far behind at this stage. The well-known *Town Crier* columnist Christopher Morley said of the Chicago production in *The Saturday Review*, "There was no longer any realization of being in a theater: simply a deep perspective of sylvestered hillsides. An unspoiled prospect of fairyland. The mind (that annoying encumbrance) was checked with hat and coat; the performance was pure sensual gift to the eye and ear. Extraordinary!" The players flashed like silver needles, forming patterns of light and darkness and accompanied by the actual scent of pine needles, blown by machines through the audience.

One problem on the tour was that Mickey Rooney was constantly playing practical jokes, which Olivia could not abide. To avenge themselves, the other actors decided to play one of their own on him: Olivia would throw a fainting fit behind the curtain during the play's epilogue; and Rooney, who fancied himself a doctor, would anxiously minister to her. She fainted excellently on cue. As Rooney came to her with the box of medication, she sat up and laughed—and he fell over backward.

But there were more serious problems on the tour. It was proving impossible for Max Arnow at the studio casting office to secure Olivia for preparations for the film. A contract was drawn up guaranteeing her $250 a week and transportation for herself and Lilian, who was chaperoning her on the tour, but no one was sure whether Olivia would be able to sign it. On November 13, she cabled *The Dream's* producer, Henry Blanke, that she was staying at the Croydon Hotel in Chicago and would wire if she changed her address. The same day, R. J. Obringer wrote to Ronald Button, Reinhardt's lawyer, saying he had arranged for Mickey Rooney to appear in the film; the letter referred to the fact that Mickey Rooney's mother had insisted on receiving an additional $500 before she would get on the plane with Mickey—a gun-to-the-head tactic typical of "show biz" mothers in those days.

On November 18, Olivia seemed to have reached a major stumbling block. She cabled that the corporation that had her under contract for the run of the play was making things impossible for her, and that she had been told it would be illegal to sign the Warner contract before the corporation released her. She was very worried that she would lose her chance for film stardom and there was a distinct edge to the words "Can you expedite matters as would like to do picture. Answer Western Union Collect." It was clear that she didn't expect Henry Blanke to pay for a return telegram.

In a telegram to Warners' dated November 19, Ronald Button stated that Olivia was refusing to sign the contract until she actually saw the release from her theater company contract to allow her to travel to Hollywood. Button insisted that such a release existed but that Marco Wolfe of the theater chain was reneging on the deal, and a later telegram indicated that Button was even questioning the deal's legality.

There were further obstructions and holdups. On November 21, Olivia had an awkward meeting with Wolfe and sent a telegram to Warners' reading: "Received summons to conference this morning with Marco and his eastern agent. Marco maintains the release given Button is valueless since conditions governing said release have not been fulfilled by Warner Bros. He also claims my leaving road show might seriously weaken cast. Do not understand Marco's obstructive tactics. Can you not bring about my unconditional and legal release?"

As her fate swung in the balance, the arguments went on. Jack Warner was so determined to have her in the cast that he himself cabled Meyer Weisgal of the theatrical company that had her under contract, saying that if there was any further delay the studio would be "damaged considerably"—an astonishing statement regarding a new and untried player.

Marco Wolfe cabled Warner on November 23 that he would do his best to release Olivia as soon as her understudy was completely rehearsed, but he urged Warner to promise that she and Rooney would return to the cast as quickly as possible.

The shooting would take over two months, and Warner advised Wolfe that, whatever happened, Olivia must be available in Hollywood by December 17 at the latest, but he promised to free her for the New York production that was to take place afterward. On November 28, Wolfe finally yielded to Warner's entreaties (and no doubt bribes) and between planes rushed over to the theater and had Olivia sign the contract that would launch her on her career. Nevertheless, Olivia held the contract back for five full days before sending it to Hollywood, advising its dispatch by telegram. She knew how to tease.

Indeed, by this act, Olivia showed that as a mere eighteen-year-old girl she was able to take on a major studio, force it to wait for her word, and compel it to value her so completely that it would go to any lengths to secure her release. Most actresses would have not been surprised if they had been passed over for a readily available contract player; and, of course, Bette Davis, who had always wanted to play Shakespeare, was waiting ostentatiously in the wings. But Olivia was strengthened by the knowledge that Max Reinhardt and Jack Warner wanted no one else for her part; that Hal Wallis and Henry Blanke agreed; and that she was indeed perfect for it. She cabled the studio from Milwaukee on December 11 that it would be convenient for her to begin work on December 17 and that she hoped transportation arrangements would be made so she could finish her Milwaukee engagement. On December 14, she announced that she would arrive the following day by TWA and would be available for calls at the Highland Hotel in Hollywood.

She quickly moved on arrival with Lilian to an apartment in the imitation French castle known as the Château des Fleurs, an apartment building on Franklin Avenue in the heart of Hollywood. The pretentious edifice had a sunken court, a wishing well, and a sundial. The apartments were high-ceilinged and airy, but very damp and drafty in winter, with tall French windows that could be opened with handles. The hallway was flagged and imposing, yet the address was not considered first-rate, not as grandly pretentious as the Château Elysée that lay slightly to the east of it.

The shooting of the film version of A *Midsummer Night's Dream* had already begun when Olivia joined the cast on December 17. The director was William Dieterle, who had played Brutus in Reinhardt's production of *Julius Caesar* in Berlin in 1920. One of the problems with Dieterle, which drove everyone at the studio to distraction, was that he relied on his wife, an astrologer, for every move he made on the set. If she decided that Mercury was in retrograde, she would not allow him to work that day; if the moon was in Scorpio, he had to change a scene accordingly. Despite the fact that Jack Warner, Henry Blanke, Hal Wallis, and Max Reinhardt combined forces to refuse Mrs. Dieterle admittance to the set, Dieterle declined to do anything until she had reappeared, complete with charts of the positions of the planets, and could tell him what he might do safely.

Reinhardt himself codirected, but he had little knowledge of the cinema and felt uneasy with the restrictions of the sound stage and black-and-white cinematography. It is unfortunate that the silent screen's use of locations had not then been carried over into talkies, because it would have been ideal if *The Dream* could have been shot in an actual forest, augmented with imported trees and plants. Instead, Henry Blanke hired a sophisticated designer named Anton Grot, who created an artificial, spangled forest on two adjoining sound stages. Hal Mohr, the cameraman, recalled years later that the forest was built up all the way to the ceiling, cutting out sufficient light, with the result that the first day's work was invisible on the screen!

As Olivia began work, there were other problems. Reinhardt, used to the theater, hated the idea of beginning work at 8:00 A.M. and insisted on rehearsing the players in the afternoon and evening, laying out the work for Dieterle the following day. In the theatrical rehearsals, Reinhardt had sat with the other players in a semicircle, working out every scene. He hated rehearsing in studio conditions. Nevertheless, he overcame his feelings to guide the actors brilliantly, especially James Cagney as Bottom and Mickey Rooney (again) as Puck. Only Joe E. Brown, as Flute, had a style too broad for Reinhardt to control. As for Olivia, she was perfection itself: Adding an extra edge to her teasing, mocking, energetic Hermia, she simultaneously subdued herself with great instinct to the demands of the camera. Hal Mohr recalled that she had that certain instinct of the fledgling star: She knew how to move in relation to the camera, and which angles were best for her. He could see this young girl looking surreptitiously out of the corner of her eye and knowing exactly where the light was. Henry Blanke told me:

> She seemed so demure and restrained. But all the time, behind that innocent gaze, I could see her watching, watching, she observed everything; when she wasn't required for a scene she would come and look at the other actresses. You felt that she could have taken over any part in the film that she chose.

Jean Muir, who played Helena, told me:

". . . Reinhardt! All right, he was very great, but he never gave any of us a chance to be ourselves. At one stage, I ventured to say, "I think—" and Reinhardt said, "I don't care what you think" and "Just do what I tell you." As for Olivia, she did everything Reinhardt told her, *exactly*, down to the tiniest touch of detail, she knew exactly what she was doing; she was on her way up, and she knew how to take orders like a soldier. . . .

The long hours of shooting were a great strain, but Dieterle was a good director, and Olivia learned from him the discipline, precision, and "centering" necessary for screen acting. At first, she was too conscious of the camera, worrying like so many actresses about her correct angle and whether she would be afflicted by unflattering lighting. The late Hal Mohr told me many years later how she took a keen interest in his camera work, unheard of in young actresses, and that she never took for granted her extraordinary natural beauty. This care for detail and presentation was at the heart of the extreme calculation and thoughtful preparation that were to mark Olivia's whole career. She was conscious of improving her voice, of modulating it to bring out the depths of an emotion. She studied her body movements with the care of a dancer, realizing that even more than on the stage, the body, greatly enlarged by the camera, could be the instrument of total expression of a thought or a feeling. She knew that under the microscopic eye of the lens, the slightest insincerity or miscalculation would be exposed, alienating the public and perhaps finishing her career. She was acutely aware that the young Ross Alexander, who played Demetrius, one of the quartet of lovers in the play, lacked the qualities of potential stardom, and even more fatally knew it. Although not bad-looking, with an acceptable figure, he was devoid of the charm, strength, and directness an audience could hook on to. Between scenes, she would try to console his brooding despair; a few years later, he and his wife would tragically kill themselves in despondency over the failure of his career.

By contrast, Dick Powell, who played the young Lysander, was a cheeky charmer who left no woman untouched and had a bounce and cockiness that enabled him to have a good career as a leading man. Although in love with the young Joan Blondell, he still made token (and futile) passes at Olivia while, in full period costume and reedy tenor voice, practicing numbers composed by Harry Warren for his next musical. Mickey Rooney fascinated Olivia much more: This brilliant young boy even survived a tobogganing accident in which he broke his leg, performing many scenes on a tricycle behind conveniently camouflaging bushes.

During the grueling weeks of shooting under hot lights, sometimes all through Saturday night, Olivia had to struggle to sustain her fitness program. With little sleep, she would rise on Sunday morning and plunge into a range of athletics including swimming, bicycling, riding, and walking. She also indulged in amateur painting. Her mother continued to teach her diction, and she studied Italian, Spanish, and French. Joan was at that time just embarking on a theatrical career, and Olivia spent every moment she could upstaging her sister and putting her nose in the air at any mention of Joan's success. Olivia herself had a dream of pursuing a career in the theater, but her mother had signed her to a binding seven-year contract at Warners' that gave her no choice whatsoever in the parts she would play.

The Beverly Hills premiere of *The Dream* was a very distinguished event, and it was followed by perhaps the most elaborate party in Hollywood history to that date—at the Santa Monica home of Marion Davies, mistress of William Randolph Hearst. The tennis courts adjoining the house were enclosed under a huge square tent of blue canvas, the walls of which were concealed behind painted trellises covered with live vines and flowers. A wooden dance floor occupied the center space, and about this were grouped 100 tables, at which the guests were served an elaborate buffet supper. Two thirty-piece orchestras alternately supplied dance and concert music. The guests were received in the main foyer of the mansion, where their wraps were checked; they were then directed through the living room, drawing room, and library to the double stairway that led to the ground floor and the improvised party room. The tent resembled a bower, where the stars, producers, and directors of Hollywood moved informally through the flower-bedecked tables.

It was a night to remember. And the reviews for both the production and for Olivia were excellent. The problem was that the public was notably indifferent; the extremely artificial presentation and the use of verse was unacceptable in the Middle West and the South, where culture was still unknown, and audiences in those areas often walked out of the theater minutes after the movie began. Perhaps reacting to this, Jack Warner never embarked on a similar venture again, and Irving Thalberg at M-G-M had cause to regret that he had imitated Warner in making *Romeo and Juliet*, with Leslie Howard and Norma Shearer.

  # *Three*

 Through the good offices
of two of her friends, the painters George Dennison and Frank Ingerson, Joan had obtained a letter of introduction to the Australian star
May Robson, who had made her name as a portrayer of kindly but
stern old ladies, much like herself. Soon after, she was to become
world-famous for her vibrant portrait of Aunt Polly in *The Adventures
of Tom Sawyer* on the screen.

At the time Joan's friends wrote to Miss Robson, the star was
preparing a Los Angeles production by Edward Chodorov of the
Broadway play *Kind Lady*, based on a short story, *The Silver Mask*, by
Hugh Walpole. It was about a gentlewoman who invites a ne'er-do-
well artist into her home; the artist gradually takes over her whole life,
introducing his predatory family and reducing her to the role of a
prisoner.

Miss Robson responded with her customary swiftness, summoning
Joan to a meeting with her. Dennison and Ingerson drove Joan to Los
Angeles; and with great trepidation, Joan was brought before the
formidable Australian actress, who agreed to give her a chance.

Determined to make good, Joan threw herself into the *Kind Lady*
rehearsals with great intensity. She listened closely to every word
May Robson spoke; she acquired perfect diction; she learned with

Miss Robson to walk tall, at least on the stage, and overcome her round shoulders; and she learned how to use her fragility, her nervousness, to the best advantage. She received very good reviews in the play; she was on her way.

Lilian was irritated by Joan's success. More than one actress in the family was too much for her to handle. Some months before, Joan had met a young U.S. vice-consul named Edward Anderson, who was on leave from Canada. He was nice-looking and well built, and had a future in diplomacy, but the trouble was that he was looking for a docile, charming wife and not a career girl. Lilian encouraged the platonic affair, feeling strongly that Joan should be married off securely, thus clearing the path for Olivia's rising career. Olivia naturally agreed. Joan became engaged to Anderson, but with grave misgivings now that she was beginning to have a career of her own.

Having done very well on stage in *Kind Lady*, Joan proceeded on a successful tour of the play while Olivia was filming *The Dream*. Since Lilian ignored her, and was devoted to pushing only Olivia, Joan managed to find refuge in something approaching friendship with George Fontaine. He relished the opportunity to put Lilian's nose out of joint by encouraging Joan, and he took Joan's tiny salary and expertly invested it. He was her business manager for many years. Joan emulated Olivia by studying at Max Reinhardt's drama school, but Reinhardt stubbornly refused to recognize her ability as an actress and never pushed her as he had Olivia. She studied diligently, but nobody seemed to feel that she would be in any way an outstanding actress.

Joan was depressed by this, and she had a further setback when her fiancé, Edward Anderson, returned from a visit to Canada in 1935 to cement the details of their forthcoming marriage. Joan, who loved poetry, recited a sonnet by Rupert Brooke to Anderson at a picnic lunch one Sunday at the beach. Anderson, bored by the recitation, told her that she shouldn't trouble her little head with highbrow matters. She broke the engagement on the spot. Already her nature as a strong and individual woman was beginning to show.

At home, Olivia continued to augment her mother's power over Joan. Olivia's money, also invested with George Fontaine, kept all three women at the Château des Fleurs. Mervyn LeRoy, the director, remembers meeting the family at the Château. He was convinced that Joan had as much talent as Olivia, and infuriated Olivia, who worked at Warners' as he did, by telling her so. LeRoy wanted Joan to see Jack Warner and obtain a contract, but neither Lilian nor Olivia would hear of any such thing. LeRoy took Joan under contract instead, and used his influence to get her a small part in her first picture, *No More Ladies*, with Joan Crawford and Franchot Tone. Joan was fascinated by Crawford's extraordinary presence, posture, and carriage, which made up for deficiencies she may have had as an actress. She learned much from watching her.

Neither Olivia nor Lilian would allow Joan to use her own name professionally. In fact, it was a condition of Joan's contracts before approval by George Fontaine that she assume his name—not legally, just theatrically.

Even though Joan had achieved prominent billing in a picture, she was still nothing more than the kid sister at the Château des Fleurs. She had to help Lilian serve tea while mother auditioned Olivia's prospective beaux. She chauffeured Olivia to Warners' over the old Cahuenga Pass; she even had to take lunch to Olivia in her dressing room. However, the alternative to taking care of Olivia's every need was to be left homeless, since Lilian never ceased to remind her that her mother and her sister were keeping her. There seemed to be no hope in the future at all, and it took all of Joan's will not to abandon her family and risk living in poverty. Her part in *No More Ladies* made no impression whatsoever, and she jokingly came to refer to the picture as *No More Parts*.

It was typical of Hollywood at the time that Olivia was rushed into a baseball comedy, *Alibi Ike*, with Joe E. Brown. Olivia was never noted for her sense of humor or for her prowess at comedy, and she yawned her way through the production, wondering if her mother hadn't made a mistake in getting her locked into a Warners' contract. The only relief in an otherwise dreary experience was going to Fullerton, California, to see the Pacific Coast League in training. Olivia learned to pitch, hit, run bases, and do spectacular slides along with the boys; but although her athletic achievements made the experience bearable, she was notably distracted, praying for a better opportunity to come along.

It did not. She next found herself in an equally tiresome concoction called *The Irish in Us*, an assembly-line programmer starring James Cagney. During the shooting of the picture, however, in the spring of 1935, Olivia learned that the studio's most lavish production to date, *Captain Blood*, was in preparation. The pirate story had been devised as a vehicle for Robert Donat, the British star who had made a success as the defiant and courageous hero of a version of *The Count of Monte Cristo*. While the studio awaited the arrival of Donat from Britain, Jean Muir was tested for the part of the Lady Arabella, the pugnacious heroine, along with an unknown young contract player from Australia, Errol Flynn. Oddly, Olivia, whose life was to be enmeshed with Flynn's, had almost met him when she came from Chicago to appear in *The Dream*. The studio had asked her to pose with him for some publicity shots and she had refused.

Jean Muir recalls that she hated doing the test with Flynn, because he would always look contemptuously at her forehead instead of into her eyes, throwing her off-guard and making her fluff her lines. He did the same thing to Anita Louise. But when Olivia, at her own urgent request, made a test on March 28, he did not treat her in a similar way. The moment he saw her, he was captivated; and the moment she saw him, she fell hopelessly and desperately in love with him. She knew nothing of his other self, his dark and sinister side; she saw only his looks: his chestnut hair; his penetrating brown eyes; his chiseled jaw; and his superb, broad-shouldered, narrow-waisted athlete's physique. He had a fresh, electrifying, primitive vitality that bespoke his origins in the pagan world of the South Seas. Although he was Australian-born, he remained Irish in his recklessness and lack of discipline, as well as in his political commitment: Already at that early stage he had been marked down by British Intelligence (MI6) as a sympathizer with the Irish Republican Army.

Contrary to most accounts, several months went by before Hal Wallis or anybody else at the studio made up their minds on casting the picture. Robert Donat dropped out in the late spring of 1935, partly because of his chronic asthma and partly because of an affair with a girl in England who refused to come to America. Olivia was tested again, and so was Bette Davis, who was furious when she learned that, again, as in *A Midsummer Night's Dream*, she had been overruled in favor of Olivia. But not even her most extravagant admirer could see her in the role of a ravishing young beauty able to capture the heart of a gallant privateer.

In May, the production was almost canceled because Jack Warner panicked at news that Cecil B. DeMille was embarking on a rival pirate film entitled *The Buccaneer*, based on the life of Sir Henry Morgan. In June, Leslie Howard and Brian Aherne were ahead in the running, but neither was available, and all attempts to secure Clark Gable and Ronald Colman from M-G-M and Goldwyn, respectively, fell apart. On June 20, in desperation, Wallis (although he recalls the story differently) called for further tests of Flynn with wig and costume. So uncertain was Wallis of the correctness of his choice that on June 27, with production due to start at any minute, he made a last-minute test of Ian Hunter, a staid and unathletic performer who was in every way totally unsuitable.

Wallis was also uncertain about Olivia. She had a badly aligned tooth, and in late July Wallis was sending notes to Henry Blanke complaining about the offending molar: "It looks bad when she smiles. We want her to get this fixed for *Captain Blood* so will you call her in and tell her to do it. There is no reason why she shouldn't do this at her own expense so have her do it. We've been talking about this for a very long time." Olivia obliged and the production got under way.

Olivia's attraction to Flynn gave a genuine warmth and sparkle to their scenes together. She told me:

> The studio was investing in two unknowns, so they had a series of rehearsals on one of the sound stages with just us and the director, Michael Curtiz and the dialogue director, Stanley Logan. Errol and I were very ambitious, we were always there ahead of anybody else. One day after lunch we sat down and we talked and I said, "What do you want from your life?" And he said, "I want success," meaning approval and money, and then he said, "What do you want?" and I said, "I want respect." By that I meant serious work well done.

And that was the difference between them: Flynn wanted to breeze his way into quick money and fame; Olivia wanted to work hard, to be taken seriously by critics, and to graduate quickly from costume drama into serious and intelligent moviemaking.

As for a romance, despite Flynn's entreaties, it was out of the question. Flynn had married the tempestuous and passionate French actress Lili Damita that June in Arizona and she was so fiercely possessive that when Flynn even looked at another woman she would throw all movable objects at him. It was a tortured relationship with only sex as a binding factor, and Flynn was totally unsuited for marriage or for responsibilities of any kind. Olivia deceived herself into thinking that the dangerous, primitive male beauty she was acting with was simply an overgrown schoolboy, cheeky but harmless, coarse-grained but decent at heart. So infatuated was she that she could even overlook the stream of foul words that poured out of Flynn's handsome mouth and the relentless sex drive that had him hoisting up the skirts of available dress extras in his portable dressing room or even (studio scuttlebutt had it) behind the flats.

There were problems all through the production. After the first few days of work, in which Flynn, as Olivia recalls, came in early and dutifully to work, he began to drink at night and tear up the late hours in fights with Lili, showing up the next morning testy and headache-ridden. Wallis sent grumbling notes to the director, complaining about Flynn's "cold" (actually a hangover) and clumsiness in the dueling scenes. He also felt that Olivia suffered from the problems Flynn presented. On August 27, he wrote to Curtiz:

> The little girl, De Havilland, is not as good as she has been in other pictures. She seems to have lost her naturalness, a sparkle, that she had in other pictures. She should be spontaneous, and bright, and light, and [have] a sparkle in her eyes, but in this picture, it doesn't seem to come out. I don't know what it is. Turn her loose in a couple of scenes, and see how she does them, and let that natural spontaneity of hers come out; because it seems now to be depressed and she seems to be "acting" too . . . . The scene between the girl and Errol Flynn should have been much more charming. When she looked up at him and said "You are hardly in a position to have anything to say about that," she should have done it with a twinkle in her eye, and not burning—apparently sore as she did it. I don't know; the whole damn thing seems to be wrong. Let's get some charm and humor into the picture, and some naturalness, and don't let everybody act so much.

Wallis had still another problem: Olivia began to take the matter of her costumes in hand, an action unconscionable in a new actress. On October 11, he wrote to studio manager William Koenig:

> I, personally, told these wardrobe people what she was to wear in the scene . . . she came up here to show me a costume which she was wearing in one of the scenes and brought with her members of the wardrobe department . . . she was to have a heavy traveling cape, much the same as the man's cape which she brought up to my office. This morning, they phoned me from the set that she was ready to work with a beautiful satin cape that made her look as though she were going to an evening party instead of a boat bound for England. This only means that they are now doing a lot of rushing around, getting out the old cape—which is a man's cape and which we will have to use because we don't want to hold up the company.

Olivia's fascination with Flynn increased on location at Laguna Beach, but she was afraid of showing any interest in him, and the moment they left location she would go to her hotel room with her mother and never even join him for dinner. One night there was a big boxing match in New York and Flynn was determined to hear the broadcast. Since he had no radio in his room, he walked into the hotel lobby dressed only in a tattered bathrobe, sank into a chair, and listened in, causing the elderly ladies to flee. Olivia watched him surreptitiously from the stairs, amused, but terrified of joining him.

In the middle of shooting *Captain Blood*, Olivia began tests for another picture, *Anthony Adverse*, based on the novel by Hervey Allen and directed by Mervyn LeRoy.

Shooting began on *Anthony Adverse* on November 16, 1935. Olivia played Angela Giusseppi, the daughter of a Scots merchant's Italian cook, who falls in love with the hero, a foundling adventurer; she becomes an opera singer and a mistress of Napoleon Bonaparte, and the mother of Anthony Adverse's child. But whereas Curtiz had driven Olivia relentlessly to give the best of herself, the small, cigar-puffing, shrewdly humorous LeRoy was like a little Caesar, more intent upon dealing with the action scenes than giving her the care and attention she needed. To make matters worse, the fact that he very much admired Joan greatly irritated Olivia.

Moreover, Olivia did not find Fredric March equipped with the same romantic appeal as Errol Flynn, whom she strongly felt should have played the part of Adverse.

March was somewhat dry and academic as a performer, stiff and lacking in athletic grace and coordination; yet for some reason he never stopped working, always looking awkward and uncomfortable in his roles, as though he wished he were somewhere else. Unlike most stars, he seemed to be ill at ease with himself, probably aware that he lacked the physique and presence necessary in a leading man. In the love scenes, he gave Olivia nothing. He seemed all too conscious of the presence on the set of his wife, the talented Florence Eldridge, who in fact was not jealous by disposition. A fine actress, Miss Eldridge lay very much in the shadow of her husband's career.

Olivia, unhappy with the production as a whole and fretful over the absence of Flynn, once again was miserable at the thought of her long commitment to the studio.

She had several rows with Wallis over her costumes: She insisted they be very low-cut to be historically correct, showing off her beautiful breasts; but Wallis knew that the Breen Office, which controlled movie censorship, would make a fuss, and that there would be further problems in Britain, where the rules were even more strict. He overruled Olivia, and she fretted and fumed.

Also, perhaps in an attempt to bring life to dull lines, she at times became excessively theatrical. Once, when there was a scene between her and Fredric March in which she had to say, "Oh, Anthony, I love you!" and she did not feel anything for March, she forced the line, sounding, as Wallis remarked in a note to Mervyn LeRoy, "as though she were back in *A Midsummer Night's Dream*." One scene in a hay wagon took an excessively long time to shoot, because Olivia was unable to convey the necessary degree of emotion in the sequence. Many close-ups had to be shot again and again because Olivia's eyes were staring blankly at her awkward hero.

Olivia was pleased at the prospect of appearing with Flynn once more in another super-colossal epic, *The Charge of the Light Brigade*, based on a fictitious but entertaining reworking of the story behind the heroic failure of the British cavalry at Balaclava during the Crimean War of the 1850s. Olivia replaced Anita Louise in the part of Elsa Campbell, a beautiful young ingenue in love with two brothers, Flynn and Patric Knowles. The hardest scene Olivia ever had to play was the one in which she had to give a ring back to Flynn, declining her love for him.

But as the production went on, Flynn, who was now more confident and cocky as a star, began to behave badly, deliberately annoying Olivia in return for her continuing to refuse him sexually. She spent much of the picture sketching the sets and characters of the film, and he would often make off with the finished drawings and hide them from her or vulgarly place them in a toilet that was lacking paper. On one occasion, he told her that an insect had settled on her bustle. Naïvely, she turned around, looking for the culprit, but couldn't see anything. Flynn took a very large flyswatter and slapped her with it, then said he must clean up the imaginary mess and wiped it off with a sponge, ruining her gown. He put a green rubber snake in her panties, boiling water in her water cooler, salt and pepper in her ice cream, and nails in her skirt in her clothes closet. At one stage, he released a mouse; the chair that she stood on had one loose leg and collapsed, toppling her over.

These pranks did not amuse Olivia. Although futile because of his marriage, she longed for a genuine feeling of romance to build up; instead, Flynn treated her like a silly girl, and the tough woman and actress in her fiercely resented this. In order to outweigh stories of a feud between them, the studio concocted an entertaining fiction in which, during a fight sequence, Olivia allegedly was struck by a blunt steel weapon glancing from an extra's shoulder and fell into a lake at Sherwood Forest near Los Angeles, from which Flynn rescued her. The story went on: "During the excitement, Flynn's right foot was burned by the explosion of a dynamite cap in the water. It had been placed there by the powderman to give the effect of a bullet hitting close to the boat."

Actually, the real experience of making the film was less colorful but considerably more harrowing. Olivia had to go eighty miles a day in severe heat to the ugly location of the Lasky mesa, where the art department had built a full-scale replica of an Indian fortress, the Chukoti Garrison. Since Joan was out of town, a studio man drove her to this desolate, windswept spot, blazing in summer heat, dry, covered in tumbleweed, and crawling with enormous black tarantulas that a careless foot could easily crush. It was impossible to keep her hair tidy, and her makeup was ruined by windblown dust. She was not consoled by Flynn or his bosom friend David Nevins (later Niven) and their obstreperous knockabout behavior. The screaming matches between the two men and Curtiz made this very Victorian young lady clap her hands to her ears. Indeed, Curtiz spent most of the picture yelling at his male cast and forcing himself against his nature not to terrorize Olivia into floods of theatrical tears.

But no trace of Olivia's discomfiture showed on the screen; once again she looked ravishing and played with great style and charm a part that in other hands would have been hopelessly insipid. The picture was more notable for its vivid spectacle of an ill-fated war than for anything else, but she made a distinct impression nevertheless.

After the picture was over, there was a ball for the British colony in Los Angeles, at the Ambassador Hotel; and Niven called her and asked her to join him, Merle Oberon, whom he was seeing, and Basil and Ouida Rathbone at dinner beforehand, followed by the dance. When she arrived there, the man who had been promised as her date was not present, but Flynn was. She was shocked that he and Niven had engineered this, since the slightest hint of a romance would be fodder for the gossip columnists, especially since Lili Damita was out of the country at the time. Furious with David, Olivia dared not turn on him as at least fifty cameras would catch her in her rage. So she insisted on taking David's arm while Merle Oberon took the other, thus overcoming the problem. During one dance, she allowed herself to join Flynn on the floor and he whispered to her, to her utter dismay, that he was madly in love with her and would divorce Lili to be with her.

She was petrified. There was nothing in the world she would rather do than have an affair with Flynn; she could not resist him. But on the other hand, to be a corespondent in a potential adultery suit would ruin her reputation with the women's clubs and damage her image of sweet innocence forever. With extreme surreptitiousness, she went driving with him in his car late at night to try to reason with him, but she had to fend off his advances and finally gave up and insisted he take her home. They did a radio program together, and after it Flynn asked her to join him on his yacht, but she knew that would be fatal; once they were at sea, she would be unable to control her feelings.

At last, Olivia told Flynn that she simply couldn't see him until he had told Lili the truth. Lili was in Morocco at the time, and Flynn assured Olivia he had written to her. But weeks went by, and it seemed obvious that he had not. Exhausted from the strain of not knowing what was happening, Olivia decided to fly to Vancouver for a vacation and, at the Los Angeles airport before she left, was astonished to see Flynn, who did not see her. He was greeting Lili, who looked ravishing in a blue sharkskin dress and white pumps, and as though it were a scene in a movie she saw them embrace passionately. It was a shock to Olivia; she was close to tears. She loved Flynn still, but she realized her infatuation for him was romantic, hopeless, and doomed.

Joan refused to take seriously Olivia's infatuation with Errol Flynn, and that irritated Olivia. Shrewder than her sister, Joan saw through Flynn and realized that he was worthless; indeed, she had no respect for Olivia in the matter and made her feelings known. Olivia was upset by Joan's failure to appreciate Flynn, and by Joan's constant reminders that Flynn was married and that there wasn't the slightest chance that his possessive wife would ever give him a divorce. Olivia could only retort by reminding Joan that her opinion was of no interest whatsoever, and that she was still a struggling and obscure beginner while Olivia was a star. Living off Olivia, self-protective Lilian insured her meal ticket by flattering Olivia to excess night and day, while at the same time according to Joan not giving her sister the slightest encouragement in her own career.

Perhaps fortunately, it was several months before the studio was able to find a suitable vehicle for Olivia, and she was free from June to November of 1936. It was mentioned in the columns that she had met and become fascinated by a good-looking, thirty-five-year-old English nobleman and automobile enthusiast, the multimillionaire Herman Alfred Stern, Baron Michelham. Michelham was heir to fifteen million pounds and to a title bestowed by King Luis I of Portugal. At eighteen, Herman Michelham had fallen in love with a middle-aged woman, who agreed to marry the boy if his father settled one million pounds sterling on her and twenty thousand pounds a year. Afterward, young Lord Michelham was very unhappy with his wife and alleged that he had been forced to marry her because she was involved with his father. There was a tremendous court case over this in which the executors of the estate sued Herman Michelham for the family fortune, claiming that he and his wife had been involved in depriving them. Michelham won the case.

To this day, Lord Michelham denies that he even met Olivia. However, the columns in both Britain and America mentioned their alleged romance persistently.

Joan was appearing in a play called *Call it a Day* at the El Capitan Theater in Hollywood while Olivia was appearing in the screen version. Both productions took place in November 1936, although the shooting of the picture ran past the end of the play's run. Joan signed a contract with Mervyn LeRoy and Jesse L. Lasky, who jointly admired her in the stage production. She was taken on by the Kahn-Green Agency and later by Zeppo Marx, brother of Groucho, Chico, and Harpo, who had retired from the screen. LeRoy and Lasky sold Joan's contract to RKO-Radio Pictures, Lasky remaining with the company and LeRoy backing out. She agreed to sign on condition that there be no reference anywhere to her being Olivia's sister.

At the same time, she, Lilian, and Olivia moved to a new address, 2337 Nella Vista Street in the Los Feliz district of Los Angeles. It was an ordinary, modest, ivy-covered house with a small front yard in a pleasant but not particularly fashionable neighborhood not far from the Cecil B. DeMille estate and Basil Rathbone's imposing residence on Los Feliz Boulevard; it is virtually unchanged today—though the ivy has gone.

Joan's first picture at RKO was *Quality Street*, directed by George Stevens and starring Katharine Hepburn. Joan was seen only briefly in the role of Charlotte Parratt, virtually a walk-on; her chief memory of the picture was of Katharine Hepburn, delightfully bossy and opinionated, ordering elaborate picnic baskets to be brought in during an afternoon break, which greatly irritated the producer and director. Kate would talk ten-to-the-dozen while the cast dared not utter a word. Joan looked ravishing in the period costumes, but she was not mentioned by more than a handful of reviewers. During the shooting, she complained constantly that she had to borrow wardrobe, car, and even beaux from her sister, and that Olivia made her painfully aware of her dependence. "We had to share the same bathroom!" she groaned to a reporter. Normally, this would have been in order, but it is easy to see that the extreme tension between the two sisters resulted in mutual resentments of territorial imperatives and priorities.

Joan never stopped working at RKO. Her second movie, *The Man Who Found Himself*, offered her her first starring opportunity; she played a flying field nurse—a real-life role she was to occupy in World War II—in love with a physician (John Boles) who has been barred by the AMA for alleged malpractice. The mistake Joan made in playing the part was that she imitated Katharine Hepburn's voice, and this seemed absurd in her case. But her performance was touching and earned her the respect of the studio top echelon. Kate Cameron in the *New York Daily News* wrote: "Miss Fontaine is as blonde as Miss de Havilland is dark, but she has the same charm and poise which makes her sister one of the most promising of the younger actresses in Hollywood." Olivia made no comment.

In 1937, Joan made *You Can't Beat Love*, about a small-town playboy, played by Preston Foster, who has an affair with a mayor's daughter with whom he is competing in a political campaign. The *New York Mirror* described Joan as the sole distinction of the movie: "She is pretty, has a winning smile, and gives an unsensational performance in a role which demands nothing more." Unfortunately for Joan, she had to swallow a bitter pill: The picture opened in New York on the lower half of the bill with Olivia's *Call It a Day*.

While Olivia prepared for her next picture, the comedy *It's Love I'm After* with Bette Davis and Leslie Howard, in the spring of 1937, she heard to her dismay that Walter de Havilland was coming to California. He arrived in San Francisco in May, when she was in midproduction. Joan was shooting *You Can't Beat Love*. Neither girl wanted to see him—Olivia because of her feeling that he had neglected her for Joan; Joan because of her terror of his incestuous feelings for her.

On May 17, 1937, Walter, clearly suffering from mental degeneration, wrote to the manager of RKO Studios, stating, "Ill effects to Joan's career will surely follow if she continues to ignore her own father. Certainly in Japan would her name suffer; parents there are always first in their children's thoughts." He then went on to say he was enclosing an original "sketch" (British for "playlet") on which he was pleased to give the studio first offer.

The manuscript he enclosed is a very curious effort. It is a playlet about incest entitled *A Hundred Years Apart*. It begins with a scene in San Francisco where Walter, just off the boat from Japan, is reading in the *San Francisco Examiner* for May 15, 1937, that Joan has been frequently in San Francisco to "be with her father as much as possible." De Havilland adds that "Really, she considers her father out of date." He then goes on to list the dramatis personae as himself; Joan; Pat, a blonde from Hollywood; and Joan again, disguised as a chaperon.

In the first scene, Joan is seen reading a letter from her father, the gist of which is that since she will not "relieve" his lonely evenings, she must find a substitute. She is to engage a flat and install a Hollywood blonde of the same age with a chaperon. "Appreciation of classic poetry [is] a desirable feature." Joan says that since father is so old-fashioned, she must try to cure him.

In the second scene, Joan and her father reach the flat, where "articles of feminine use" have been deposited. The father gives the concierge of the building money not to interfere with the "proceedings." Nervous about what is going to happen, Joan makes herself up as Pat's chaperon, disguising herself as a woman of fifty-five. They enter the apartment that evening, and Pat tells Walter that her chaperon doesn't count and is there for appearance's sake only.

Walter shows them into the bedroom and Joan removes her disguise behind closed doors. Later, Pat goes into the kitchen with a bathing suit and an apron on; Joan in disguise inspects the dinner table and goes to the room, where she removes all clothes except her bathing dress, veil, gloves, muff, and beach slippers. Pat emerges with the soup, and Joan joins them, both women still in bathing suits. Father tries to discuss poetry with Pat, but her answers are slangy and show complete ignorance. Walter gives her rhymes and a limerick to read ("There was an old man of Kentucky . . ."). Pat dances on the table, throws cushions, and kisses father "for Joan."

Now bath time arrives for Walter. He prepares the bath and is singing in his tub when the girls throw eggs through the transom, Pat standing on a chair. Afterward, Walter finds both girls settled in his bed, and on it are Joan's instructions, which read, "Practice fait accompli and prove possession is nine points of the law." But no sooner does Walter attempt to obey his daughter's instructions than the two women order him out of the room. He seizes a hairbrush and threatens early Victorian treatment in return for their unwillingness. Both ignore the warning, but after one lash of the brush, Pat flees shrieking. Joan receives a stroke and also leaves the room. The two girls bolt Walter into his own bedroom with nails.

At breakfast, they tease him with even scantier bathing suits, and Walter is also wearing trunks. After breakfast, Pat produces Joan's final instructions, which order a "double dose of Victorian special." Whatever the "special" is, the girls yield to it. All ends well, with Joan's true identity revealed.

This crude, incestuous farce caused shock waves in the studio and fed the fires of those executives, led by Ned Depinet in New York, who had no enthusiasm for Joan. On June 19, 1937, Robert Sparks, one of the production chiefs, wrote his colleague Sam Briskin that he had received a letter in the form of "a confused and rather bitter lament" from one Walter de Havilland and didn't even want to mention the playlet to Joan. He added, "It seems rather bad to have anything like this passed around concerning one of our players for whom we have great hopes. Do not allow any publicity." Briskin returned the material with a note saying, "We regret that there is no purpose for which the studio could use the manuscript submitted."

It seems incredible that a patent lawyer and representative of the Japanese government would have descended to such semipornography, but it is clear that the strains of mental and moral weakness that emerged in the de Havilland character through inbreeding were working their way out in him in his sixties.

Olivia longed to share her feelings with Bette Davis, her costar in *It's Love I'm After*, because Bette's own father had been a patent lawyer and had been mentally disturbed. But Bette, perhaps because she resented Olivia taking her parts in *The Dream, Captain Blood*, and *Anthony Adverse*, refused, according to Olivia, to talk to her for the entire length of shooting. They were soon to be friends, but certainly not yet.

In 1937, in contrast with Olivia, Joan was enjoying working in pictures. RKO, under production chief Pan Berman, was a much more relaxed and informal studio than Warners', and there was an atmosphere of friendliness that spread out from its genial chief executive. Joan wasn't fazed by the fact that she had only a plain, modestly furnished dressing room, very far from the luxurious on-set quarters of Katharine Hepburn and Ginger Rogers. She found pleasure in the relaxed RKO schedules—schedules that were perhaps too relaxed, since the studio constantly floundered in financial problems and was threatened by take-overs so often that the employees frequently wondered if they would be able to collect their weekly paychecks.

Joan rose early each morning, dropped Olivia off at Warners'—a long and complicated drive in those days from Los Feliz to the Cahuenga Pass to Burbank—and then drove to RKO in Hollywood. She enjoyed the bustling, gossipy atmosphere of the makeup room, presided over by the jolly Mel Berns, who kept up a rat-a-tat conversation about everything and everybody in town while he was applying the makeup and while costume assistants came in with the dresses that the performers would wear that day. Full of fun and laughter, Joan was entirely at home with the RKO family.

The effortless sparkle of the Astaire-Rogers musicals reflected the atmosphere in which they were made. But a tiny revolution took place in the summer of 1937 when it was announced that Ginger Rogers would not be making the next Fred Astaire picture, *A Damsel in Distress*, directed by George Stevens. According to Astaire, the reason was that Ginger was tired of simply being an adjunct or second fiddle to him. But according to Vernon Harbin, who was on the studio staff at the time, Astaire himself wanted a change because he was beginning to feel a need to assert himself, to prove he could carry a picture on his own. In fact, whenever possible, Fred had introduced solo dances that were far beyond Ginger's range.

Ruby Keeler was mentioned as a possible partner for Fred—an absurd idea, since she was the worst star dancer in the business, with large feet that she would anxiously watch lest she trip up, and an excessively coy manner that was already dated by 1937. There was also some talk of Jessie Matthews, a British star of great charm and gaminesque appeal. But finally it was decided to have the picture created almost entirely in solo dances for Fred, and Joan was cast as the British girl, with only one sequence in which she got to dance with Fred.

Joan was petrified at the prospect of that one scene; her level of dancing was scarcely beyond that of shipboard fox-trots and school ballet lessons. She had to go through training under a brother of Ruby Keeler's, but the results were poor and the studio finally abandoned all thought of having her tapdance in the picture. Instead, she was to do one dance at the RKO ranch near Malibu under the direction of choreographer Hermes Pan. With great kindness and sweetness of character, he guided her through the routine and was far too polite to comment on her inadequacy. She was painfully aware of it anyway, constantly feeling the tension of someone who was stepping into Ginger Rogers's dancing shoes. She had difficulty timing her movements to the Gershwin music, and was so nervous at one run-through that she even started to lead.

In other respects, she was well cast in the movie as a member of the British aristocracy, and she was able to make suggestions to the art director to improve the British costumes and decor—despite the fact that she had never been to London. She found the director of the film, George Stevens, very attractive, but he failed to respond to her, which made her feel even worse.

Olivia was notably rude about Joan's efforts as a danseuse. She didn't help matters by saying to a columnist, "My sister has decided to become an actress too. It has ruined the close-knittedness of our family life. It's bad enough, at first to have me an actress, with hours upset and schedules changed; now it seems as if when I have a moment to rest she is at the studio, and the sweet closeness of our relationship has slipped away." The "sweet closeness" was, of course, a figment of Olivia's imagination.

Joan's efforts in *A Damsel in Distress* left everyone at RKO unimpressed—indeed, Ned Depinet, the accomplished New York head of RKO, was convinced Joan was a dead loss on the screen. And the reviews didn't help. Joan had to read such remarks as that made by the powerful Regina Crewe in the *New York Journal*: "The missing link between a smash Astaire hit and just good film fun is . . . Ginger Rogers!" Kate Cameron in the *New York Daily News* stated: "An Astaire picture isn't itself without Ginger." And Frank S. Nugent in the *New York Times* delivered the death blow: "What more can one ask of in an Astaire show? Miss Rogers? Don't be a pig!"

This was a calamity for Joan, made worse by the fact that neither Lilian nor Olivia showed her the slightest sympathy. She was humiliated by their indifference to her plight, and there were many violent scenes at Nella Vista. She went through further humiliation when neither George Fontaine nor her mother would buy her a dress for the Pantages Theatre premiere of *A Damsel* and she had to be dressed up by studio wardrobe. Moreover, her escort was a young man who was dating Olivia. And when Joan started to dance with Astaire, a woman was heard stating loudly, "Isn't she awful!"

Olivia at the time was making the epic *Gold Is Where You Find It*, in which George Brent stood in inadequately for Errol Flynn. It was a story of California in the 1870s, the clash between the wheat farmers and the hydraulic miners who were cutting a path through the agricultural regions.

Whereas Olivia, dazzled by Errol Flynn, had just about tolerated the drudgery of playing insipid young women totally unlike herself in the previous historical epic romances, she had now lost patience entirely with the kind of formula material in which the studio was casting her. But she rather enjoyed the town of Weaverville where the picture was made. She was amused by the town's ramshackle, meandering inn—the fact that she had to carry her own luggage to her room because there were no bellhops; that the taps coughed an occasional spurt of rusty water; and that if she wanted a cup of coffee, she had to go to the kitchen and fix it for herself. Stars in those days were accustomed to being treated like royalty, so she couldn't help laughing when she entered the hotel café for the first time and the blond waitress with piled-high hair walked over and vigorously pumped her hand, saying, "Hi, Olivia! Gee, we're glad to see you! I'm off in ten minutes and if you want a second helping you're going to have to ask the cook!"

Much of the time, Olivia was housed in a tent city twelve miles from Weaverville and sixty miles from the nearest major township; the location could only be reached by a twisting one-way mountain road along which portable showers, electric generators, refrigeration units, and dressing rooms had to be shipped. If a local citizen had embarked on the road in his jalopy or truck, the entire procession, trembling on the brink of a precipice, had to back down laboriously to make way for him.

The tent city was arranged in four parallel rows of twenty tents each, with streets between the rows. Inside the tents, studio propmen set down redwood flooring on the earth. Olivia had a tent to herself, with private shower and washroom; an army of hairdressers, makeup and costume people occupied the tents around her. She arose at 5:00 each morning, breakfasted at 5:30, and began shooting at 6:00.

Unseasonable fog and days of rain proved a constant irritation. Olivia was annoyed not only by the meaningless dialogue she had to speak but by having to cope with the difficult roads, the downpours, and the chilly nights without proper heating. Other scenes were shot at Perris, California, where the temperature was 108° that summer; because the dry heat caused moisture to disappear from faces and arms, the actors playing workers in the fields had to be sprayed with water to provide realistic perspiration.

Hal Wallis was as fretful over Olivia's makeup as Sam Briskin was over Joan's costuming. He was critical, too, of her performance, telegraphing Curtiz on September 10, "Lips are much too red, lower lip is much too heavy, lines were read too schoolgirlish. Don't let this girl play it like a high-school play." Makeup was always a problem in Technicolor films, and Olivia was irritated when Wallis called to tell her that he was angry she had deliberately changed her makeup on location. She emphatically told him that he was wrong. He fired off an angry memorandum to the Westmores, makeup specialists, saying, "We were congratulating ourselves last week after seeing her closeup test here and thinking it was the best Technicolor makeup and the most beautiful shot that we had ever seen. Now we find that the girl gets on location, works in a few scenes and we have to make retakes because the stuff is so bad. Personally, I can't begin to figure out why these things happen, but there must be a reason for it somewhere." Many shots had to be redone, which stretched Olivia's patience to the limit. She was even recalled to the studio from hundreds of miles away to have new tests taken, which were shipped back to the cameraman with severe instructions that he match their quality.

Olivia, who yearned for intelligent roles that would bring out her capacities as an actress, was furious over these production trivialities. Many female stars, concerned only with their beauty, hair, makeup, figure, and costuming, would have mooned for hours over possible flaws in their presentation on the screen. Olivia, confident in her beauty, wanted only to bring some realism and depth to the naïve and empty characterizations given to heroines in those days.

While shooting *Gold Is Where You Find It*, Olivia had to memorize a whole new part for the most ambitious picture ever made by Warners' up to that time, the role of Maid Marian in *The Adventures of Robin Hood*. Gone was all hope of even a brief respite after the grueling ordeal in the mountains and scorched plains of *Gold Is Where You Find It*. Robust and athletic though she was, and at the height of her youth, Olivia felt herself being slowly but surely worn down as she sat up night after night with her new pages of dialogue.

There was still a further problem to face. Margaret Lindsay, who played an ingenue in the picture with an excessive amount of wriggling and squirming, proved to be very distracting, and it was rumored that Lindsay was casting longing glances in Olivia's direction. All in all, Olivia gave a sigh of exhausted relief when the entire deadly rigmarole of this film at last ground to a halt.

But there was a worse ordeal still ahead of her as she embarked for wardrobe tests for *Robin Hood* and traveled north to shoot the picture at Bidwell Park in Chico, California. Her pleasure at working with Flynn again—she still held a candle for him—was undercut by the presence of Lili Damita, who was there through much of the shooting, jealously keeping an eye on Olivia. Moreover, Flynn had started to drink heavily and was more uncontrollable than usual.

A consolation was the location itself: Bidwell Park had been selected by the director, William Keighley, some weeks before; it was the nearest thing to a fairy-tale version of the real Sherwood Forest in which the Robin Hood legend was set, filled with live oaks, sycamores, wild vines (not normally found in England), ferns, and rich plantings of ash trees. The art director had augmented the forest with plaster of paris trees and rocks and had festooned telephone poles with artificial leaves. Because the grass and brush had been removed due to fire hazard, artificial grass had to be put down and scores of bushes, ferns, and flowers planted only for the length of shooting to satisfy the local fire laws. A great camp was built, with a setting of an outdoor feast centered on the largest living oak tree in the world, 92 feet high, with a spread of 149 feet and a trunk 28.6 feet in circumference, named after the British botanist Sir Joseph Hooker.

The units were housed in four enormous tents set up near the gates of the park. Each morning at 5:00 A.M., Olivia would leave her lodging in a local inn to make her way to the great marquee where the hairdressing and makeup departments, with rows of brilliantly lit dressing tables, were waiting for her and the rest of the cast. She would then walk to another tent where she was dressed in the marvelous clothes designed for her by Milo Anderson. Unexcited though she was by her dialogue, she was as eager and curious as ever, and the propman, the cockney Limey Plews, recalls that she insisted on going through the prop shops looking at the collection of 10,000 arrows, long and crossbows, battleaxes, lances, daggers, maces, lutes, armor, imitation ducks, twelfth-century furniture, plates, knives and forks, and stables of trained horses.

Olivia had youth on her side; her many vexations and frustrations over the issues of Michelham, Flynn, and motion-picture scripts never became totally overwhelming. After all, she was now earning a great deal of money; the fan mail was pouring in; and the setting of Bidwell Park was an inspiration. What was more, she could feel her Norman ancestry stirring in her veins as she enacted or saw enacted many scenes that might have been part of the lives of the earlier de Havillands.

The atmosphere darkened as the film went on. Hal Wallis, restless and irritable as ever, was annoyed by what he took to be excessive slowness and lack of macho drive and vigor in Keighley's direction; and he much regretted that he had not allowed Michael Curtiz to finish *Gold Is Where You Find It* first and then proceed with the direction of this new picture, which called for Curtiz's special touch. The cast—Flynn, Olivia, and the others—all resented the fact that Keighley lay under a cloud.

As for Flynn, his behavior grew worse and worse, and when he was drunk he turned into a monster who allegedly would make love to any living thing. Ann Robinson, who stood in for Olivia, remembers an extraordinary scene in which Errol tried to break down the door of Olivia's room and rape her. It was only with the greatest effort that Jim Fleming, Flynn's devoted double and friend, managed to control him; tough as she was, Olivia was frightened by the terrible outbreak of rage and violence on the other side of the door.

Fog and rain delayed shooting that fall, and Flynn's lateness on the set and inability to work some days, and Keighley's meticulous slowness, put the movie well behind schedule. Back in Hollywood, Errol began rewriting dialogue, much to Hal Wallis's annoyance; and when Olivia approved the changes in a scene in her castle chamber, the producer became utterly furious. One welcome break in the strain and monotony of the shooting was the big archery tournament shot at Busch Gardens in Pasadena. Olivia was fascinated by the reproduction of the twelfth-century scene, with scarlet banners flying, a rich gold-trimmed canopy, and the gallant contestants aiming at their targets.

Nevertheless, stimulated though she was, Olivia was frequently tired, even worn out during the shooting; and when Keighley was fired by Wallis and replaced by Curtiz, she exploded and demanded Keighley be restored. But Wallis was adamant and when Olivia made the mistake of going to Jack Warner over his head, her effort boomeranged and she was ignominiously ordered back to work. She played the banquet-hall sequence in Nottingham Castle with barely simulated enthusiasm, and even the captivating sight of Flynn striding into the hall with a deer slung over his handsome shoulders couldn't raise her pulse at that stage.

The production, at first so glamorous, now seemed merely interminable. What was more, even when it was over, there were tedious retakes to be made and close-ups to be cut in, always the bane of even the most hardworking and resolute actors. Dubbing, too, was a problem, particularly because of the constant array of natural sounds in the film, from birdsong to hooves to the rustle of trees in the wind and the thudding of arrows into their targets.

The resulting movie was magnificent, however, and a personal triumph for both Flynn and Olivia. There was no question that it was tormenting for Joan to realize that Olivia had become an absolutely first-rank star with this production. Nor was Joan consoled by the script the studio sent her for the Kiplingesque epic *Gunga Din*, in which she had to play the useless part of a planter's daughter in India—the picture was an imitation of *The Charge of the Light Brigade*. Fortunately, she didn't yet realize that she would be doomed temporarily by that otherwise much admired production, to be shot in the spring of 1938.

Meanwhile, so relentless was the studio pressure that Olivia, whose only thought now, the columnists insisted, was to get to England to marry Lord Michelham, had to go right ahead and make a trivial comedy, *Four's a Crowd*, with Flynn, in which she had nothing to do but speak foolish lines and envy the broader but more finished comedy talent of Rosalind Russell. While, in a desperate effort to emulate her sister, Joan trained under Max Reinhardt at his Hollywood Drama School and understudied the actress Margo in the school's production of *Faust*, Olivia more or less walked through *Four's a Crowd*.

Lilian made the bookings for the trip to Britain. Olivia could barely sleep, thinking of the journey ahead, and on February 28 she did the unthinkable and walked off the picture at 6:45 P.M., stating that she couldn't work one minute longer. Hal Wallis was beside himself, but Olivia would not come back. Moreover, Flynn announced, along with Olivia, that he would leave the picture the moment it was done and would refuse to make any retakes. Therefore, all additional shots were squeezed into a handful of days, and Olivia, her weight down to less than a hundred pounds, her face drawn, and her stomach afflicted with possible preulcerous pain, had close to a breakdown.

So serious was her condition that the studio doctor, W. R. Meals, wrote to Wallis that if Olivia continued to overwork she could be rendered permanently ill. A cardiogram showed severe arrhythmia and fibrillation that could result in permanent myocardial damage. She also had low blood pressure and was anemic. He advised that she be spared as much energy expenditure as possible, and not have to work long hours at night.

The studio ignored this instruction, and Olivia responded with continual lateness and uncooperativeness and again refused to work at night. The studio manager, Tenny Wright, was so distracted by her behavior that he went over everyone's head and sent a note to Jack Warner reading: "I suggest this matter be turned over to the Actors'

Guild to have them police Miss Havilland." Jack Warner told Wright to talk to Max Arnow of the casting office and have him inform Olivia "that when she has a noon call, we have the right and privilege to work her for eight hours."

It was only when Olivia's agent, Leland Hayward, screamed at Jack Warner on the telephone that the studio relented slightly, but Olivia was in very bad shape when the production ended.

Since the breakup of her engagement to the young diplomat Edward Anderson, Joan had been without a regular beau; but she now became interested in the fading Hollywood star Conrad Nagel, an idol of her childhood.

Nagel was born in 1897 in Keokuk, Iowa, son of the dean of music at Highland Park College in Des Moines. In his childhood, he had displayed oratorical gifts and was an admirable singer and actor who emerged in stock companies with great success. Exceedingly handsome, with wavy gold hair, intense blue eyes, and a chiseled profile, Nagel was immediately successful on Broadway, and made a great hit in *Forever After*, with Alice Brady, a play that made him a national star. He married a flautist's daughter, Ruth Helms, in 1919. He was a keen spokesperson for Equity and fought vigorously for improved union conditions for actors.

Nagel went on to make an impression in motion pictures, his photogenic face and perfect physique surviving the cruel eye of the camera. Cecil B. DeMille was delighted with him and cast him in *Fool's Paradise* as a man suffering from blindness. He was cast by M-G-M, over the authoress's objections, as the hero of Elinor Glyn's extravagantly romantic *Three Weeks*; and as a result of his triumph in the part, he emerged high in the M-G-M roster of stars.

However, he fought with Louis B. Mayer because he was known to be working for better union conditions, and he helped to form the Academy of Motion Picture Arts and Sciences. In a major controversy over the academy's foundation, in which Nagel was overruled in taking the view that it should represent labor interests, Mayer smashed Nagel's career. He hated Nagel for having strengthened the unions, and Nagel's wife blamed him bitterly for his fall into obscure motion pictures. Nevertheless, he sustained his downfall with grace and style.

When Joan met him, Nagel was just divorced, a man whose only consolations were his money, his enduring looks and physique, his circle of loyal friends, and his belief in the Christian Science teachings of Mary Baker Eddy. Joan greatly respected him for his courage and steadfastness in supporting the cause of struggling actors. There is no doubt that he was very devoted to his daughter and was afraid that his affair with Joan might undermine his strong personal relationship with the growing girl. Joan's problem was that she still was secretly in love with George Stevens and tortured by George's affair with Ginger Rogers. It was scarcely the best possible basis for a relationship, but once more Lilian encouraged the match, and Olivia casually agreed that it would be good for Joan to marry Nagel.

When Nagel invited Joan to northern California on a duck hunt, a fashionable sport of those days, Joan accepted eagerly, happy to get away from the tension-ridden atmosphere at Nella Vista. They stayed at the Santa Barbara residence of the Anheuser-Busch beer heir Gert von Gontard. One night, when Joan got up to go to the bathroom, the tank broke, and after struggling futilely with the washer, she knocked on Nagel's door. He gallantly turned plumber, then escorted her back to her room and decided quite coolly it was time to relieve her of her virginity.

It was an unpleasant experience. Joan suffered pain that was more severe than normal for first intercourse. The pain recurred almost as intensely every time Nagel made love to her on the duck-hunting trip. Back in Los Angeles, she went to see a doctor, who told her that she had a cyst on her ovaries and that until it was removed she would not be able to enjoy physical relations. For some reason she does not explain, Joan did not go ahead and have the operation. For the infatuated Conrad Nagel, it must have been unpleasant to know that Joan would not be able to have pleasure in bed. He was a kind and considerate man and it must have dawned on him that there wasn't much future in the situation.

He was worried still more as time went on about his daughter, Ruth, and this combination of feelings made him tell Joan he had to go east. She was disappointed, and Lilian was even more upset; now she would have Joan on her hands indefinitely. Nagel simply drifted away, and the affair fizzled out. Joan was alone once more.

# *Four*

In March 1938, Olivia
and her mother boarded the French liner *Normandie* under the assumed names of Mrs. George and Lavinia Halliday, en route to England from New York. The columnists still insisted the purpose of the
trip was to see Lord Michelham. When they arrived in England,
Lilian and Olivia tried futilely to dodge the press. Even then, Lord
Michelham denied he had ever met Olivia and insisted that all he
knew of their affair was to be found in the columns. Olivia was worn
out, so thin and gaunt that her condition was widely commented on.

She proceeded on a tour of villages, feeling wrung out and miserable, while Joan was equally depressed in Hollywood. Jules Levy, of
RKO, said Joan had "very little promise" and that the reaction of the
salesmen to her was unfavorable and that she should be dropped.
Executive Leo Spitz wrote in another memo, "She has had ample
opportunity to prove herself: I doubt whether she will ever make the
grade." An attempt was made to cast her in a film called *Smashing the
Rackets*, but on June 7 she flatly refused to go for her wardrobe and
was suspended. Frances Mercer played the part instead.

Apparently producer Pandro Berman took pity on Joan, because
she did go into *Gunga Din* after all on June 22. Shooting continued
until September 24, and a note in the studio files shows that she was

still paying her income to George Fontaine, who retained power of attorney as her business manager.

Joan traveled with her costars Cary Grant, Douglas Fairbanks, Jr., and Victor McLaglen to the same windswept location Warners' had used for *The Charge of the Light Brigade*. The temperature was well over 100° by late morning each day and the winds blew a blinding dust, aggravating Joan's sinus problem and causing her severe headaches and streaming eyes. It was a rough shoot: A tent city was set up, and the plumbing and electricity were primitive; the sweat ran down Joan's face, ruining her makeup; the period costumes were heavy and clung to her stickily; she had to rise at dawn each morning and work until well into the evening. It was difficult to play the part of a cool, genteel daughter of a tea planter, a girl in love with soldier of fortune, Douglas Fairbanks, Jr., without showing her extreme discomfort.

She was bored and irritated by many things, but she was able to sustain herself because of her strong attraction to George Stevens. Bereft of Nagel, Joan was still unable to obtain from Stevens any more interest than he gave to arranging a battle line or setting up an elaborate prop. Her frustration was added to by the fact that Stevens was unbearably slow and would make take after take of a scene until everyone was exhausted. He was of Indian background, and sometimes he would simply sit, impassive, stocky, imperturbable, and the cast would wonder when he would give them some direction.

Pan Berman finally snapped. The financial backers of this troubled studio were screaming because of the dragged-out shooting, and Pan, who hated confrontations of any kind, had to go up to Lone Pine and demand that Stevens speed things up. Stevens flared; there was an unpleasant quarrel in front of the cast and Stevens threatened to walk off the picture. But somehow the matter was smoothed over.

Joan was lonely on location. Cary Grant was often visited by his girlfriend, the beautiful Phyllis Brooks, an edgy, difficult actress with a sharp tongue whom most people didn't like and whose career never went very far; and Douglas Fairbanks restlessly missed Marlene Dietrich, with whom he had had a prolonged affair. These tensions among the leading players took a heavy toll on Joan, and when she returned to Hollywood she was in a very bad temper indeed.

Meanwhile, Olivia had returned from England, more rested now—she had slept most of the way back on the ship. On the voyage to England, she had met Brian Aherne, the handsome, tall, blond actor who had appeared with her in a film called *The Great Garrick* just before *Gold Is Where You Find It*, and now that she was back, they dated occasionally. But there was still no attraction between them and, perhaps expressing a certain sense of humor, he began to date Joan instead.

Olivia, with her customary strength and resolution, decided to rebuild her life from scratch. In the beautiful early summer of 1938, she went to the beach; acquired a suntan; learned to ride a surfboard; played tennis and Ping-Pong, scrambled to the top of the navy's giant twin-motored planes at San Pedro; sped down to Ensenada, Mexico, to go shark fishing with Victor Jory; and even, to appease the studio, played a set of lawn tennis with her sister and Conrad Nagel.

She also walked through another meaningless film, *Hard to Get*, and forced herself to do *Wings of the Navy*, an elaborate air-force recruiting propaganda picture, mostly shot at Pensacola and San Diego. It was a Hearst production, made jointly for the newspaper tycoon's Cosmopolitan Pictures, and had many spectacular scenes involving flights of giant navy multimotored patrol and bombing planes. Olivia was disappointed that a minor illness prevented her from going to Pensacola, Florida, on the special *Wings of Navy* train. She recovered quickly enough to fly there, but the reason she didn't finally go is conveyed in a telegram from Hal Wallis to the director Lloyd Bacon in Florida on July 8, 1938: "Please try definitely to do without De Havilland there as will save considerable money." This cost-cutting meant that she missed her opportunity to make the journey and the studio publicists had to work overtime to make up stories about her adventures on location—winning a swimming contest and judging a beauty contest among other fictitious episodes.

During the shooting, Olivia became friendly with the famous stunt aviator Paul Mantz, former adviser to Amelia Earhart and close friend of Howard Hughes. He told her, to her great fascination, of Hughes's extraordinary exploits in the air. Indeed, while Olivia was shooting *Wings of the Navy* that July, Hughes was making his famous round-the-world flight. He had just gotten over a disastrous affair with Bette Davis and, insecure in his personal relationships and afflicted with recurring problems of impotence despite his macho image, he had nervously returned to a relationship with Katharine Hepburn. On July 10, he began the round-the-world flight by dipping his wings in a romantic gesture over Hepburn's country home at Old Saybrook at the mouth of the Connecticut River. He flew over Boston, Nova Scotia, Cape Breton Island, and Newfoundland to Paris, where he arrived a record sixteen hours and thirty-eight minutes after leaving

New York. He flew on in difficult conditions to Moscow, then to Yakutsk in northern Siberia, to Fairbanks, Alaska, and Scranton, Pennsylvania, back to New York, having made the entire trip in three days, nineteen hours, and seventeen minutes.

Seven million New Yorkers welcomed him home; but Hughes, chronically shy, slipped through the official greeter Grover Whelan's fingers, evaded the beloved Mayor Fiorello La Guardia, and rushed to Katharine Hepburn's Turtle Bay town house. However, when he saw the great crowd of press men at her front door, he asked the taxi driver to take him to the Drake Hotel. The next day, the reluctant hero was given a ticker-tape parade through the city; a million people jammed the sidewalks and gathered in the windows and on the rooftops to greet him. Another great reception followed in Houston; his father's town was, if possible, even more ecstatic than New York.

Stimulated by Mantz, Olivia followed Hughes's progress with fascination. She longed to meet him, but she knew that he was almost certainly in love with Katharine Hepburn and she dared not hope that there would be any chance of starting a relationship. She may also have heard, via the studio grapevine, that Hughes had a sexual problem, and she may have decided to avoid getting herself into yet another complicated situation. Mantz, playing matchmaker, tried to figure how best to bring Olivia and Hughes together, probably feeling that while Davis and Hepburn were challenging, Hughes would be taken with the fact that Olivia was intensely feminine. There was no immediate meeting arranged; but Mantz remained bent upon arranging it.

That September, Olivia was offered a part in a Paramount production, *Kentucky*, but she refused it just hours before Jack Warner, not knowing of her decision, declined to loan her. Instead, much to her fury, she was cast in still another Errol Flynn epic, *Dodge City*, a story about the Santa Fe Railroad and the struggle of its pioneer owners, drivers, and crewmen to cut a path across the virgin prairies. Olivia was cast as a newspaper girl reporter, the younger sister of William Lundigan. *Dodge City* was partly rebuilt at the studio, partly on location near Modesto, California, where the dusty plains in late summer and early fall substituted for Kansas. Longhorn cattle were rounded up from a wide area, fences were pulled down, and there was a careful mocking-up of an early railroad train in order to give the film the look of authenticity. By the time the studio had completed its work, Colonel Richard Dodge himself would have been at home in the environment. But Olivia, who had formerly obtained consolation for her superficially written parts through her interest in careful studio crafts-manship and location work, was now utterly bored and fatigued by the whole thing.

Her stand-in, Ann Robinson, whose marriage that summer to Warners' first-aid chief, Paul McWilliams, Olivia had attended as bridesmaid, recalls that Olivia was extremely testy, irritable, even filled with fury during the entire shooting; her annoyance gave an edge, not quite called for by the script, to the part of the pioneer newswoman.

Flynn, despite her later statements, was no longer the object of her affections, and his behavior had ceased to charm her; when he walked onto the set late on the first day of work limping from a twisted ankle suffered in his hasty departure from a married woman's room, she was utterly furious.

Fortunately, Paul Mantz was present through part of the shooting to take her mind off Flynn and his crony. Mantz took her for flights in his plane, which encouraged her later to obtain her pilot's license; and on the way back to Los Angeles, he told her that he had finally set up a date for her with Howard Hughes, via the well-known pimp Johnny Meyer. This wasn't exactly the romantic setting Olivia had in mind; but when Hughes sent his personal plane to bring her to Hollywood, she couldn't help but be impressed.

The ever-eager Louella Parsons had spies everywhere, and one of her legmen reported that he had seen Olivia stepping out of the Hughes plane at the Burbank airport. Foolishly, Louella, who was usually a little more careful, announced in her column that Hughes and Olivia were engaged to be married. This assertion greatly annoyed Olivia and she was about to call Louella to demand a retraction when the phone rang in her bedroom at Nella Vista. She at first thought it was a gag when a grating but oddly appealing voice said, "This is Howard Hughes speaking. Now that we're engaged, don't you think we ought to meet?"

Although she recalled later that their first date together was on New Year's Eve, 1938–39, in fact it was earlier, because shooting on *Dodge City* ended early in December.

With some unease, she accepted the invitation to dine with Hughes and they went to a dinner dance at Victor Hugo's, a place to enjoy music and to dance to the popular fox-trots and rumbas of the day. They drank champagne at a corner banquette and Hughes was charming, shy and gangly. Always a romantic, Olivia felt that his reputation must be undeserved and the sense of possible weakness in him brought out the maternal in her, which he shrewdly played on with a seducer's skill. She asked him about his round-the-world flight and he told her of his feelings when he flew. This was undoubtedly thrilling to a twenty-three-year-old woman and it went to her head; but when he took her home, very much later, she didn't ask him in. First of all, it wasn't customary in those days for women to take the lead in such matters; and second, her mother and jealous sister would have made any journey to the bedroom extremely precarious.

So the relationship ticked along on a basis of more or less pure friendship, as Olivia fell more and more in love with Hughes and he began to have visions of breaking his usual rules and marrying her. She was fascinated by his leaky, shabby Chevrolet, his sneakers worn with dark baggy pants and hideous patched navy blue coat, or white canvas trousers that looked as though they had been cut out of a yacht sail with a blunt pair of scissors. And he always wore a battered felt fedora, with holes in it, in an attempt to cover his already thinning hair at thirty-three years of age. He often forgot to shave, to cut or manicure his nails, or to use a deodorant. Nevertheless, his world flight, his millions, his famous gallantry, and his gangly shyness added up to an irresistible mixture and their dates continued.

There was also excitement for Olivia's sister: Joan had been offered the part of Melanie in *Gone with the Wind*, which David O. Selznick was adapting into the headiest brew in Hollywood history. She had originally read for the part of Scarlett O'Hara, which she wanted desperately to play; herself newly gay, mischievous, witty, and delightfully dangerous, she resented the saccharine parts she had been playing even more bitterly than Olivia resented her own, and she knew she was far less suited to them than Olivia could ever be. She saw herself improbably as Scarlett, because she herself was a rebel and not exactly virtuous; but she overlooked the fact that the training of Walter de Havilland and George and Lilian Fontaine had given her a polished elegance that would have made it impossible for audiences to accept her as Margaret Mitchell's hoydenish heroine. When Joan went to see *Gone with the Wind*'s director, the witty, opinionated George Cukor, and said that she wanted to read for Scarlett, he exploded with laughter, saying, "Oh, no, no, no! Scarlett! Impossible, darling! Melanie, yes, perhaps. Would you read for it?" To his amazement, Cukor saw a tigress leap out of the delicate Dresden figure before him: "Melanie!" she snapped. "If it's a Melanie you want, call Olivia!" And she stalked out.

Hardly able to believe this outburst, Cukor recalled later that he suddenly thought, Maybe Olivia would be the perfect choice after all! She fit Margaret Mitchell's description of a demure, brown-haired, brown-eyed, sweet, good but firm and decisive woman; and he felt at once that she possessed the strength of Melanie—a strength that enabled her to survive fire and Union sword and painful childbirth and deprivation of property with decency intact. He was surprised to find when he mentioned her to Selznick that Jack Warner had offered her in a package along with Errol Flynn as Rhett Butler and Bette Davis as Scarlett; Selznick had rejected this, viewing Flynn as far too "light," lacking in body and range as an actor, to carry off the Butler role, and Warner had refused to separate the elements in the package. Selznick nevertheless agreed that Olivia would be acceptable as Melanie, only expressing concern that her "British origins" might possibly cause some criticism in the South.

When Cukor called Olivia at Nella Vista and asked her if she would like to read for Melanie at his house in West Hollywood, she was overjoyed. She had read the novel, along with seemingly everyone else in America, when it had been published three years earlier; and unlike almost every other actress in Hollywood, she had had the sense not to see herself in the part of Scarlett. Moreover, she admired Selznick for the taste and skill of such movies as *A Tale of Two Cities*, *Viva Villa*, *David Copperfield*, and *Dinner at Eight*, and Cukor's direction of the latter production, along with that of *David Copperfield*, and of Garbo's performance in *Camille*, had impressed her equally.

Howard Hughes shared her enthusiasm and, unbeknownst to her, called Selznick and told him that there was "no other Melanie in the world." Selznick could not fail to listen to America's hero—but just to be sure, Hughes also called the genial Jock Whitney, who was deeply involved in the production both financially and personally. Jock and Liz Whitney were pleased by the idea, and the normally phlegmatic Liz called Selznick personally to urge the choice on him.

There was, of course, a certain tension in Olivia's mind as she drove herself to Cukor's house, with its famous oval living room, on Cordell Drive. If Jack Warner found out what she was doing, via the grapevine, her career would be in jeopardy. Her exclusive contract forbade her to negotiate with any other studio, and Warner was still stung by Selznick's refusal of her as part of the Flynn-Davis package.

There are two versions of what took place at Cukor's house. According to his own—and he was adamant about this—he gave Olivia a scene to memorize on the telephone and she came in letter-perfect.

But she told me with equal certainty that she didn't know what she was to read until she reached the house and he gave her the script with marked lines. They seem to agree more or less on the rest of the episode, which had its comic aspects.

It was, both recalled, a fine Sunday afternoon in early January 1939, and Olivia had smartly worn a dress of Victorian design selected by her and Lilian as it expressed Melanie's modesty, deportment, and reserve. It was made of black velvet with a white lace collar, short puff sleeves in the then current mode, and white lace cuffs. The setting was Selznick's drawing room, furnished in English mahogany, with an "English" bay window and drapes—not unlike the library set in *Gone with the Wind*. Cukor, who as a rule disguised his homosexuality, suddenly and hilariously assumed skittish airs: He swished his portly figure across the room and "became" Scarlett, clinging to the curtains with such dramatic emphasis as Margaret Mitchell's distracted heroine that it was all Olivia could do not to burst out laughing. But she controlled herself and played the scene with such poised, demure, wide-eyed sweetness, such firmness and austere but very feminine deportment, that there was no question in Selznick's or Cukor's mind—she *was* Melanie. Selznick, who always played coy when it came to giving a decision on any actress for his beloved project, simply lost all control and blurted out, "Well! I guess that's it! You're Melanie—you're the one!" Olivia beamed and could scarcely restrain herself from throwing her arms around the great producer; it was almost certainly the greatest moment in her entire life.

No sooner had Selznick spoken these words than he suddenly made an unexpected gesture: He ushered Olivia into the combined playroom and projection room next to the living room, a chamber with yellow walls, a golden couch, and other furnishings in traditional Hollywood desert beige. Irene Selznick, David's wife and the daughter of Louis B. Mayer, was sitting on the couch as they came in; she said she had eavesdropped and was "thrilled" by Olivia as Melanie. Without warning, Selznick then issued an instruction and the lights went out. Olivia found a chair, and to her amazement the red velvet curtains at the end of the room parted and she found herself looking at Andrea Leeds, Anne Shirley, Frances Dee, Elizabeth Allen, and the other actresses who had tried for the part of Melanie. The tests were truly embarrassing and Olivia scarcely knew where to look. All she could think of was why Selznick had been so tasteless as to show her the tests, and also whether perhaps he might feel tempted to change his mind. She decided that if he changed it, she would tell him that he was crazy.

Perhaps he was trying to convince himself he had made the right choice. When the ordeal was finally over, he said to Olivia, "Okay. Now how are we going to persuade Jack to let us have you?" It was a realistic question, and there was no easy answer.

Olivia returned to Nella Vista with thoughts whirling about in her head. She didn't know whether to sit the whole thing out or to besiege Selznick with calls to see what Warner's decision was. For days, she suffered the torments of the damned and life at Nella Vista with mother and Joan became worse than ever. Hughes promised to do his best with Warner, and Leland Hayward also promised. The days and sleepless nights wore on and on. For all her composure, Olivia came close to falling apart.

Jack Warner flatly refused to even consider releasing Olivia. When Hayward called her with the news, Olivia flew into an unrivaled tantrum. She went to see Warner, who deliberately kept her waiting for an unconscionable amount of time. When at last she made her way into his appropriately purple-furnished grand office with its sunken living room and said, "I *must* be Melanie," his face broke into a smile. "Olivia, you don't want to be in the picture at all," he said. "It's going to be the biggest bust in town," and he started playing with a model railway. Olivia was flabbergasted. She knew perfectly well that *Gone with the Wind* would be the greatest picture Hollywood had ever—and perhaps *would* ever—make. She fell silent, shocked into speechlessness, while he moved on to his next point: "You don't want to play the part of Melanie anyway. The only part worth anything in the whole goddam book is Scarlett!" Finally, Olivia's throat unlocked. She exclaimed, "No! I'm not interested in Scarlett! The part I want to play is Melanie because there is something about her that is right for me, and there is something I want to say through her that I feel is very important to say to people!"

Warner suddenly found he had a pressing appointment; he had prearranged—as he always did on such occasions—for his assistant to call him with word that a very important exhibitor in London was calling and wouldn't wait. Olivia made her exit with as much dignity as possible.

Of course, Warner's chief reason in refusing Olivia the chance of a lifetime was that when she returned to the studio as a huge star she would want much more money than the $1,000 a week she was getting and she would no longer be willing to be a foil to Errol Flynn.

She went home and conferred with Lilian; she consulted Howard Hughes; she went to see Walter Plunkett, the great costume designer for *GWTW;* and she also talked with Hazel Rogers, Ben Nye, and Monty Westmore, the trio in charge of makeup and hairstyling, because she knew they had advance scripts and she not only could memorize the part of Melanie but also could study the costume sketches and makeup designs.

Knowing that any further meetings with Jack Warner would be futile, she recalled that Lili Damita had used her influence over Jack Warner's attractive wife, Anne, in order to secure Flynn his chance in *Captain Blood.* It was known that Anne exerted a benign influence over her husband and that she often spoke up for Warner contract players, starting with Bette Davis, who were disillusioned and disappointed by his treatment of them. Olivia called Anne on the pretext of extending a seemingly innocuous invitation to afternoon tea, then a fashionable custom. They met at the Brown Derby on Wilshire Boulevard, where she poured her heart out to Anne, and Anne promised to help.

While Anne tried to find the appropriate night for pillow talk with her husband, Selznick, insecure as always, began running the batch of tests again for Melanie. Since they were all clearly inappropriate, he began to think about Marsha Hunt, a very pretty girl who had read for Melanie at a very early stage. In Olivia's footsteps, Marsha went to Selznick's house and gave a reading that was so tender and touching, so refined in its sweetness, that Cukor uncharacteristically clapped his hands together in applause and hugged Marsha in rapture, saying, not for the first time, "I have found my Melanie!" He forbade her to say a word about it, however, and actually that devious man was still determined to use Olivia if possible and would use Marsha only if Jack Warner proved an immovable obstacle.

Then at last salvation arrived for Olivia. Not because Jack Warner had yielded to Anne's blandishments or shown a crack in his platinum heart but because he needed James Stewart for Laurence Olivier's part in a film version of the current Olivier hit *No Time for Comedy*, and Selznick had Stewart under personal contract for several films in a row. Oddly, Olivia had dated Stewart, and would soon become more seriously interested in him; and, of course, Olivier was involved with Vivien Leigh, who was now the hottest choice for Scarlett. In all events, fate was on Olivia's side—she was "meant" to play Melanie, and now she would—but she never would forgive Jack Warner for his behavior. She rushed home to tell Lilian and a very unhappy and irritated Joan her news, and celebrated with Howard Hughes that night—albeit platonically.

She also—very shrewdly—cabled Margaret Mitchell, even cleverly remembering to address the author by her married name. The cable, dated January 13, 1939, read, "Dear Mrs. Marsh: I am not at all envious of Rhett because thanks to you it was Melanie, ma'am, that I wanted! But seriously, I feel it a great honor to have been selected to enact one of the roles in your book, the title of which escapes me at the moment." This throwaway, with its ironic reference to the then worldwide announcement that Clark Gable had been cast as Rhett Butler, was published in the Atlanta *Constitution* the day after it was sent, by arrangement with Selznick's flack Russell Birdwell.

Miss Mitchell replied on January 30, apologizing for taking two weeks to respond to the wire, expressing her pleasure in it, and explaining that the cast announcements had kept her busy night and day and that she had been flooded with letters and telephone calls. She added, "The letters I have received and personal comments I have heard indicate that your selection for the part of Melanie has met with general approval . . . I'm sending my sincere good wishes to you. I know better than anyone else how difficult a part Melanie's will be. She's one of my favorite characters in the book and I am looking forward to the day when I will see you portray her on the screen." This letter became one of Olivia's most prized possessions.

Olivia formed a friendship with Vivien Leigh. She was fascinated by Vivien's taste and style; her ambition; her sparkling, sometimes feverish green eyes; her exquisitely carved features; and the resolution that carried her, despite shaky health, through the months of shooting. It was an odd coincidence that both she and Vivien were British; but discussing the parts with each other, they recalled that Vivien was part Irish, and Scarlett was Irish-American, and that Melanie's southern accent was close to certain British regional dialects, and that British people were more understandable in terms of accent and mannerisms in the southern states than in the North.

Olivia and Vivien drew closer during their many hours of dialogue-coaching under the guidance of young Will Price, who later married Maureen O'Hara. He spoke with a very appealing, essentially Georgian accent, although he was in fact born in Mississippi; and he made Olivia and Vivien understand the nuances, the subtle shadings of Georgian speech. He was assisted by Selznick's chief aide, a charming alumna of the Atlanta *Constitution*, Sue Meyrick, who was general factotum at every level of the production, and by the historian Wilbur Kurtz, an authority on the South during the Civil War.

Olivia did not meet Clark Gable until they began work, but she had met Leslie Howard, who jokingly told her that she had stolen the role of Melanie from him—a particularly amusing quip since, despite his somewhat effete appearance, Howard was a stud beside whom Gable was a mere Howard Hughes. She was struck at once by the fact that neither Howard nor Gable liked the picture or their parts in it. Gable felt that he simply wasn't equal to the part of Rhett Butler and that he didn't have the necessary conviction in the material's genuineness to carry it off. Howard thought the movie ridiculous, despised Hollywood, and was aching for his lover, an English girl who was destined to die young, breaking his heart. It is possible that Howard also correctly suspected he was too old and, although handsome, not nearly rugged enough to play a soldier and the object of Scarlett's burning attentions. As he often remarked to friends, the entire picture was a sustained example of a kind of literary coitus interruptus, in which the heroine endlessly went to bed with the wrong man because Ashley Wilkes would not give her a tumble. He used to say wryly that the idea of Scarlett so desperately chasing this slender gentleman of leisure, when she could have had the husky Gable for the asking, stretched the audience's credulity to the limits.

Of course, it was just this modesty and self-mockery that made Howard charming and far more irresistible to Olivia than the moody, humorless, and self-conscious Gable, who seemed quite unaware that he was possessed of a magnificent physique and stunning good looks that the world of women swooned over. Even the enchanting Carole Lombard, with whom Gable was in love, had difficulty restoring his troubled ego. He was so embarrassed by the scene in which he had to cry over his daughter's death in a riding accident that Olivia herself had to intervene to show him there was nothing unmasculine about this response to a tragedy.

By contrast, Olivia was at home with her role from the first moment. Apart from the fact that Melanie was plain, Olivia was totally one with the character. As Margaret Mitchell wrote in *Gone with the Wind*, "She looked—and was—as simple as earth: as good as bread, as transparent as spring water. . . . There was a sedate dignity about her movements that was oddly touching. . . ." In order to render herself less attractive, she had chosen a hairstyle out of two possible choices that would make her look less beautiful, and Cukor greatly approved her decision. She adored Cukor. He had a strong rapport both with her and with Vivien Leigh, partly attributable to his homosexuality; he was one of the very few gay directors in Hollywood. Olivia had never been able to relate to homosexual men before, and now that she had found such empathy with a man of this character, she was dismayed, as Vivien was, by Clark Gable's outright contempt for him. During Cukor's lifetime (he died in 1983), it was impossible to mention the real reason why Clark Gable hated Cukor, and a shocking episode has had to go unrecounted. The cameraman Lee Garmes told me:

> We were deep into shooting, all inspired by Selznick, I believe, and very happy with Cukor and his sensitive approach to the subject. But Gable was growing daily more restless, convinced that Cukor was giving all of the attention to the girls and ignoring him completely. He was aching for Victor Fleming, who was working on *The Wizard of Oz* at Metro and to whom he could relate: Fleming was a man's man and liked to talk about women, chase them, and bed them, and he liked his generous swigs of scotch, would follow football and baseball, and liked to box and work out in a gym, and he boosted Gable's ego by telling him what a stud he was: The two men were part of the Club of Manhood in Hollywood. Cukor was interested in costumes and jewelry and hairstyles and had never been near a race-track or a diamond or a gym in his life.
>
> Finally, one horrible afternoon—I'll never forget it—Gable suddenly put his hand up and stopped the shooting. He shouted furiously, "Fuck this! I want to be directed by a man!" Everybody froze. You could have heard a hairpin drop. Not a living soul on the set moved or uttered a word. Vivien and Olivia were deathly pale and walked to a corner. Cukor stood there trembling and finally made a clumsy, shattered exit.
>
> Frantically, we all called Selznick, who for once in a million times was not on the set. Feeling ill, we watched him talk to Gable. It was obvious Cukor was finished—and, indeed, even if he hadn't been, there is no way he could have ever gone on with the picture.
>
> It was a cruel slight that Louis B. Mayer gave Cukor *The Women* as his next picture—but a blessing in disguise as he did a great job of it. And Joan Fontaine was in it!

The news that Cukor was fired came as a severe shock to both Olivia and Vivien. In full costume, dressed for a scene of mourning, they rushed to Selznick's office and stormed at him, demanding not only that Cukor be restored but also that Gable apologize. This gesture, however, was very naïve in the circumstances: It was Gable whom the public had chosen as Rhett, and who, as the very person-ification of American strength and virility, would ensure the picture's commercial success. Selznick turned from his hysterical stars and went to the windowseat of his office. He was adamant finally that he would not change his mind.

To replace Cukor, Selznick plucked Victor Fleming out of *The Wizard of Oz* through Irene's intercession with her father, Louis B. Mayer—which meant that Fleming never directed the greatest scene for which he ever received credit: the *Over The Rainbow* sequence, shot by King Vidor. When a miserable Olivia discussed these events with Howard Hughes, he said, "Don't worry, everything is going to be all right. George and Victor have the same talent, only Victor's is strained through a coarser sieve!"

There was a certain amount of truth in the statement, since neither Cukor nor Fleming had a very marked individual style or could be described as an artist in the strict sense of the word; they were just serviceable Hollywood craftsmen, whose styles were virtually insep-arable in the final film. Essentially—and this is probably what Hughes meant—*Gone with the Wind* was Margaret Mitchell's creation as visualized by Selznick; Selznick—not Cukor, Fleming, or the other directors who worked on the film—was its authentic progenitor.

Days after Cukor's dismissal, Olivia lost her one source of moral support when Hughes went off to Key West, Florida, to work with director Howard Hawks on a screenplay based on a Hemingway novel, *To Have and Have Not*. In raffish Key West, Hughes got out of hand, mingling with gangsters and Mafia members, international ad-venturers, and amateur spies in a dangerous and glamorous context. Every Sunday he would sail in from the keys with a boatload of riffraff and telephone Olivia on the ship-to-shore line. Against what sounded like the entire Gulf flowing down the line, the high-pitched thin voice—the voice of someone rapidly going deaf—would whistle in her ears, and it was hard for her to make herself understood in reply. In a peculiarly perverse gesture, Hughes would send Olivia thirteen white orchids each week: She was superstitious and, although she appreciated the gesture, it made her feel uneasy.

Now that he was absent, she realized that he was psychologically incapable of the sustained relationship she wanted with a man; that there was no future in the situation for her. Moreover, he made clear to her on the phone that while he wanted to marry her, he wouldn't be ready until he was fifty years old—seventeen years hence. He would not marry her until she was finished with her career, and in fact wanted her to give it up now to devote herself to him. When she expressed surprise at this, he said that from puberty he had planned his life like a play in four acts: the first for flying; the second for building planes; the third for planning the future of aviation; and the fourth for marriage and retirement. Fond as she was of him, Olivia didn't feel like being the star of the fourth act in his life and she decided she would have to weigh the situation very carefully when he returned.

Meanwhile, the shooting of *Gone with the Wind* went on—and on. Selznick worked through the nights and slept through the mornings, which he abhorred, arriving on the set at noon and making himself a thorough nuisance to everyone. Olivia more and more regretted the loss of Cukor. He had been so clever with her in such sequences as the childbirth scene, in which she had convincingly portrayed labor pains by watching them at his instructions in the delivery room of the Los Angeles County Hospital; he had even twisted her ankle under the bedclothes to make her wince convincingly. Fleming, by contrast, treated everyone as though he were a martinet on a parade ground and never gave her any personal guidance.

In desperation, Olivia and Vivien decided to moonlight with Cukor, who gave them "black market" direction for weeks before he started on *The Women*. Whenever Olivia felt uncertain about interpretation, she would go to his house on weekends or dine with him at the Victor Hugo. As a result, her acting maintained its range and depth. But word of the secret meetings got out and Fleming made both actresses' lives hell. At one stage, he screamed at Vivien, "Miss Leigh, you can stick this script up your royal British ass!" Vivien herself used every four-letter word in the book—a shock to Olivia, who was more genuinely ladylike.

There was the growing feeling in Hollywood that the film was going to be a disaster. Olivia felt that the whole town was against the picture from the moment the popular Cukor was fired and that there wasn't a soul in Hollywood who wished her or anyone else in the picture well. Selznick was fighting upstream, but his motor drove him through everything, and Olivia was sustained by his energy. Equally important, with Cukor's careful guidance, she began to feel that she had captured Melanie's confidence, her faith in life, and her forgiveness of Scarlett. So completely was she involved in her part that she would wear her center-parted hairstyle to bed at night for weeks on end, and, exhausted, she would spend her noon break doing nothing but going over her lines in the fresh air, trying to recuperate from the many hours under the scorching Technicolor lights.

She never ceased to be amazed by Vivien. Despite her misgivings about Gable, Vivien would spend her lunch hours playing a board game she loved, called Battleship, with him. A kind of nautical version of Monopoly, it involved considerable skill and strategy, but so complete was Vivien's control that she could actually stop in the middle, play a scene as Scarlett, and then return to finish the game without a tremor. Gable, on the other hand, would grumble loudly about being interrupted and have to work his way up to the scene. Olivia would sometimes join the game, but drove the others mad because she had to have ten minutes' notice in advance of every sequence she was in so that she could stand before a mirror in costume and think her way back into the characterization.

While the torments of *Gone with the Wind* went on, George Cukor was rescued from the disgrace of his dismissal by being engaged to direct a version of Claire Boothe Luce's celebrated stage play *The Women*, about the ripples set off in a shark pool of bitchy New York women by a chance remark made by a manicurist in a beauty salon. Cukor, who continued to like Joan and often laughed with her over her losing Melanie to Olivia, cast her in the small part of an innocuous wife, the only decent character in the picture other than the betrayed society woman played by Norma Shearer. Cukor told me:

> This was a picture in which every part down to the smallest called for real actresses. Make no mistake about it, no mere movie queens could carry off this movie! Joan had a thankless part, the only thinly written one, but she played it with great naturalness and breeding—a word that seems oddly old-fashioned today but I can't think of another that quite does it. She held her own with the big ones; I knew she was going to move ahead.

Joan very carefully watched the big stars of the picture. Rosalind Russell had a strong comedy technique, playing with an exaggeration that teetered on the edge of self-parody, while Joan Crawford as the husband-stealer used her great sex appeal and toughness to very good effect. In her later work, Joan Fontaine incorporated much that she had learned from these stars.

Meanwhile, Olivia, although she knew that *Gone with the Wind* would "make" her, began to weary of the great epic by the late spring and early summer of 1939. She heard that she was already being seriously considered for the role of Mrs. de Winter, the mousy, dowdy heroine of *Rebecca*, which the feverish Selznick was contemplating even in the midst of the hysteria of *Gone with the Wind*. She was very intrigued.

# *Five*

 Jack Warner's deal with Selznick specified that Olivia would be finished by April 12, 1939, when she would be called for costume tests, wig, and makeup on *The Knight and the Lady*, later entitled *The Private Lives of Elizabeth and Essex*, in which she was to play the insignificant role of a lady-in-waiting to Bette Davis's Virgin Queen. In mid-April, Warner and Hal Wallis grumblingly agreed that Selznick could have her until May 4 but that she must come in for the tests for two days when she wasn't needed for *GWTW*. Simultaneously, they insisted she read a script for the Samuel Goldwyn picture *Raffles* which they were loaning her for. So she not only had to think about *Elizabeth and Essex* and *Rebecca* and *Raffles* as well and go in for difficult tests with complicated Tudor costumes but also prepare for that same *Raffles*—a light comedy in which she would be merely a foil for David Niven as E. W. Hornung's famous gentleman cracksman—when all she should have been doing was giving her entire mental and emotional attention to the part of Melanie.

With Howard Hughes constantly bothering her as well, his phoned requests for marriage seventeen years hence as eccentric as always, she was quite at her wit's end and frayed badly during a scene directed by Sam Wood in which she had to read from a novel by Dickens to a group of nervous war wives concealing a wounded Ashley Wilkes from the soldiery.

While *Gone with the Wind* was still being shot, Olivia, in a fury, did the unthinkable: She turned up on the set of *Elizabeth and Essex* on May 24 and announced, just as the whole company was being lined up, that she would not utter one word on this picture until she had completed her role in *Gone with the Wind*.

Curtiz, who was directing, turned on her in a rage and shouted at her, to which she replied that he, Hal Wallis, and everyone else at the studio had agreed to this arrangement and that she had no intention of obeying director's orders. She screamed and yelled at everyone in sight, and Bette Davis, who had begun work only two days before, became so angry at this unprofessional behavior that she came perilously close to smacking Olivia's face. Bette simply was not aware of the circumstances and incorrectly assumed (she discovered the truth soon afterward) that Olivia had finished work on *Gone with the Wind* and was being intransigent. As for Errol Flynn, he burst out laughing at Olivia's tantrum and went off the set to have a drink with his cronies in his dressing room; he thought his part as the earl of Essex was a joke anyway.

Olivia was taken aside by the set manager, Frank Mattison, who walked her into the alley on Curtiz's instructions, trying to calm her down. Suddenly, she broke free and ran to her dressing room. He followed her there and she yelled that she had given Jack Warner and Hal Wallis the names of several actresses who could play the part instead of her, and she repeated her statement that she would not play any lines of dialogue until finished at Selznick's. She pointed out that doing *Gone with the Wind* decently was a solemn responsibility, and she also wanted to make the best of a secondary role in *Elizabeth and Essex*, but it was impossible to perform two different characters at the same time and she assumed that this had been worked out with Selznick. She said she would not be missed from the throne-room scene and that she should be eliminated from it and saved for later scenes. Mattison promised to discuss the matter with Robert Lord, the associate producer, and Curtiz, both of whom were determined that she would do the scene. She then said she would play the scene provided she did not have to speak. As a result, the entire day's work had to be scrapped and reshot; and it was only when Jack Warner called Olivia and threatened fire, brimstone, and destruction that she came to heel and did play some scenes.

She exploded once again on June 10, at 5:15 P.M., during the rehearsal of a scene between her and the actress Nanette Fabray. She told Curtiz that she would not work one minute after six o'clock, and Curtiz shrieked at her that unless she stayed and finished the sequence he would cut it out of the picture. She turned to the whole company and crew and announced, to the utmost dismay of Bette Davis, who had worked very hard on the scene, that she would be happy to see it go. She made so violent a display of hysterics that Frank Mattison dismissed the company at 6:15, and indeed the whole of that sequence had to be redone and the one following it scrapped.

Miss Davis responded with an equal lack of professionalism, suddenly announcing that she would not shoot the picture in the sequence called for by the schedule. To add insult to injury, Errol Flynn got drunk, crashed his car off Sunset Boulevard, and was off the set for a week. And when Olivia played a lute and sang a period song, Jack Warner decided no one could understand a word of it and it had to be completely redone.

Throughout the shooting, Olivia was constantly back at Selznick's doing retakes. When Hughes returned that June, she was utterly shattered and exhausted and in no condition to cope with his peculiarities. Furthermore, he then did something that really broke the back of their relationship. After she had gone to considerable trouble to see him at the air show in Los Angeles in the midst of all her different schedules, he took her up to his house on Muirfield Road and told her that he could not marry her until his late middle age. She had had enough of this nonsense and said that she was not going to marry him ever. Then, two weeks later, in an attempt to appease her sister who was dating Brian Aherne, she and Hughes cohosted a party for Joan at the glamorous Trocadero overlooking Hollywood on Sunset Strip. Hughes danced with Joan after dinner, and Joan talked to him meaninglessly in order to cover up her nervousness. Deafer than ever, he could barely hear her through the noise of the band—and then, without warning, he proposed marriage to her!

It was an outrageous gesture. Having failed to win Olivia's hand, he now wanted Joan's. Joan was shocked, but allowed Hughes to slip her his phone number. She was intrigued enough to meet him the next day at Don the Beachcomber's in Hollywood, which at that time had a charming little tropical garden. He repeated the proposal, and Joan, who was not attracted to him in the slightest, finding his whining voice, near-deafness, shy behavior, and awkwardness totally unattractive, returned to Nella Vista and told Olivia everything. Olivia, already hysterical after the episode on *Elizabeth and Essex*, turned on Joan with unparalleled rage and charged her with being responsible.

At the same time, Joan's affair with Brian Aherne deepened. Handsome, very charming, well over six feet, with blond hair as wavy and golden as Conrad Nagel's, Aherne was thirty-seven years old in 1939, some fourteen years Joan's senior. Like Nagel, he had polished manners; a slender, well-made figure, and great presence. Born in Kings Norton, England, in 1902, he had risen to success on the American stage, largely through his performance as Robert Browning opposite Katharine Cornell in *The Barretts of Wimpole Street*. He was certainly not in the first rank of Hollywood stars, but was considered a reliable and useful leading man who could fill most parts without causing any untoward competition with his leading lady. He had a somewhat cool and haughty manner, and was tight with money and shrewd with investments.

He had, of course, met Olivia on the ship that carried her to England; he had recently gotten over a complicated romance with Marlene Dietrich. Joan had seen Aherne on and off, and she slowly but surely fell in love with him. In the meantime, plans were progressing for her first major screen part, in Daphne du Maurier's classic *Rebecca* —the same role for which Olivia had originally been considered.

The preparations for this picture by David O. Selznick had gone on throughout the shooting of *Gone with the Wind*. He had planned *Rebecca* as early as 1937, soon after the great success of the novel, and he had approached Alfred Hitchcock, who was famous in Britain, to direct the film. Hitchcock accepted, and Ronald Colman was offered the starring role of Maximilian de Winter, the troubled husband tortured by memories of his dead wife. Colman, afraid that the element of suspected murder in the story would affect his image with the public, declined the part. William Powell begged for it but was finally ruled out as too American. Olivia was ruled out to her annoyance. Loretta Young was seriously considered for the role of the heroine, the sensitive and nervous young girl who marries de Winter and finds herself in a menacing and overpowering household. But she, too, seemed excessively American.

Olivier was hired in the early summer of 1939, and his lover, Vivien Leigh, was most eager to play Mrs. de Winter. But her screen test was bad; she was too deeply involved in the role of Scarlett O'Hara to change character for the test. In July, Selznick again decided to approach Olivia, although he was put off by the problems of dealing with Jack Warner and with Goldwyn, to whom, of course, Olivia was promised for *Raffles*. He was worried, too, by the fact that Leland Hayward, Olivia's agent, was also the husband of Margaret Sullavan, who was in the running; and if Selznick mentioned de Havilland to Hayward, it might upset him. Amusingly, Selznick put in a memo to Daniel T. O'Shea, one of his vice-presidents, on August 1, 1939, "There might be a problem in Miss de Havilland . . . because of her sister, Joan Fontaine. . . ." He mistakenly believed that Olivia would object to taking the part because Joan was being considered for it.

Later in August, Olivia was, to her great anger and disappointment, ruled out a second time because of the impossibility of dealing with Goldwyn and Warner. Joan was tested several times and finally she was left with Anne Baxter as her only competition.

The choice was given to George Cukor. Joan was lucky; Cukor, of course, had been responsible for her first casting in a film, in *No More Ladies*, and was very pleased with her in *The Women*. He ran the tests and said that she was undoubtedly his selection. Olivia's response is unknown.

Selznick, however, called Joan in and asked for just one more test. He told her frankly that he was afraid she could not sustain the part and might be monotonous through the entire picture and he needed to be finally convinced by seeing her in three or four key sequences. Joan refused. She was in great pain from an impacted wisdom tooth and was scheduled to have the tooth extracted the day after her meeting with Selznick. Moreover, she told Selznick, she was to be married right after the extraction and dared not postpone the wedding, afraid of displeasing Aherne. This was very smart of Joan: By being unavailable, by not rushing in to do the test, she provoked Selznick to feel more strongly about her. But then he began to think some more, and for a time he leaned toward Anne Baxter.

While Selznick was at last making up his mind. Joan's marriage to Aherne took place on August 19, 1939, Olivia decided (perhaps under pressure from Warners' publicity department) to attend the wedding as bridesmaid. The best man was the Hollywood producer Buddy Leighton, and among the ushers were the British character actor Alan Napier, the well-known society sportsman Tim Durant (who seemed to be present at everything in those days), and the Rumanian director Jean Negulesco. The whole group flew to Monterey—very fashionable for weddings in those days—and stayed at the deluxe Del Monte Hotel. During the wedding rehearsal at St. John's Chapel, the parson suggested to the couple that they kneel down beside the marriage bed and pray before they had sex. Joan and Brian dissolved into helpless mirth before the blushing minister.

The arrangements for the wedding were undertaken by Lilian Fontaine, who splurged (with Joan's money) on everything from a special organist to a swarm of limousines. But neither prospective bride nor groom was in good shape: Joan had had the troublesome tooth extracted and her face was tender and swollen; Aherne was sniffling and sneezing with a nasty cold. Olivia behaved peculiarly. Seeing the playboy Pat di Cicco at a pre-wedding-day party, she raved to Joan and suddenly took off with him to a romantic encounter in the night. Meanwhile, Aherne told his roommate, Jean Negulesco, that he had suddenly decided not to go ahead with the wedding; he apparently wondered if he hadn't allowed himself to be swept away by his romantic attraction—Joan was after all very young and on the brink of a career. But Joan was adamant that she would not give up the wedding. She tossed and turned most of the night; she recalled later that Olivia suddenly turned up at three o'clock in the morning to announce with glee her affair with di Cicco. Joan was too nervous to mention Aherne's wedding nerves.

The next morning, the guests left the hotel to go to the wedding ceremony; Lilian characteristically held everyone up while she looked for a missing brooch. At last, the ceremony took place. At the altar, Aherne said to Joan in a whisper, "That's the last time you'll ever keep me waiting." Having forced himself to go ahead with the wedding, he was furious that Joan herself was late, not accepting that Lilian was the cause.

The elaborate wedding breakfast that followed severely depleted Lilian's savings. The couple, by now less than madly in love, drove off to San Francisco. Still in pain from her extraction, Joan was in a very bad mood. Matters were not helped that night when Aherne discussed his romance with Marlene Dietrich with Joan; he jokingly asked if he could possibly take Marlene's daughter out occasionally, but Joan reminded herself that Maria was only ten years old.

The honeymoon couple were canoeing at Benbow Lake, north of San Francisco, when Joan's agent, Jimmy Townsend, received the call from Selznick that confirmed her casting in *Rebecca*. A bellboy signaled her from lakeside, Brian paddled in, and Joan rushed to the phone. She was amazed by the news. Aherne was cool. He wrote later that he was appalled to discover that his new bride would now be emerging as a star. He said to her, instead of hugging her and congratulating her, "Why not? You might as well do it for that money!"

*       *       *

Meanwhile, Olivia was going through a difficult time herself. She somehow managed to finish *The Private Lives of Elizabeth and Essex* despite the fact that Bette Davis, still utterly furious over Olivia's outburst on the set that June, said not a word to her for days on end and would come into the great throne room of Elizabeth's court, deliver an elaborate "good morning" to everyone, and pointedly omit Olivia. In addition to Bette's snubs, Olivia had also to deal with Curtiz's continuing rudeness and the summer heat, made worse by her period costumes and by the lights used for Technicolor, which made her feel she was on fire. She also had to change from Elizabethan clothes into Civil War costumes and go back to Selznick for retakes on *Gone with the Wind*. These proved exhausting and tedious, especially since Olivia felt she had played herself out as Melanie. To add insult to injury, she started work on *Raffles* at the beginning of September.

In the meantime, Olivia desperately tried to secure her future with the irascible Jack Warner by begging him to have lunch with her; but he was unavailable and unforgiving. On July 18 she sent him a long, rambling letter on blue stationery, very carefully typed—most uncommon for a star, since most used their own handwriting—and, even more unusual, with no personal monogram or letterhead, not even an address.

The letter said, "It is a shame that you are so busy this week that it is impossible to arrange a luncheon engagement. I should have enjoyed the experience so much." She went on to say that she wanted to straighten out the matter of *Elizabeth and Essex*; that when Warner had called her on the phone, full of indignation, she had wanted to talk to him in person, rather than discuss so vital a matter through such an unsatisfactory medium. She said she knew how easily a misunderstanding could be created between a producer and a performer by a prejudiced word from an overzealous middleman, and that tragedies could result from such misinterpretations; she was sure Warner would agree with her that what could correct this "threatening evil" was complete directness and honesty, and the directness and honesty must not be encumbered by a go-between. She charged the go-between in this instance (obviously, production manager Frank Mattison) with being a troublemaker.

She went on to discuss the "solemn responsibility" of *Gone with the Wind* and her need to do her best, despite everything, on *Elizabeth and Essex*—"a bad performance on my part could weaken that film perceptibly." She said it was impossible to play two different characters at the same time; that she had been given a call two and a half weeks ahead of the arranged starting date and had been desperately nervous, her vitality gone, her "tummy doing nip-ups" on the fatal night when she had "limped" onto the set to struggle through the scene.

She said, obviously referring to Curtiz, "I found that a certain man who means well wanted to get this charming scene over in a hurry—and then, *bang*! he said something very tactless, and to my horror I found myself shaking from head to foot with nerves, and unable to open my mouth for fear of crying—which would never do in front of so many people." She said she was sure that if Warner had been on the set, he would have dismissed the company rather than shoot the scene so late in the day, and that "you understand that any actress, no matter how talented she is, is dependent very seriously upon her appearance and her vitality for the quality of her performance. When those two things leave her, whether it is after five years' work or at the end of the day, she has nothing to rely on." She begged Warner to remember this fact and not listen to any mischief-maker. She wanted "to make the air between us quite clear again," she said, and felt she owed him this quiet explanation. In closing, Olivia said she would appreciate a note from Warner telling her he understood that she was "absolutely on the level." She assured him that nothing was further from her desire than to add to his cares and responsibilities, "For you have a tremendous business to conduct, one that you have built to outstanding success and complexity, and your time is not to be wasted with trivialities."

This somewhat mealymouthed letter was quite in reverse of Olivia's true feelings. She felt abused and disgraced by being exploited as an actress and as a woman, and she was very far from feeling the kind of glamorous self-satisfaction and excitement that the public in its innocence imagined the stars felt day by day. She read fan-magazine articles about herself, illuminated with sepia-toned photographs smiling blissfully into the camera, with increasing stupefaction, feeling, like so many performers, that she was reading about somebody else. There was a chasm between the public's fantasies of her and the reality of her headache-ridden, depressed, overworked, and near-sleepless existence in the home she still lived in on Nella Vista.

The reshooting of *Gone with the Wind* continued even during the humdrum work on *Raffles*, and, exhausted and still angry about losing *Rebecca*, Olivia had to go back for retakes on both *GWTW* and the new picture as both Selznick and Goldwyn expressed their dissatisfaction with her work and wanted her to play it again with more emotion and commitment. She was quite drained by late November, and was only partly revived by meetings with two men who were soon to fascinate her deeply: James Stewart and John Huston.

Of the two men, James Stewart was the first with whom she became romantically involved. He resembled Howard Hughes in being tall, gangly, and shy, and in being a keen aviator; but there the resemblance ended, since, unlike Hughes, he was a stud, famous for his sexual performance in a Hollywood that crudely judged men by such a standard. Curiously, the lives of the two sisters again had a common thread. Olivia, like Joan, was involved now with not only a flier but a man who, like Aherne, had been enamored of Marlene Dietrich. That fall of 1939, Stewart was involved with Marlene in a romance during the making of *Destry Rides Again*. The film's producer, Joe Pasternak, recalls that during breaks between sequences, Marlene would invite Stewart to her dressing room. Marlene was so impressed with his visits that one day she gave him a present in front of the whole cast and crew of the picture and he had to unwrap it then and there. It was a life-size figure of Flash Gordon.

Olivia met Stewart after the picture finished shooting; Marlene had grown tired of Stewart as quickly as she had wearied of Brian Aherne. Olivia, however, was fascinated by him; his slow drawl, his relaxed manner, and his seeming indifference to everything almost disguised a commitment to his craft that disclosed itself in many fine performances. She had admired him in his Frank Capra classics, *Mr. Smith Goes to Washington* and *You Can't Take It with You*, in which he had costarred with the jittery and hypersensitive Jean Arthur; and now she was excited to see the rough cut of *Destry*, not in the least jealous of Marlene, but glad that Stewart was free now for her.

While Olivia was busy with *Raffles*, Joan, who was reading the *Rebecca* script, lived with Brian Aherne at his house on North Rodeo Drive in Beverly Hills, trying to make the most of a marriage that was very far from being the romantic daydream envisioned by readers of the fan magazines.

The house was white, in the Georgian mode, with a rolling lawn and daffodils growing along a brick walk. It had an elegant white four-pillared portico, a spreading tree on the front lawn, and flowering creepers that crawled up the wall. The garden blazed with bougain-villaea, roses, and daffodils.

Joan filled the house with blossoms and redecorated parts of it, including her own bedroom, dressing room, and bath; she laid silver wallpaper into the panels and painted them with apple blossom designs; her dressing room was done in pink. The dining room, furnished with imitation eighteenth-century Chippendale, she left untouched, as well as the hallway with zinnias crowding a brass bowl, grandfather clock chiming away, and everywhere displays of English sporting prints. The bar was lined with photographs of good friends, including Nigel Bruce, David Niven, Douglas Fairbanks, Jr., and Ronald Colman.

Joan very much wanted children, but her gynecological problems prevented her from conceiving. She was always active: When visitors came, she would never sit in a chair but would walk around restlessly, sitting on the floor, perching on chair arms, fooling around with books or phonograph records or table-tennis paddles; she would never cease talking, then suddenly go off to sunbathe in a special canvas enclosure; and then she would put on music and listen enraptured for a few seconds, only to remember something else and rush off to the kitchen or the telephone. She was edgy, restless, and mercurial. Her great friends were Reginald Gardiner; Basil and Ouida Rathbone, who gave extravagant parties that left them perennially broke; and David Niven—before he went to Britain to join the commandos. Joan and Brian had a glass bowl on the cocktail bar where everyone was encouraged to put coins for British war relief.

Joan ran the household with great expertise. George Fontaine was still taking good care of her money, and she was careful about paying bills, kept a record of everything, and was very strict with the maids. Only the butler, whom she later charged with being a male Mrs. Danvers, and who had been with Brian Aherne for years, dared try to usurp her power; but unlike the fragile Mrs. de Winter in *Rebecca*, Joan was a formidable adversary and soon had him in hand.

Breakfast, lunch, and tea had to be served exactly at the appointed hour or the unfortunate servant would receive a come-uppance. The fires always had to be lit at a certain time, and the ice had to be placed in an ice bucket at cocktail time. Joan personally supervised the placement of cigarettes, matches, and ashtrays everywhere, and a petal fallen from a flower would greatly irritate her.

She ate like a marine, but with her high metabolism she never gained an ounce. Her dinners were always British in character and included such dishes as steak and kidney pie, roast beef and Yorkshire pudding, cottage pie, and shepherd's pie, all accompanied by roast potatoes and lashings of cabbage or spinach, and followed by sweet desserts like trifle.

The house was cleaned on a military scale, and Joan would personally control these boot-camp operations as strictly as George Fontaine had done. Shelves had to have white paper ruffles; table napkins (always called "serviettes") had to be neatly rolled in monogrammed silver rings; and knives, forks, and spoons were arranged in descending order in a manner that even Emily Post would have approved.

Brian Aherne found it difficult to adjust to Joan's numerous changes in the household. Aloof, cool, but often stern and irritable, he was hard to understand and himself had a streak of the martinet. He was exasperated when, shortly before Christmas, at their first big party, his secretary, Miss Honeywell, told him that Joan was giving her instructions to redecorate the entire living room. Aherne said this was totally unnecessary, but Joan roamed about, dictating endless notes, and at eleven o'clock, just five days before Christmas when there were many social events, the decorator arrived. It was maddening. Aherne had chosen the living room's rich blue wallpaper; she ordered it stripped down and replaced with gray and off-white. She also asked for all the sconces to be replaced with crystal, and had the curtains pulled down and the Empire sofa recovered in red. The effect was bold and striking, but for a man as stiff and inflexible as the very British Brian Aherne to see his home completely reworked by his wife was intolerable.

Joan forbade him to enter the room until the decorating was complete, and she put severe pressure on the decorator by insisting that he and his team have the room ready by Christmas Eve, only four days later. They worked around the clock to achieve her purpose. When the guests arrived, she theatrically threw open the doors to a Dickensian scene of ropes of evergreen, clusters of candles, a mistletoe bough, motifs of holly and ivy, red berries twinkling from every sconce, and the entire room softly ablaze with candles. Aherne's only comment was that at least his own room and study had been left alone. He had compromised with her when she put a new commode next to his bed, but in no other respect.

On the surface, the household was transplanted British: calm, imitation upper-middle-class. Anyone wandering into the house would have heard the gentle, hollow tiptap of Ping-Pong balls, the spring and snap of a game of bagatelle (a British pin table sport), the clack of a croquet mallet tapping a ball through a hoop on the lawn, and the cries of famous guests echoing from the cocktail bar as Joan told one of her famous raucous jokes.

Yet beneath this surface life of clean-limbed, athletic, true-blue British charm, beyond the gracious exchanges and the leisurely Sunday afternoons, a lethal tension was building between the young couple. Stern and inflexible though he may have been, Aherne had met his match in the equally tough but changeable and fast-moving Joan. Joan grumbled to friends about Brian's allegedly "inconsiderate" love making. Olivia could console herself for the fact that Joan had married first with the cool remark to reporters that "Joan and Brian have every chance of remaining happy—because they're alike!" They were indeed: Joan would complain if Brian left his pipe smoldering in an ashtray; while he would reprimand her for her round shoulders, ordering her to stand up straight as though holding a broom behind her back by her elbows.

As the tension increased, Joan found herself in a kind of *Rebecca* situation: She was convinced that Brian was still mesmerized by memories of his former mistress, the stage actress Claire Eames, who had died young several years before. Not only did Joan have to put up with the allegedly Mrs. Danvers-ish butler, but she also had to tolerate the echo, almost the scent, of Claire Eames in the house. She would find mementos of Claire when she was obsessively cleaning Brian's room, and she would feel more than a twinge of jealousy.

Worse problems arose out at Aherne's Thunderbird Ranch; it was in the desert at Indio and lashed by stinging winds that unbearably aggravated Joan's sinus problems. Aherne loved the hard light, the razor-edged shadows of the desert, but Joan loathed the place. Her sensitive freckled skin responded badly to the fierce sunlight, and she began to wheeze from the fine grains of windblown sand. Thunderbird was as grim for her as Manderley for Mrs. de Winter. When Aherne sat engrossed in the morning paper at breakfast, ignoring her streaming eyes and nose and loud complaints, she could have hit him.

Worse than anything, he had the traditional Englishman's attitude toward a wife. It was hard enough playing a scene with Laurence Olivier in which he would condescend to her, treat her as a silly little goose who should not trouble her head too much, but she came home to a husband who uttered these sentiments in real life. And Joan was not the mouse she portrayed on the screen. She was the mouse that roared. She fought back with the barbs that became her trademark. She was, in her own mind at least, "liberated" before her time: She wanted total independence and she wanted her mind to be acknowledged. She wasn't the type to sit like her screen persona in a cashmere sweater and sensible tweed skirt with her hair in a bun and horn-rimmed glasses perched on her nose while she read the latest Louis Bromfield novel. She was an ambitious, driving, imposing woman.

The truth is she was emphatically not what Aherne had foreseen when he married her, and he began to long for a mousy housewife who would simply run the household and perform her duties as a hostess under his gentlemanly guidance. He would return tired from work in a picture to find Joan still not at home.

Their life together slowly dissolved into arguments. A break was needed, and at last they found one in flying. With her typical determination, and anxious to save her marriage, Joan overcame a terror of heights to join Brian in his private aircraft, a two-seater that could make bold hops across the American continent. He had a map in his den of airplane routes of the United States and had them all memorized.

Joan, who had always wanted to be a man, rejoiced in any kind of masculine activity, and suddenly Brian found himself attracted to her again because she could fix a sputtering engine or twirl a reluctant propeller as expertly as he. She was never happier than when she was dressed in dungarees, covered in oil, solving some tricky mechanical problem.

The worst moments in Joan's marriage were the nights. Sexual intercourse was still very painful, and it is interesting that for two solid years she did not have an operation to cure the cystic condition. It says a great deal about the state of her psyche that she did not feel a feminine impulse to experience pleasure, and perhaps it says much about the essence of her feelings toward Aherne that she didn't seem to feel it essential to enjoy complete fulfillment with him.

In 1939, Joan was busy making *Rebecca* while Brian was making *Vigil in the Night*—ironically, for Joan's former romantic idol, George Stevens. On the first day of the *Rebecca* shooting, Hitchcock greatly annoyed Joan by saying, "Here comes the First Lady of Guernsey!" Throughout the making of the film, Hitchcock continued to refer to Joan that way.

The movie closely followed the book. Selznick believed that the audience wanted to see its favorite scenes on the screen and would not tolerate too many changes. Hitchcock had planned the whole picture down to the last shot, storyboarding it in detailed sketches with cameraman and art director; he had directed it in his head before he began. Joan felt like a puppet in his hands, and he would take no nonsense from her; when she acted sickly and hypersensitive, he would sit immobile, his face getting redder and redder, his hands folded over his ample stomach, and then he would order the First Lady of Guernsey to go on with her work. He addressed her rather like a competent secretary.

He was irritated by Joan's excessive expressions of shock—her overdone slack-jawed stare as she discovered the Gothic secrets of Manderley, the Cornish mansion in the story—and he complained to Selznick, who urged him to be patient and to keep trying. Hitchcock encouraged the British players to be cool and distant to Joan, since he wanted to help her portray a girl who was out of her element in a British household; and he was certainly aided in his purpose by Laurence Olivier, cast as the mysterious Maximilian de Winter, who was still smarting that Vivien Leigh had been turned down in Joan's favor and asked that Joan be fired.

Olivier hated Joan in the part. His irritation, edginess, and coldness toward her unfortunately marred his performance, since it was all too obvious that even his professionalism could not overcome his feelings, and the romantic scenes between them were not always convincing. Only Joan's delicate, if sometimes overacted, portrayal succeeded in giving the love scenes a degree of romantic interest; and Olivier's sheer charm, good looks, and carefully modulated voice may have caused audiences to see a warmth in his playing that really wasn't there. On one occasion, he was so irritated with Joan that he actually fluffed a line—unthinkable for a British actor—and shouted "Shit!" Hitchcock said, with cold jocularity, "Watch it, Larry. Joan's a new bride." Olivier, who of course knew that perfectly well, asked to whom Joan was married. When she told him "Brian Aherne," he snapped, "Couldn't you do better than that?"

Judith Anderson, who played the sinister housekeeper Mrs. Danvers, who terrorizes Mrs. de Winter, recalls that at times Joan seemed to want her to be menacing in order to get into her characterization. She told me:

> There was a crying scene she had to do. It involved shedding real tears; glycerine tears wouldn't do. Suddenly, without warning, she said, "Slap my face!" I was shocked. I said, "What do you mean, slap your face?" I told her I wouldn't do it, and to my amazement she went over to Hitchcock, who wasn't too pleased with her trying to make such an arrangement, and she

said to him, "Slap my face!" And he lit out and gave her a great big smack and she sat down and humped her little shoulders and out came the tears.

Joan was surprised to see that Judith Anderson, though the perfect picture of black-garbed menace and resolution on the set, was a very insecure and nervous actress ill at ease with motion pictures. In one scene, in which she had to open various wardrobe doors and, with more than a hint of lesbianism, run her hands over Rebecca's dresses and furs to humiliate the young and unfashionable bride, Judith proved unable to go ahead at all. She said she felt Mrs. Danvers should "see" Rebecca in the scene. Hitchcock thereupon opened the closets for her and caressed a rich chinchilla coat with extraordinary conviction, "becoming" not only Mrs. Danvers but also Rebecca, despite his portly figure. Judith and Joan broke up at his hilarious feminine movements.

At last, Olivia saw her performance in *Gone with the Wind*. Although shown in rough-cut, without the music of Max Steiner to hold it together emotionally, the picture still seemed powerful. Her performance as Melanie would soon electrify the world, earning her almost as good reviews as Vivien Leigh's Scarlett. Indeed, her playing was as good as Leigh's—in a less obvious, less clearly rewarding part. Kindness and sweetness of character are perhaps the most difficult characteristics for any actress to portray, since they can so easily become cloying; but under the guidance of Cukor and the later coaxing of Victor Fleming and Sam Wood, Olivia succeeded in creating a human being, strong, brave, and decent without being sickly, weak, or self-pitying.

She was at her most touching in an early sequence in which, with Ashley, she gazes down on the young gallants and their ladies fair at the furbelow feast in the garden of Twelve Oaks and says, commenting on a South that is already doomed, "It's a whole world that wants only to be graceful and beautiful." Olivia was good also in the bazaar scene when she removed her wedding ring for the support of the troops and placed it gently in a basket, to be followed by hypocritical Scarlett making the same gesture; and in the sequence with the Yankee deserter, when she awkwardly pulled a Confederate sword from its sheath, a gesture that invariably brings a gust of tense but affectionate laughter from any audience; and above all in the childbirth scenes, when her agony and concern for Scarlett and for the unhappy maid, Prissy, are touching and persuasive. She provided an admirable counterpoint for Scarlett, and Margaret Mitchell and the adapters most shrewdly split the audience's identification between the two characters since so many of Scarlett's actions seem harsh, bitchy, alienating; whenever the audience loses contact with Scarlett, they can fasten happily on Melanie instead. For this reason, Olivia's performance was as important as Vivien Liegh's. And fine though Hattie McDaniel was as Mammy, it is unfortunate that Olivia did not receive the Academy Award instead of Miss McDaniel the following February.

Olivia always claimed in interviews that she was forbidden by the studio to go to the premiere of *Gone with the Wind* in Atlanta and went anyway. The truth is, a memorandum dated December 12, 1939, indicates that she was given official permission to attend, providing she turned up on December 18, three days after the premiere, to appear in a film called *Married, Pretty and Poor*. However, Olivia had no intention of coming to the studio for wardrobe and makeup tests for this picture. First, the title was absurd, laughable for a star of *Gone with the Wind*. Second, the story, though a touching account of the lives of the underprivileged, later retitled *Saturday's Children*, offered no particular advantages to an actress; the main male parts, due to be played by John Garfield and Claude Rains, eclipsed the female.

Unfortunately, Olivia neglected to tell the studio of her refusal until just before she left for Atlanta, and she was suspended without salary, losing a total of $10,416 at a rate of $1,250 a week. Jack Warner was furious and she left under a cloud, but she was quickly picked up by the excitement of the occasion. David Selznick had chartered a plane with the title of the film emblazoned on one side and all of the leading players aboard, with the exception of Leslie Howard, who, hating the production and back in Britain for the war effort, was glad to be absent from the occasion. Also on the plane was Laurence Olivier, who was determined to find some way to sleep with Vivien Leigh after the completion of *Rebecca*, which he despised and barely mentioned in his memoirs. In order to cover for his affair with Vivien, which was not supposed to be public because both were married, Olivia was scheduled to be his companion and would ride with him in the motorcade.

When the plane arrived, there was a crowd of photographers and reporters at the airport, and the stars walked down three flights of red-carpeted steps to a blaze of popping bulbs. The day was chilly and overcast, but everyone was laughing happily, joking with each other as they drove in a fleet of automobiles to the Georgian Terrace Hotel. A million people were lined up on the streets to greet them, and Olivia, with her famous companion, was seen pointing excitedly and counting the rows of spectators—eight deep.

The next night, there was a huge costume ball in the Atlanta Armory; a special escort was to pick up Olivia and Vivien, who were to meet in Vivien's room at nine o'clock. The famous hairdresser David flew in from Antoine's in New York to dress Olivia's hair, and she wore a rich gown of pink tulle and two pink camellias. But when she went to Vivien's room, there was no answer. Knowing that Vivien tended to be mercurial in her habits, Olivia, herself seldom punctual, panicked. She called Selznick's room and publicist Russell Birdwell's, and neither was in. She called the front desk and the clerk said that everyone else had left. By now hysterical, Olivia said, "Call a cab!" The clerk told her there were no cabs as the whole city was involved for the occasion. Olivia said, "All right, get the police!"

The police van arrived, and Olivia suddenly found herself behind bars. Siren screaming, the van made its way to the armory, and Olivia hurled open the doors and jumped out, brushing aside the ushers. Just as she walked up the aisle, the mayor of Atlanta said, through the public-address system, while the spotlight went to the stars' box, "And now, Melanie Wilkes—Miss Olivia de Havilland!" Everybody screamed with laughter because the mayor had not been briefed on Olivia's absence and her seat in the box was empty. "Here I am!" Olivia called up from the aisle. The spotlight faltered, then swung to her as she waved her arms in the air. The entire audience burst out with applause and affectionate laughter, and the ball was ready to begin.

The next day, there was an elaborate reception, and then the premiere. Olivia clasped her hands together with such intensity that the knuckles turned white as the rich heavy curtains parted and the rolling title of the movie slowly progressed across the screen. Even the credits were exciting. Each panel played against evocative scenes of the Old South, ranging from fields plowed at sunset to a blaze of pink blossoms. The movie, accompanied by Max Steiner's score, with its full-blooded rendering of southern themes, had a weight, a rhythm, an electric force that carried the spectators with it and quite overwhelmed them. For the elite audience brought from the finest homes in Georgia, the movie was especially pleasing, and even the most persnickety people present, including those whose immediate kinfolk were in the Civil War itself, could find little fault with it. In scene after scene, the spectators responded to Clark Gable's shrewd, disillusioned, witty, and forceful Rhett Butler; to Vivien Leigh's scheming, heartless, yet irresistible Scarlett; to Hattie McDaniel's monumental Mammy; and to Olivia's touching, firm, decent Melanie.

Olivia was "made" at last. Never again would she accept ill treatment; in her now was born a new and more determined creature, willful, resolute, and capable of ruthlessness if anyone stood in her way. More than ever, she was furious with the system that would try to press her to return from this glorious and glamorous occasion to such foolishness as *Married, Pretty and Poor*. And there were bitter aloes as well: Jack Warner sent no telegram of congratulation, no flowers, not a word, only a cold and rude reminder that her suspension would continue unless she made a film called *Flight Angels*, which was scarcely more than a B picture. His shortsightedness and stupidity prevented him from realizing that he now had a huge name on his hands for whom he should at once construct a major vehicle. To him, Olivia was a minor player who had gotten too big for her boots.

On her return to Nella Vista—where Lilian, who had, much to Olivia's despair, chosen not to see the film, was waiting with trivial housekeeping matters to discuss—Olivia received a telegram from Warner saying:

> Perhaps I should not be surprised at all by your behavior because your present attitude is my anticipated reward for permitting you to play in outside pictures. Am certainly amazed at your neglect and apparent refusal to answer the telephone calls of Mr. Wallis and myself. Please remember you are under contract to this company and accordingly I believe it would be good taste for you to answer our phone calls. Please telephone me immediately at the studio in order that I may personally hear your assurances that you are reporting to the studio tomorrow for work.

Olivia was astonished by the telegram because she had in fact been on suspension since December 12 and had just been told the day before that Anne Shirley would replace her in *Married, Pretty and Poor*. Baffled, she called Leland Hayward, and he told her that the studio bosses were ignoring the suspension because they were dissatisfied with Anne Shirley. Indeed, Olivia had scarcely put down the phone when a revised script arrived at her house. She was ordered to report at once to casting director Steve Trilling—or else. When she told Trilling on the phone that she would not be coming, Warner flew into a rage and her contract was suspended on the spot.

On December 21, in a note to Morris Ebenstein of the New York office of Warners', studio legal boss R. J. Obringer wrote of the problems with Olivia—"difficulties I am sure you realize every time someone pats an artist on the back after a successful picture." Olivia was not allowed to do any publicity, and Jack Warner personally sent a note to Obringer three days after Christmas also forbidding her to appear for Joan's former lover, Conrad Nagel, on the Gulf Screen Guild radio show of the Motion Picture Relief Fund, playing Bette Davis's role in *The Petrified Forest*.

Meanwhile, Olivia continued to date James Stewart, with whom she attended the *Gone with the Wind* premiere in New York City. There can be no doubt that their romance was a far cry from her aborted affair with Hughes. They went to "21," where Olivia had her first bourbon old-fashioned, and to all the shows they could fit in. They were the talk of the city, the gossip columnists enjoying a field day as Olivia hugely enjoyed her suspension.

During this period, *Rebecca* was released; and although Lilian and Olivia were indifferent, Joan was delighted with the results. She was excellent in the film, memorably supplying the opening narrative, "I dreamed I went to Manderley again," and playing with a carefully modulated sensitivity and skill the delicate transition from mouse to lady of the manor. In the early scenes, she was eager, naïve, awkward, totally put-upon by the relentless American tourist Mrs. Van Hopper, expertly played by Florence Bates; at Manderley, she showed a slow but sure strengthening of will and purpose in the face of her husband's callousness and the open contempt of Mrs. Danvers, her strength emerging most forcefully in the scene in which she tells the housekeeper, "I am Mrs. de Winter now." In the second half of the picture, Joan more than held her own with such players as Gladys Cooper, C. Aubrey Smith, George Sanders, and Reginald Denny.

The picture was a kind of mirror of her own life, of her own transition from a shy wren to the composed lady of Rodeo Drive, with her sensible sweaters and tweed skirts, her severe hair and expertise with flowers and menus. She had at last broken free of her parents and their questionable influences; now she was a match for Olivia. Her reviews were very strong and she was nominated for an Academy Award.

Selznick now saw her as a very big star. But on the verge of her triumph, Joan was suddenly stricken with severe pains and became feverish and ill. The ovarian cyst that had made the physical side of marriage to Brian Aherne a painful duty had flared up and she was rushed to Good Samaritan Hospital in Los Angeles, where she underwent emergency surgery. Her doctor, John Vruwink, put her on the critical list and she lay in severe discomfort in the intensive-care unit.

*Rebecca* had its premiere the following night, and a blight was cast over the occasion by Joan's condition. Brian Aherne dragged an unwilling Lilian off to the premiere, leaving Joan to fend for herself. When Louella Parsons came up to Lilian at the Ciro's party later that night, she gushed to her radio audience, "This must be the moment of moments for you as a mother, Mrs. Fontaine! Now, not only one daughter but another is to be found in the firmament of stars!" As she gurgled on, Lilian turned to a block of ice. Finally, she said to the eager microphone, "Joan may be phony in life, but she's almost believable on the screen."

Louella, who was unaccustomed to dealing with reality on any level, shrank before this all-too-true expression of the personage who had given Joan and Olivia birth. Lilian only once more saw one of Joan's pictures, *Jane Eyre*, of which she said, "She was defeated by her beauty."

Hearing the broadcast in her hospital room, to which she had gone from the intensive-care unit, Joan scarcely felt any better. But she rallied bravely, and began to talk to studios about possible roles for which Selznick planned to loan her out. Just to rub salt in Olivia's wounds, Warner deliberately offered Joan the starring role in *The Constant Nymph*, which Olivia wanted more than anything and which had originally been scheduled for Merle Oberon, who had suffered a severe reaction to sulfa drugs and was out of the running. Joan was excited, but there was considerable delay on the script, and Merle refused to give up and fought fiercely to play the part.

While the matter was kept in abeyance, Olivia, who would have been perfect for *Nymph*, was greatly chagrined to find that she was being cast in an innocuous light comedy, *My Love Came Back*, a remake of Walter Reisch's appealing romantic farce *Episode*. The director, Curtis Bernhardt, new to American films, was on tryout with this picture and was not entirely at ease with American methods. Olivia was far from in a good mood when she was handed the script, in which she portrayed a talented, high-strung violin student of the Brissac Academy in New York, who walks out on her music teacher, played by the cuddlesome S. Z. Sakall, only to be accused of being the girlfriend of Charles Winninger, president of the Monarch Music Company.

Olivia mirrored the part in real life. To prepare for the role, she began taking violin lessons from Professor Konchester, who also taught her fellow actress Jane Wyman; but studio records show that whereas Jane mastered the violin at least to the point of handling the fingering and bowing on a dummy instrument, Olivia had no patience for the task and flounced out of her lessons like the girl in the picture, refusing to continue the unequal struggle. As a result, Curtis Bernhardt, a cool, expert German who disliked incompetence, became very annoyed and decided on some other method of disguising the problem.

At first, the makeup department made a mask of Olivia's face to put over that of a professional violinist. But when they tried it on the violinist, she announced that she could neither see nor breathe. They then thought of getting a double who could more or less play the instrument, keeping her in semidarkness or silhouette, until someone pointed out that the script showed the musical scenes taking place in brightly lit classrooms, and that if this procedure were followed, it would mean that not only the audience in the college concert sequence would be in darkness but so would the stage; indeed, nobody would have been able to see any of the other players either.

Finally, after one catastrophe after another, a propman came up with the idea of placing a real violinist behind Olivia, embracing her in a manner that must have given considerable pause to the front office as she scraped and fiddled around the actress.

This experience only increased Olivia's aggravation and she disappeared from the set for several days that spring, feigning illness and going into tantrums at Nella Vista. The easygoing Jimmy Stewart, with whom she was continuing her affair, patiently put up with her outbursts of fury and tried to stop her from consuming such ill-balanced meals as pretzels, hot tea in a beer mug, and Bavarian chocolate cake, which in later years aided her trend toward plumpness. She was, with Melanie under her belt, extremely imperious, haughty, and overconfident, and the late Curtis Bernhardt told me that she never stopped complaining about everything from morning to night. She no longer felt it necessary to act a sweet nothing off as well as on the set, and Jack Warner dreaded her attempts to reach him and avoided her like the plague.

Shooting of the picture finished in May 1940. Olivia's temper, however, was not improved by word that not the slightest effort was being made to prepare a special vehicle for her in the wake of *Gone with the Wind*, and it took all of her willpower to resist walking out and taking another suspension when she was told she would have to submit to the drudgery of yet another Errol Flynn concoction, *Santa Fe Trail*. Her triumph as Melanie had not made the slightest difference to her status at Warners'—in fact, by June her relations with the studio had deteriorated so far that all letters to her were sent via Leland Hayward. She fired him impetuously and hired Myron Selznick, David's peripatetic brother, believing perhaps that he had a better liaison with Jack Warner; but right after that, Myron was banned from the lot and Olivia was even more in the doghouse.

Joan, meanwhile, was busy preparing to work on *The Constant Nymph*, Merle Oberon having been forced finally to withdraw. Olivia, however, was clearly determined to get the part, and indeed on June 10 her name suddenly appeared above Joan's in the prospective cast list, with Vivien Leigh slightly ahead of her. The producer, David Lewis, had long meetings about the matter with the charming and amusing director, Edmund Goulding. Goulding was in a considerable bind, not sure whether to cast Olivia or Joan and knowing how ruinous it would be to any actual or potential friendship with one or the other sister, no matter what decision he made.

At the same time, Joan was going through a miserable period in her marriage. She had grown as overwrought and nervous about her husband as Mrs. de Winter had been about hers. Having long looked forward to a vacation with Brian, she was scarcely encouraged when he took her to Hartford, Connecticut, not for a visit to the local and very important dogwood ceremonies but to see the aunt of his dead mistress Claire Eames, who was herself now dying of cancer. Joan was badly shocked when she saw pictures of Brian and Claire in the living room. Even though it was to be expected, it was a painful reminder of the "Rebecca" in her life.

Both Joan and Olivia were involved in competition in flying that summer—Joan with Brian, and Olivia with Jimmy Stewart, who rejoiced in taking her on hops over southern California and even out to sea. Both had Fairchilds (and Olivia wasn't pleased to see that Stewart's plane had a Warner engine). Joan and Brian flew for British war relief, and Brian made a mistake on radio by telling the audience, referring to British Royal Air Force pilots, "I have a message for our boys. Keep your peckers up!" Fortunately this gaffe went unnoticed by most Americans.

Joan was compensated for this strenuous tour by learning of her nomination for the Academy Award for *Rebecca*; but back at the house on Rodeo Drive, she already started to foreshadow her future role in the film *Suspicion*. She was tortured with jealousy as she kept finding perfumed notepaper, matchboxes from nightclubs and hotels she had never been to, and even a handkerchief that wasn't hers around the house. But all attempts to have Aherne explain this failed, and his habit of referring to her as "a little goose," reminding her that she shouldn't "trouble her little head," scarcely improved matters.

Joan's only consolation was that she and Brian could at least enjoy flying. She acted as Brian's navigator, telling him when he was off course, poring over map after map. Often, they would land and have lunch in small farmhouses, Brian in flying togs, Joan windblown and disheveled in coveralls. They both loved to swim and would plunge into hotel pools wherever they went. They would talk constantly about friends, books, games, music, and the theater, and about their determination to dress for dinner in black tie and evening gown, even when they were alone.

Aherne bought a Fairchild 24, a high-wing monoplane with a Ranger motor, painted black and red with gray upholstery and a checkerboard tail. He took many joy rides with Joan and their friends the writer Charles Bennett and his wife, Maggie, crisscrossing California, Nevada, and neighboring states. Charles and Maggie had their own plane and sometimes they would bumpily follow each other over mountain ranges in every kind of weather.

Joan and Brian also flew further afield, intrepidly crossing the continent to such favorite spots as Cape Cod, Nantucket, Chesapeake Bay, Williamsburg, Roanoke, and Kittyhawk. A particular pleasure was landing on the private airstrip in Bluebell, near Philadelphia, Pennsylvania, owned by Brian's close friends Abby and Connie Wolf. Abby Wolf was a distinguished Philadelphia Main Line lawyer, and Connie was a remarkable woman in her own right—a pilot, balloonist, and enthusiast for everything, possessed of irrepressible energy. Joan, Brian, Abby, and Connie would take off for trips in the Wolfs' seaplane, land on lakes in Maine, put up in lodges or camp and cook out, and fish for trout and bass. Connie Wolf recalls that Joan would enter into the spirit of things, but her moods would vary drastically, from excitement to sickliness and depression, depending on what she could get out of the situation.

Charles Bennett told me that one night Joan and Brian and Maggie and he were guests at an elaborate dinner party at the home of writer

Lenore Coffee. Among the guests were Ronald Colman, Edward G. Robinson, and Sir Charles and Lady Mendl. Joan became bored and drew Charles aside, suggesting in a whisper that they go into the next room and pretend that Charles was David Selznick chasing her around his desk.

They went to the living room and the chase began. Suddenly, Joan tripped and fell against a table, sending a Ming vase crashing to the floor where it broke into pieces.

The other guests came in, led by the hostess, who fled to the bathroom and passed out on the floor. Brian Aherne announced that the accident wasn't his responsibility and left the room. Edward G. Robinson said in a learned manner that he was sure the pieces of the vase could be reassembled. Eventually, Joan and Brian and the Bennetts went to Rodeo Drive and laughed the episode off for the rest of the night.

The next day, Bennett wired hostess Lenore Coffee taking the blame. She called him, saying that she appreciated his action as that of a perfect English gentleman. But she sent Joan the bill.

# *Six*

Olivia began shooting
*Santa Fe Trail* in July 1940. Her relationship with James Stewart was
not really gathering momentum; she felt increasingly that his request
to marry her was somewhat frivolous, and that, like Hughes, he
wanted many women and would never be able to settle down with
one. With her shrewd instinct for male psychology, she knew that
most men—no matter what they pretended—were anxious to reassert
their sexual egos through other women and needed constant flattery to
sustain their virility—a flattery that a strong and independent woman
like herself would be unwilling and embarrassed to give. Thus, powerful and important men tended to marry either for convenience and
social status or for the pleasant, mindless companionship of fluffy,
thoughtless creatures who would never for an instant suspect the
double, triple, or quadruple lives their husbands enjoyed leading.
There was no way that any secrets could have been kept from someone as intelligent as Olivia. Whereas some women of strong intelligence, very much in love with their husbands, would have shut their
minds off from the truth, bold and imperious egotists like Olivia
would be so all-consuming and possessive that nothing would escape
their attention.

That was true of Joan as well. Like Joan, Olivia knew that the man she was in love with was like all other men. And she would prefer to remain independent and unmarried rather than share a man with anyone.

The shooting of *Santa Fe Trail* proved long and tedious, relieved only by the presence of Raymond Massey, who fascinated Olivia as he brought to life the remarkable character of John Brown. For two and a half months, in conditions of suffocating heat, Olivia, Errol Flynn, director Michael Curtiz, and the two hundred-strong cast and crew laboriously moved from West Point to Agoura, Providencia, Buffalo Flats, Busch Gardens, Sun Valley in the Santa Susannas, Lone Pine, and Bishop, experiencing rugged conditions all the way. The production was spectacular and handsome, including an admirable re-creation of Harper's Ferry, Virginia, and the United States Arsenal at the time of John Brown's raid; and the burning of a large Kansas barn and the escape from there of black slaves, a sequence that almost cost the lives of five black extras and caused violent criticism within the unions.

During the hard riding, hard fighting, and general struggle of the production, there were several mishaps: Flynn was cut by a saber thrust, and a blank cartridge seared Raymond Massey's right leg. The dozens of horses suffered badly on the trip wires and some had to be shot. The ASPCA made serious charges and the insurance people screamed. The dust in the cavalry-charge and freight-caravan scenes was so severe that it had to be damped down by giant oil-tank trucks converted into multicapacity water sprinklers. Olivia's dress was often soaked through, causing her to run furiously into the dressing room. Her stand-in, Ann Robinson, says that Olivia was at her wit's end night after night, separated from James Stewart, busy resisting the advances of Van Heflin, and realizing there was no chance of interest from Ronald Reagan, who was happily married to Jane Wyman and expecting a child. Her only consolation was the chance of returning to Stewart on an occasional weekend for flying lessons, and romance.

As for Flynn, Olivia gave many interviews where she mentioned his extreme nervousness and tension. She couldn't understand it, but the reason was that the FBI was constantly following him, checking up on his secretly known Nazi connections, connections that Jack Warner apparently chose to ignore but which were well known to Charles Einfeld, the cunning publicity boss. Indeed, soon after *Santa Fe Trail*, Errol Flynn was to compound his earlier treason to Great Britain and Australia by actually helping the Nazi spy Dr. Herman Erben to get across the border into Mexico when there was a federal warrant for Erben's arrest. Had any of this been known to Olivia, she would undoubtedly have dismissed it from her mind. It is interesting, however, that when Bette Davis was asked about it, she would not deny it. Higher placed in the studio echelon, she must have got wind of the facts.

Olivia again greatly irritated Hal Wallis by taking a hand in the matter of her costumes, as she had done in previous pictures, encouraging that irascible but entertaining Australian Orry-Kelly to make her clothes more elaborate. Wallis grumbled, replacing Orry-Kelly with Milo Anderson, whom he liked no better. He was annoyed that in one scene Anderson was making Olivia's wedding dress absurdly fancy; no such garment, he felt, would have been suitable in the Old West, especially since she was traveling by train through dust, with open windows. She was made to wear a hat that was more 1940 than 1853 in style, and he felt the hat should be a bonnet. Wallis was a stickler for making everything subdued, realistic; he was convinced that otherwise audiences would lose their belief in the story.

Many scenes had to be redone because Flynn, distracted by political problems and worried about the fate of Herman Erben, was drinking at night and flubbing many lines. Olivia was greatly relieved when the production ended; and for once almost looked forward to her next film, the charming *One Sunday Afternoon*, later retitled *The Strawberry Blonde*. When Ann Sheridan turned down the part of the other woman in this pretty Gay Nineties story, the young and inexperienced Rita Hayworth took over, and the picture made her an overnight star. Olivia adored her; then at the height of her beauty, Rita was painfully shy but intelligent and sensitive. And Olivia always very much admired James Cagney, enjoying the experience of working with him once again. Even Olivia had to laugh at the antics of Joey, an organ-grinder's monkey that played a significant part in the action and was constantly slipping its chain and running up extra girls' skirts. The matter became serious when one girl sued Warners' for $20,000, claiming the monkey had bitten her in a particularly sensitive place, and Warner issued a memorandum to the propman, Limey Plews, reading: "Effective today, any monkey found in the studio will get stuffed"—an unfortunate double entendre. Scenes were rewritten to exclude the monkey. Errol Flynn took the creature home and delighted in watching it relieve itself over his guests.

Throughout the shooting of *Strawberry Blonde*, and despite her pleasure in the story, Olivia tended to be late on the set—an unforgivable sin in Hollywood. And then, in the midst of the production, disaster struck. The benighted Walter de Havilland arrived from Japan and gave a press conference aboard the *Tatuta Maru* in San Francisco harbor, repeating his early complaints of his daughters' neglect. He had apparently run afoul of the Japanese government, which was suspicious of him because he was friendly with a group of Englishmen who had been arrested and charged with espionage at the time; and it is possible that he had some connections with British Intelligence, because, Joan testified later, he seemed to have advance knowledge of Japanese intentions in joining Germany in the war against the Allies. She says that he foresaw Pearl Harbor as early as November 1940, but this is unlikely, since plans to attack Pearl Harbor were almost certainly not envisaged that early. Still, it is certain that Walter de Havilland was under suspicion as a former government patent lawyer and could not return to Japan; he told reporters that he had an income of "just $80 a month," that he was looking for "a cheap place to live," and that he would write a book entitled *Early Days When the Family Was Together* for private circulation.

Asked what her response was to his arrival, Lilian, who was then visiting with friends in Saratoga, issued a statement that read: "This news comes as a surprise to me and my daughters because during the twenty-one years that have elapsed since our separation and divorce my daughters and I have had only one contact with him. The girls and I came in 1919 to America, where I have brought them up."

The falsity of this statement is certainly surprising, since in fact, as we know, Joan spent a long time with her father in Japan in the 1920s and Lilian had visited with him after the great earthquake to settle the details of the divorce. It is clear that Lilian wanted to disguise these facts in order to eliminate any possible connection between herself and her ex-husband, who increasingly showed signs of eccentricity inherited from the de Havillands.

On November 8, 1940, Walter de Havilland wrote to Warners' from the Oban Hotel, 6364 Yucca Street, Hollywood, on stationery with the de Havilland crest on the left-hand side, modified to show an armored hand waving an arrow surmounting a coronet, three replicas of the castle in France, and the framing motto handed down from 1066, *Dominus fortissima turris*. In the letter, Walter referred to an original cable (which no longer exists) sent from Japan; he said that since the cable proved "useless in diverting Olivia from a course injurious to your interests," he would only mention that her "heartless and unfilial behavior" had lost her much favor in the Far East, where mutual family support is "a sacred duty" and children would help their father "however deep a criminal he might be!" He added that the damaging publicity (for Olivia—he didn't specify Joan) was regrettable, but that he could not avoid "interviews wherever I go." He then made a direct threat that when the small sum allowed him by the Japanese government was exhausted, "as it soon will be," there would be publicity of a startling nature "and again very adverse indeed to your interests." He regretted that the studio was unable to influence Olivia into "taking the course the public of every nation expects of her." And he added a curious, quite gratuitous footnote: "Olivia gets her clear enunciation from her father, her looks from *his* family."

This letter was, of course, not answered.

While *Strawberry Blonde* was still shooting, Walter de Havilland, unable to get any response from his daughters, who flatly refused to see him, checked into the Hotel Barclay on West Fourth Street in downtown Los Angeles and wrote a letter on November 22 to William R. Wilkerson, publisher of *The Hollywood Reporter*, the prominent trade journal of the film industry. In the letter, he stated that he hoped Wilkerson would help him restore "normal" conditions with his daughters; that owing to their mother's desertion, they never saw their father between the ages of three and fifteen; that their minds were poisoned throughout childhood against their father by their "half-Jew mother . . . no wonder the world over Jews are not wanted!" He added that "though the girls know I am here they make no reply to my plea for a real Xmas spirit"; and that because he had a Japanese wife and refused to leave her, they regarded his marriage as "a social barrier." He said that although his daughters knew his income was less than $80 a month, they were willing to accept popular opprobrium rather than show nobility of character and accord him decent treatment. They had refused to save his business in Japan when he had appealed to them, he lied, and this fact had shocked the Japanese immensely, doing Olivia much professional harm. He added: "The best publicity for the girls would be an 'old age' pension for their father—nearing seventy."

Wilkerson was a loyal servant of the industry, but instead of replying to the letter, he forwarded it to the studio publicity chief, Charles Einfeld, who, of course, promptly buried it in a file. Einfeld spent his life covering up the unfortunate private matters of the stars, and, like the RKO publicity boss Perry Lieber before him, knew that any inkling of such a note would cause untold damage in the eyes of the public.

A new problem lay ahead for Einfeld. On December 11, the *Santa*

*Fe Special* train left Pasadena for Santa Fe, New Mexico, via San Bernadino, Barstow, Needles, Seligman, Winslow, Gallup, Albuquerque, and Lamy. A double crew of chefs and waiters was in attendance to give the best possible service, but a special note sent to all passengers stated, "Because of the great number of guests on the train, it will not be possible to serve meals in rooms." There was a barbershop in the rear lounge car, which had Pullman couches, a cocktail bar, and venetian blinds on the windows. There was a shower bath, and the barber would arrange to have suits or dresses pressed. There was also a ladies' dressing room in the observation car and two lady hairdressers as well as special wardrobe assistants. A note added, "Did you forget your toothbrush, powder or paste, razor blades, etc.? Call on Alton McDermott, First Aid, in car 700, the Observation Car. He also has relief for headache, tummy ache, skinned shins, after effects, etc."

Olivia and all the other cast and crew carried identification cards, and she and the others were requested to make appearances on the rear platform of the Observation Car at every stop. A public address system had been specially installed because "We know you do not wish to disappoint the crowds gathered for a glimpse of the players and urge that you extend your fullest cooperation. A fifteen minute call will be made before arrival at these cities enroute. It will be your signal to come to the Observation Car to be introduced and to say a few words. For the convenience of the press, we have installed two high speed teletype machines and one Morse Key in the Observation Car. . . ."

When the train rumbled out of Pasadena that night of December 11, 1940, Olivia was in an unusually good mood. Whatever she might have thought of the picture, there is no doubt that the occasion was a tremendous one and the *Santa Fe Special* was a marvelous train. But something curious happened on the way to Santa Fe.

According to an informant's statement in the Federal Bureau of Investigation Special Files on Errol Flynn and his henchman, pimp, and bodyguard, Johnny Meyer, a certain woman was given a Mickey Finn by Meyer and, while unconscious, was sexually assaulted by Flynn. The report goes on to say that when she came to and realized what had happened, she attempted suicide—by what method is not made clear, and the woman's name is blacked out by internal FBI censorship. Among the actresses aboard were Nancy Carroll, Martha O'Driscoll, Irene Hervey, Rita Hayworth, Jean Parker, and Elizabeth Wilson.

No sooner had the train arrived in Albuquerque than Olivia was stricken with appendicitis and rushed back to Hollywood by plane on a stretcher, in considerable agony. A photograph shows Olivia, flat on her back, arriving at the Union Air Terminal, smiling wanly at Brian Aherne and Joan, who is seen clutching her hand. Olivia was taken to Good Samaritan Hospital immediately, and it was suddenly stated that no operation would be necessary. Years before, Rudolph Valentino had died of peritonitis because of neglected appendicitis.

Jimmy Stewart rushed to Olivia's side. Walter de Havilland was conspicuous by his absence, but Joan, herself ill at the time from what was described as "fatigue and lowered resistance," was admitted to the same hospital, where she read the script for her new picture, Alfred Hitchcock's *Suspicion*. On December 16, following a blood count and other tests, Olivia was released from the hospital; she would be "operated on after the holidays." She returned to work on *Strawberry Blonde* and was to proceed with *The Bride Came C.O.D.*, which instead went to Bette Davis. She was also offered the part of the heroine in *Affectionately Yours*, later taken by Merle Oberon. Then came an intriguing opportunity to make a picture for Paramount entitled *Hold Back the Dawn*, a story about would-be emigrants from Mexico to the United States, extremely well written by the new team of Billy Wilder and Charles Brackett.

Olivia had finally had her appendix removed at the turn of the year, but she was drastically weakened and had a long and difficult recuperation. Since the atmosphere was tense at Nella Vista, with her mother constantly fretting over her, and Walter's behavior adding to her distress, she had moved in with a new friend, Geraldine Fitzgerald, and her husband, Edward Lindsay-Hogg. One day, she accompanied Geraldine and Edward to lunch at Charles Brackett's, so weak that she had to be carried into Brackett's house. She was very impressed with him and wanted to work with him, but she was very nervous about asking Jack Warner for permission to play in the Paramount film after the horrible experience of dealing with him over *Gone with the Wind*. On that previous occasion, James Stewart had been a godsend, because of Jack Warner's need to have him for *No Time for Comedy*, and now Warner wanted Fred MacMurray. Olivia was fortunate again, and Warner, in the early spring of 1941, had to grumblingly agree to the exchange.

The script of *Hold Back the Dawn* was on a higher level than that of any picture Olivia had appeared in other than *Gone with the Wind*. There was a curious parallel to the Errol Flynn story in it. The hero, played by Ray Milland, was a soldier of fortune serving the cause of the Loyalists in Spain. Flynn had posed as a Loyalist supporter, bringing an imaginary $1,500,000 from Loyalist sympathizers in Hollywood headed by Fredric March and James Cagney, neither of whom would have given Flynn a nickel to put in the telephone. Using this disguise, he and his companion, Herman Erben, had gone behind the lines to spy for Franco. Apart from Kim Philby's adventure as a Communist agent behind the Franco lines, it was the most audacious (if amateurish) espionage mission of the entire Civil War.

In Wilder's script, Claudette Colbert played an American war correspondent modeled on Martha Gellhorn, third wife of Ernest Hemingway; Gellhorn had met Flynn at the Hotel Florida in Madrid and suspected him of gross irresponsibility in not properly serving the Loyalist cause. Olivia played an American schoolteacher, and Charles Boyer a ruthless Rumanian adventurer. There were parallels in the story also with the *Photoplay* writer Katherine Hartley (also known as Ketti), who had become involved with the former European boxing champion Kurt Frings and would later marry him. Frings could not enter the United States until Ketti arranged it, and in the interim she got to know all those people waiting desperately in Tijuana for a chance of entry. She wrote the novel on which the film was based.

The movie ran into trouble from the outset, with the Mexican government and the U.S. State Department demanding that Paramount clean up the story to remove slighting references to Mexicans, Mexico, "wetbacks," and the seedy environment of Tijuana. From the beginning, Billy Wilder and Charles Brackett fought with Mitchell Leisen, the film's sophisticated director, over his constant changes in the writing. When the shooting began that spring of 1941, Wilder also clashed violently with Boyer. A scene showed Boyer—first introduced as an elegant, Homburg-hatted man of the world—lying miserably on a flophouse bunk in rags, teasing a cockroach with his cane. As he talks to the cockroach, he uses the terms of Immigration officers from the State Department: "Where are you going? What is the purpose of your trip? Let's see your papers."

Boyer refused to play the scene. Somber, humorless, and literal-minded, the great French star refused "to ask a cockroach for his passport." Wilder became hysterical. Running out of the studio, dodging the Melrose Avenue traffic, he burst into Lucey's, the famous Hollywood restaurant and alleged pickup joint where Boyer was having lunch, and demanded to know why Boyer would not play the scene. Boyer dismissed this obscure new writer with a wave of the hand. Back in the office, Wilder began beating desks and chairs with a cane, screaming, "I'll kill him! I'll kill him! I'll beat out his brains! No, he has no brains! He's an actor! I've got a better idea—if that bastard isn't talking to cockroaches, he gets no dialogue!" And he told Brackett that they must rewrite the whole of the last part of the picture to emphasize Olivia de Havilland. Interestingly enough, the changes were approved by William Dozier of the writers' department, who later married Joan.

Olivia made the most of the part of the schoolteacher, Emmy Brown, working out a severe hairstyle and unglamorous clothes, which only served to enhance her beauty. She worked closely with the first drama coach she had come across, Phyllis Loughton, a forceful woman who later became mayor of Beverly Hills. Paulette Goddard was under Phyllis's instruction and would not make a move without her. One day, Phyllis saw Olivia chew gum and then spit it out. She said sternly, "Olivia, you know that isn't nice. Pick up that gum!" And Olivia obeyed.

Each day, Olivia would study the next day's scenes with Phyllis. Sometimes she resented the discipline; at Warners', dialogue directors just listened to the performer reading the lines to check the pronunciation of the words and to make sure they were learned, but Phyllis concentrated on characterization, greatly complementing Leisen's direction.

Olivia adored Mitchell Leisen, who reminded her a little of Cukor in his excellent taste, great charm, and extraordinary feeling for the needs of an actress. She gave one of her best performances in the picture; she was nominated for an Academy Award.

Meanwhile, Joan, disappointed that her illness had somewhat undermined her career, was greatly relieved and thrilled that she would be appearing in Alfred Hitchcock's *Suspicion* that spring. The story was ideal for her, and also took the edge off losing the Oscar for *Rebecca* to her friend Ginger Rogers in *Kitty Foyle*. *Suspicion* was a potential field day for her, in the role of a young wife who becomes increasingly certain that her handsome husband is a murderer. The husband was played by Cary Grant, who was oddly distant and impenetrable during the shooting. Far more experienced than he had been when she had made *Gunga Din* with him, he was finicky now, irritating Hitchcock at times by insisting on the exact lighting of his face in every sequence.

Some of the problems arose from the fact that Hitchcock was ill and had embarked on the film without a satisfactory script. Also, he almost lost his cameraman, Harry Stradling, to another studio, and that upset him, too. He was in a restless, miserably edgy mood, and whereas he had been very considerate to Joan in *Rebecca*, he gave her little or no attention on this new production.

Without Olivia's self-sufficiency, Joan looked for support from her director and, finding none, took ill again, with the same general weakness, anemia, and depression. On April 23, studio executive Harry Edington reported to his superiors, "As you know, Joan Fontaine is off again today. I know we have pounded Selznick in the past to get some relief, but from the amount of time this girl is taking off, and the amount she is upsetting our production, it does seem that Selznick should be willing to give us some kind of relief on the situation. Do you think it is worth trying again?" He was referring to the fact that Joan was on loan from Selznick to Hitchcock and her old studio, RKO.

Selznick, however, certainly was not about to provide recompense for the ailments of wilting stars. Joan struggled through the picture, irritable, out of sorts, and disappointed with the absurdly rewritten ending. In one version, the wife committed suicide rather than expose the truth about her husband, but the preview audience laughed this climax off the screen and a worse ending was tacked on, in which all of the heroine's suspicions turned out to be unfounded. This meant that the entire movie was nothing more than a dramatic cheat and a tease, its carefully built-up suspense meaningless—like one of those pictures in which a series of melodramatic incidents turn out to be the figments of a dream.

Both Olivia and Joan were nominated for Oscars in these two pictures—and both were totally exhausted when the films finished shooting. Olivia was consoled by her great friendship with Geraldine Fitzgerald; Joan, however, didn't please her by flatly refusing to play in the new Errol Flynn film, *They Died with Their Boots On*, to be shot by Raoul Walsh that summer, thus compelling Olivia to accept it.

Fed up with Brian Aherne and living her part in *Suspicion* in private, Joan abandoned the marital bed completely and moved into her own room. In an attempt to patch up their relationship, Aherne became romantic again, but it was useless and Joan set off for a South Seas vacation—rather oddly, in the middle of a war—in July 1941, just five months before Pearl Harbor. Aherne flew over the ship, the Matson Line's S.S. *Mariposa*, dipping his wings in farewell. On board, Joan breathed a sigh of relief at the last sight of him and went off to mix with such well-known passengers as the authors Gene Fowler and Charles Nordhoff and James Norman Hall; she had a lighthearted shipboard fling with the dashing and attractive department-store heir Tom Wanamaker. She enjoyed Samoa, Tahiti, and the other tropical ports, not missing Hollywood at all.

Meanwhile, Olivia had indeed been offered the starring role opposite Errol Flynn in *They Died with Their Boots On*, which Joan had turned down. She had no interest in the film—which was to be a highly artificial version of the life and career of George A. Custer, culminating in the battle of the Little Big Horn—but she couldn't face another suspension and another fight with the studio, and proceeded with a shrug to the tedious task. She had to turn down an offer from, of all people, Howard Hughes, to appear in a comedy directed by Leo McCarey, and this, too, didn't please her.

Olivia was cast as the fictitious Libby Bacon, daughter of the banker Samuel Bacon of Monroe, Michigan. As a publicity stunt, the director, Raoul Walsh, was made a brother of the Sioux Nation in a ceremony conducted toward the end of production. The ninth white person ever to receive such an honor, he was given the name Thunder Hawk—and he proved to be a Thunder Hawk on the set as well. A difficult and cantankerous man, with a fierce temper, he nevertheless directed the film with enormous energy and skill. It was a fine production, perhaps the best of the Errol Flynn cycle apart from *Robin Hood*, and strategically released at a time when thousands of young American males were being trained for commissions and hundreds of new units were being formed. The picture, shot partly at West Point, was a thinly disguised recruiting poster, intended to stir public belief in military heroes; all the more ironic that Errol Flynn should have appeared in it.

Olivia began the script readings in a very poor state of health. She was staying with friends that June of 1941 at the Burgess estate in Pomona, New York; the affair with Stewart was virtually over and, like Joan, she was suffering from weakness and lack of vitality, unable to do anything except lie around all day and try to get up some strength. When her agent, Jimmy Townsend of the Myron Selznick office, called to tell her she was wanted for the part of Maggie Cutler, secretary to the irascible author and broadcaster Sheridan Whiteside in *The Man Who Came to Dinner*, she burst into tears and said that although she would love to do the part, there was no way she could come back; that she was feeling excessively frail. Later, Bette Davis played the role.

On June 18, the day the studio received her reply from her agent, Hal Wallis instructed legal boss Roy Obringer to wire Olivia to report five days later in Hollywood. Obringer sent a note to Warner of amazing coldness even by the studio's normal standards. It read:

> Even though she promised to return by airplane, she could prove she was too ill to venture the hazards of airplane travel, any court would hold this would be an excuse for her not to travel by air, and it is therefore much safer to give her the additional Saturday and Sunday so she can travel by train, and thus eliminate any possible alibi that she was excused from traveling by airplane and we could not therefore suspend her as of Friday.

When this ultimatum was conveyed to her by Jimmy Townsend, Olivia's response was to announce that there would be no question of her coming at all. She was thus suspended without salary on the spot.

An extraordinary situation followed. *The Male Animal*, a comedy with a college setting and some political overtones, was embarked on and Olivia was cast in it. But she was still slated for *They Died with Their Boots On*. It is clear from this that the studio not only expected her to crack after two weeks of suspension but also would punish her by making her do the unheard-of—star in two pictures at the same time. Although character performers sometimes went from set to set, making films back to back, stars very rarely did. An exception was Robert Cummings, who worked part of the day that year in *It Started with Eve*, a Deanna Durbin comedy, and part of the day in period costume in the heavy melodrama *King's Row*.

*They Died with Their Boots On* and *The Male Animal* were indeed shot at the same time, and Olivia, who had fought back from illness and deep depression, found herself more overworked than at any other time in her life. To compound the situation, Joan, because she had had the common sense to turn down *They Died with Their Boots On*, was vacationing at that time in the South Seas.

Olivia had to play the innocuous heroine of *They Died with Their Boots On* and the energetic protagonist opposite a difficult and edgy Henry Fonda in *The Male Animal* on alternate days or even sometimes on the same day. She had to change from period clothes to modern and back again; her hair had to be redone again and again, her makeup changed; and at the same time, with both pictures shot out of sequence as usual, she had to try to give dramatic backbone to her

characters. She had to move from the rough and tough martinet behavior of Walsh to the elegant Broadway effeteness of *The Male Animal*'s director Elliott Nugent. From rugged locations on *Boots*, she had
to be driven back to the studio at hair-raising speeds to act in the other
movie—and then schedules had to be rearranged because Flynn was
ill, and there were holdups when a young and handsome heir to an
estate accidentally fell on a sword and it ran him through, fatally
wounding him. It is not surprising that when Olivia was offered the
part of the tormented Cassie Towers, victim of a syphilitic father in
*King's Row*, she burst into tears and refused to play it. Even the studio
had to admit she couldn't undertake it.

It was the most complicated time of Olivia's life. While Joan wandered a ship's deck in moonlight with the very attractive Tom Wanamaker, Olivia was struggling with the dust and heat of the California
hinterland, contending with her mother's frequent fits of temperament at Nella Vista and with long hours in an airless, suffocating
studio with temperatures in the hundreds, and crying often not only
from exhaustion but from the loss of James Stewart. It seemed like a
nightmare; and when the makeup melted with perspiration and ran
down the collar of her period dresses, Olivia felt she wanted to die.

Incredibly, so tough was she at heart, so ironclad in her professionalism, that she somehow managed to cope with everything and
proceed, after she had finished *They Died with Their Boots On*, to con-
centrate exclusively on *The Male Animal*. It was a pleasant, undemand-
ing role shot largely on location at Pomona, on the campus of
Midwestern College, but the September heat grew worse and worse,
and Pomona was exceptionally dry and stifling.

Her one consuming ambition was to make *The Constant Nymph*
instead of Joan. Jack Warner for once agreed with her that she would
be excellent as the music-loving girl in the picture, despite the ordeal
with the violin in *My Love Came Back*. She promised faithfully she
would learn to master the piano, and assured him that she had some
knowledge of the instrument. How she proposed to fit the complex
training involved into her other schedules was far from clear. And
now she was plunged into a new and equally problematic situation.

She was cast in yet another movie, *In This Our Life*, to be directed
by John Huston. It was a story of warring sisters, based on a gloomy,
repetitious novel by Ellen Glasgow; and had it not been for an acci-
dental circumstance, it would have been started in the middle of *The
Male Animal*. But Bette Davis, who was to appear in the movie with
Olivia, was in the midst of costume fittings when she received word

that her husband had been stricken with pneumonia in Minneapolis and she flew by private plane arranged by Howard Hughes to her husband's bedside, holding up the tests (unconscionably, from Jack Warner's point of view). She was not ready to work until November, but that still left no time whatsoever for Olivia to prepare for this new and taxing part. She had no break between pictures at all; and she was still more furious because she wanted to play the ruthlessly selfish sister, oddly named Stanley, but instead was cast as the good sister, Roy. It became very distracting to rehearse with Bette, using men's names (the father in the story had always wanted boys); and Bette was in a very bad mood—worried about her husband's condition, not pleased with the script, and sleeping so poorly that she was in a terrible state of nerves.

Olivia also was on the verge of a complete breakdown, and on November 3, when she came in to try on the costumes for the test, she told Orry-Kelly she thought they were terrible and shouted at him and stormed out. He himself was a hot-tempered Australian and the screams and yells were heard all over the studio.

She swept into producer David Lewis's office and declared, mysteriously, "My costumes aren't unusual enough!" He asked to see the latest sketches, thought the costumes perfectly all right, and instructed Olivia to proceed with them. Undoubtedly, she should then have left the picture and gone on suspension, but she was an obstinate fighter and it was days before she finally gave in and accepted the designs, which were only slightly modified to her specifications.

Every day, sometimes together, sometimes alternately, Bette and Olivia threatened to walk off the picture. The only break in this torment was that Olivia was sworn in as a U.S. citizen in mid-November, but the studio flatly refused to allow her to interrupt the shooting to take the oath of allegiance on Young and Rubicam's "We, the People" radio program on November 15.

To add still further to Olivia's tension, she fell tormentedly in love with the brilliant and demonic director of *In This Our Life*, John Huston. Huston was physically the same type as Howard Hughes and James Stewart—like them, he was underweight and towered over Olivia. His background was already filled with excitement: The son of the great actor Walter Huston, he had emerged as a young contract writer at Warners' whose work had a Hemingway-like sharpness and spareness, and he had made his sure mark as a director with *The Maltese Falcon*, which was destined to become a classic of the screen. The picture was notable for the extraordinarily ruthless humor and hardness of the direction, which reflected not only the mood of Dashiell Hammett's original novel but also Huston's uncompromising intelligence.

In truth, despite the physical similarities, Huston was a far cry from the insecure, sexually confused Hughes and the gangly, somewhat adolescent, cheerful if shy James Stewart. He was a more considerable personality in every way than either of those men. He was profoundly read; he had an intellect; he was a hunter, a fisherman, a man's man with an extraordinarily rugged sensibility and a passion for nature in its wildest forms. Despite his thinness, he had huge hands and shoulders and could take on any man in a fight. He was afraid of nothing and took no nonsense from anyone.

To an intensely feminine woman like Olivia, he was the answer to a dream. But it was a dream that was shot with nightmare aspects. First of all, he was married. Second, while capable of expansive humor, of great storytelling and wavings about of an outsize cigar, he could also retreat into black silences, brooding silent rages. But she stood firm: In many ways, Huston for the first and last time met his match in a woman. It was inevitably a charged, electric, explosive affair that in fact tilted the balance of the film and destroyed it. The picture was saturated with the neurotic strains of the relationship, and Huston was as disaffected with Davis, Dennis Morgan, and George Brent, and with the meaningless dialogue and situations, as he was infatuated with the tiny, invincible, wide-eyed actress.

Again and again, Olivia was ill from utter exhaustion and lack of sleep, from the strain of an emotional relationship at its peak and the cumulative effects of the most harrowing year of her life. On the morning of November 15, 1941, at 7:30, Bette Davis called studio manager Tenny Wright and said she was too ill to come to work. Irritable but cracking his typical jokes to cover his annoyance, Huston continued with the celebrated icy glint in his eye to direct Olivia, Frank Craven, and Charles Coburn. By noon, Olivia was close to collapse and announced to everyone at large that she couldn't work one minute beyond noon; that she had been ill all the previous night, and that this was Saturday and she "desperately" needed to rest; that she could not follow the schedule in shooting all that night; and that Sunday to her was sacrosanct. Somebody said snippily on the sidelines, referring to her upbringing under George Fontaine, "Why should it be sacred? The goddam bitch is an atheist anyway."

Whether Olivia heard the remark is uncertain, but in all events she walked off—and Huston, who wasn't noted for his warm concern on the job, allowed her to leave and canceled shooting for the rest of the day. He flatly refused, however, to follow studio instructions and take up another scene on the spot with actors brought back from their tennis or golf, and in the end he drove after Olivia and brought her back. He was already disgusted with the production—it was a far cry from *The Maltese Falcon*, in which he had enjoyed lunch every day with the actors, led by Humphrey Bogart, at the Toluca Lake Country Club. Here he was at odds with everything.

Moreover, Hal Wallis was dissatisfied with Olivia's performance, as he so often had been in the past, and a scene in which her character had to talk about making a visit to Baltimore he objected to so strongly that it had to be completely reshot. He charged her with not acting the scene positively or determinedly enough, and he added, "I didn't particularly like her performance in the entire scene. There seems to be an epidemic of Hepburn performances in the picture. The whole first part of the scene, with that faraway manner of speaking, the monotone delivery, etc. . . . I would have liked to have seen it played more naturally."

Before she reshot the sequence, Olivia rushed off the picture and took ill again; Huston had to drive all the way to Santa Barbara to get her back on the set.

And then came the last straw: Literally between shots, she was handed a script for *The Gay Sisters*, about three heiresses to the fortune of a man who went down on the *Lusitania*. It consisted largely of quarrels in boardrooms, and she turned it down, as Bette Davis had the day before, risking suspension to do so; she had had enough of sibling rivalry in *In This Our Life*, many scenes of which all too disagreeably reminded her of her life at home with Joan. And she wasn't pleased by the way the studio publicity boss, Charles Einfeld, played up those unfortunate parallels.

As for Bette Davis—Olivia's relationship with her was as peculiar and ambiguous as ever. On the first day of work, Davis came up to her and, without the slightest mention of the disastrous experience on *Elizabeth and Essex* and her complete boycotting of Olivia on the set, said, her eyes starting, puffing away at a characteristic cigarette, "You are one hell of an actress!" Olivia was consumed with conflicting feelings: admiration for Bette, fury over Bette's behavior on *Elizabeth and Essex*, jealousy, and a need to lean on her for advice and for her even greater strength.

Some nights, after a particularly bitter fight on the set and a clash with her demon lover, Olivia would go to Nella Vista with Bette.

Joan and Olivia as children (Charles Higham Collection).

Olivia in 1977
(AP/Wide World Photos).

Joan with Jason Robards in *Tender Is the Night* (Charles Higham Collection).

Olivia with her son,
Benjamin, 1963
(AP/Wide World Photos).

Montgomery Clift, Ralph Richardson, and Olivia in *The Heiress* (Charles Higham Collection).

Joan and Olivia in the 1940s (Charles Higham Collection).

Lilian Fontaine, the mother
of Olivia and Joan, 1947
(AP/Wide World Photos).

Olivia with Max Reinhardt and
Jean Muir (Hollywood Bowl, 1933)
(Charles Higham Collection).

Laurence Olivier and Joan in *Rebecca*
(Charles Higham Collection).

Joan with Alfred Hitchcock and
Judith Anderson, 1940
(Culver Pictures).

Cary Grant and Joan in *Suspicion*
(Charles Higham Collection).

Joan receives an Oscar for *Suspicion* from Ginger Rogers, 1942
(AP/Wide World Photos).

Joan with Lilian and
Brian Aherne, 1940
(Culver Pictures).

Joan with Deborah Kerr,
Anthony Bartley and
William Dozier, 1947
(Culver Pictures).

Olivia with husband,
Marcus Goodrich, 1946
(AP/Wide World Photos).

Olivia with husband,
Marcus Goodrich, 1947
(Culver Pictures).

Joan with Richard Ney and
Lilian Fontaine in *Ivy*
(Charles Higham Collection).

Olivia with John Lund
in *To Each His Own*
(Charles Higham Collection).

Olivia with Celeste Holm in
*The Snake Pit*
(Charles Higham Collection).

Olivia after her divorce from Marcus
Goodrich, 1952 (AP/Wide World Photos).

Olivia with second husband, Pierre Galante,
1955 (AP/Wide World Photos).

Joan with her daughters, Debbie and Martita, and her
husband, William Dozier, 1950s (Culver Pictures).

Olivia wins an Oscar for *The Heiress*, 1950 (AP/Wide World Photos).

Olivia with her daughter,
Gisele, 1958
(AP/Wide World Photos).

Joan with her daughters,
Debbie and Martita, 1951
(AP/Wide World Photos).

Joan after her divorce from
William Dozier, 1952
(AP/Wide World Photos).

Joan and producer Collier Young
before their wedding, 1952
(AP/Wide World Photos).

Joan with cartoonist Charles Addams, 1962 (AP/Wide World Photos).

Lilian was away in Saratoga, and the two actresses would have a light supper and get into a hot tub to try to soak out the tension. Bette could sympathize—she had had a similar experience when she had been wildly and hopelessly in love with William Wyler and at the same time had been working for him in *Jezebel*, *The Little Foxes*, and *The Letter*. Moreover, Bette had also enjoyed the dubious pleasure of nights with Howard Hughes. But, as Olivia said later, Bette, for all her good intentions, scarcely helped by reading favorite passages from the Holy Bible to Olivia as she lay in the hot water sponging herself and trying not to go insane.

It was an odd scene: the neurotic, overwrought, saucer-eyed Bette reading through the Book of Job, with its lists of torments stoically endured, while the ravishingly pretty, twenty-five-year-old Olivia did her best to be a good listener.

Meanwhile, Jack Warner and Hal Wallis refused to take no for an answer and literally ordered Olivia not to make a Twentieth Century-Fox picture, *Rings on Her Fingers*, and to do *The Gay Sisters*—or else.

Throughout most of December, Bette was ill with influenza and various other sicknesses, and Olivia was also ill—retaking scene after scene to satisfy Hal Wallis; feeling her affair with Huston rapidly crumbling before it had really had a chance to begin; and knowing that just as Bette had been threatened by Wyler's strength, so she was threatened by Huston's. She also felt threatened by his marriage, and by rumors that he was having affairs with other women; he was notoriously promiscuous and women apparently found him irresistible. By Christmastime, Olivia was scarcely sleeping at all.

Finally, John Huston had had enough and Raoul Walsh took over for the retakes. And then—Pearl Harbor erupted. The entire company and crew were devastated, assembling on the Monday after that fateful Sunday in a state of complete shock and despair. But so grim was the studio pressure that they had to go on working that day, and, incredibly, Olivia was handed another script that very afternoon—for *Saratoga Trunk*, from the novel by Edna Ferber. Furthermore, one day later, she was told that willy-nilly she would have to make a picture at Columbia on loan-out the following spring. It is scarcely surprising that the performances of everyone in the picture of *In This Our Life* was bad, hysterical, and that everyone suffered from the confusion and lack of confidence of the director.

For Olivia, the New Year of 1942 started on a sour note: It was then that she learned that Joan, not she, would star in the coveted *Constant Nymph*. Joan had been appearing in *This Above All* for Anatole Litvak, costarring Tyrone Power, and dates had been switched around by Selznick to allow Joan to make *Nymph*. Within an hour of completing her last day's shooting on *In This Our Life*, Olivia was ordered to report to Orry-Kelly for *The Gay Sisters*, and when she refused, she was told to report for *Saratoga Trunk*! Hysterical again, Olivia sent Wallis the following wire from home on January 5:

> Mr. Townsend [Jimmy Townsend, her agent] . . . told various people at the studio that I am exhausted and need a vacation badly. I do not understand the text of this wire [requesting me to report to wardrobe], particularly since I have given the studio excellent cooperation this year and have every right to expect consideration and understanding. . . . In spite of an operation and illness I have done five pictures in a year and now need four weeks rest as you I am sure can see and as my doctor Verne Mason, after an examination, has advised. Would you speak to Mr. Obringer.
>
> Thank you and best New Year wishes.

Somebody scribbled at the foot of her telegram an icy "Four weeks' suspension without pay." A telegram was then sent to her saying she would be on illness suspension. She sent another telegram expressing shock at the illness suspension as she needed to rest after this "extremely arduous and busy year"; that she could have taken the rest between *Boots* and *Male Animal* and *In This Our Life*, "but this I did not do because I knew it would cause you great inconvenience and perhaps cost you thousands of dollars." She ended by saying, "Please ask the studio to reconsider their first thought and recommend I be put on suspension. Which seems to me to be the only fair thing to do. All the best."

Wallis sent a note to Warner saying, "There is some merit to what she says," referring to the overlapping of *Boots* and *Male Animal*, and suggesting she be given a layoff vacation. Grumblingly, Warner agreed; but at the exact end of the two weeks, he sent word that Olivia, who was virtually bedridden and deathly ill despite the good news of her Oscar nomination for *Hold Back the Dawn*, was expected to come in for period-costume tests on *Saratoga Trunk*.

Meanwhile, Joan was nominated for an Oscar for her role in *Suspicion*. Indeed, in the long difficult months of struggle, when Olivia was at her wit's end, Joan was having a rewarding time. It was a great advantage to be under contract to David Selznick, because he had the luxury of being able to prepare pictures carefully, with some time in between each film, and in the meantime could loan out his performers, often through his brother's agency, and could give them some opportunity to consider seriously what roles they wanted to play. Unlike Warner, he was a civilized, decent perfectionist and Joan more and more grew to appreciate him, and her good fortune compared with Olivia's in working with him. The one irritant was that he made a great deal of money with the loan-outs while holding her to a far too modest salary. She worked as a nurse's aide to help the war effort, learning much about medicine from Red Cross training films. While she and Brian Aherne lived in what was now a marriage of convenience, she found it was good to lose herself in the long hours of drudgery. She was received at the White House (for the second time), and now there was the excitement of *The Constant Nymph*. She took no pleasure in succeeding Olivia in the role of Tessa, but she enjoyed the challenge of acting a child with pigtails and a simple cotton dress; she adored Charles Boyer and his wife, Pat Patterson, and was mesmerized by Boyer's excellence as an actor; and she loved the fact that the director, Edmund Goulding, would rehearse all the actors in the morning and shoot in the afternoon, and that he would reduce everyone to laughter (except the somber Boyer) by playing out the parts of herself and Alexis Smith in full.

The studio files show that Joan was popular at the studio, far more popular than Olivia. In fairness, the reason clearly was that Joan, despite her long months in the hospital, was not nearly as exhausted as Olivia and had a far more reasonable boss and an acceptable schedule. Both sisters by now were in complete agreement on one point: that the presence of Walter de Havilland on the scene was totally insufferable. He was shunted off to house imprisonment with his wife in Colorado for the duration. The official reason given was that he had volunteered to share her imprisonment. Olivia and Joan, backed by the studio publicity departments, studiously avoided all mention of their now seriously confused father, and it was to be many years before they saw him again.

On January 27, 1942, Olivia was called for a new test on *Saratoga Trunk*. She told Jimmy Townsend she was too ill to go ahead with the test and asked if there was time to cancel the crew. With hours to spare, Townsend called Steve Trilling in Casting, who canceled everything he could, but union rules forbade the bulk of the crews being canceled. Townsend told this to Olivia, who said she would waive the two days' salary due her for preparation for the test; she felt that this would balance the expense Warner had suffered because of her illness. Impatiently, Warner decided to postpone *Saratoga Trunk* and fire Olivia from it; the star part was later played by Ingrid Bergman.

On February 12, Olivia advised Warner she would have to have further rest following her month off because she was still in a state of exhaustion, with very low blood pressure, a depressed energy level, and a threatened breakdown. She wrote to Jack Warner, "You must believe me when I say I was up most of the night last night to force myself to do what you have asked me, with great graciousness, to do [referring to retakes on *In This Our Life*]." She added that although she wished with all her heart she could, she could not; and that this had nothing to do with any artistic pretensions Warner might suspect her of having, but was due rather to dread of a recurrence of the horror she experienced during her nervous illness, which she had told him about during their last meeting. She concluded: "I know this is a very intangible promise but because of your kindness and graciousness I hope to make up to you for the difficulties I have caused you."

The letter was very far from representing Olivia's real feelings. Indeed, as her ten-year contract came up for consideration, she began laying down strict rules, encouraged by Jimmy Townsend—rules that many players in those days were seeking: no more than three pictures a year, with the right to do one outside and a fee of $75,000 per picture.

Warner was pondering this without much good humor, but wondering if he might not be forced to yield, when Olivia infuriated him again.

# *Seven*

While Joan was making *The Constant Nymph*, which Olivia had longed with all her heart to play—a very important part in a remarkable motion picture—Jack Warner, instead of offering Olivia an equally significant vehicle, offered her *George Washington Slept Here*, a silly comedy with Jack Benny that would have caused her to undergo numerous indignities.

Olivia flatly refused to play the part under any circumstances—and despite her nomination for the Academy Award for *Hold Back the Dawn*, she went to the presentation ceremony in February in the worst possible humor. Brutally, Academy head William Wyler placed her opposite Joan at the long, overcrowded table. There was needless cruelty in this, and the room at the Biltmore Hotel was in a hubbub over the fact that the two sisters were in direct competition. Joan had not really wanted to be there; she didn't believe she could possibly win for *Suspicion*, and she had an early call the next morning—in those days the awards involved a dinner as well as the presentations and tended to drag on into the small hours. Olivia, however, had insisted on her presence for some reason, and had even arrived with a saleslady from Magnin's with a selection of possible dresses for Joan to wear at the ceremonies.

Some say that the Academy's decision in the "Best Actress" category that year was the most eagerly awaited in the history of Hollywood. Olivia and Joan were fourth and fifth respectively on the list of nominees, which also included Bette Davis for *The Little Foxes*, Greer Garson for *Blossoms in the Dust*, and Barbara Stanwyck for *Ball of Fire*. Olivia and Joan tried not to look at each other, nor Brian Aherne at them, while their names were read out. Ginger Rogers was handed the special envelope, and, like many before her, she clumsily broke the seal and found herself looking at the card upside down. She was, she said later, hoping that neither actress would be chosen, that it would be either Bette, Greer, or Barbara. With some trepidation, she announced, "And the winner is—Joan Fontaine for *Suspicion!*"

Joan should have been joyous, filled with excitement, but instead all the misery of her childhood rushed back and she looked at Olivia in utter terror. What Olivia's feelings were can only be imagined. After the horrible year at Warners', the impossible schedules, the degradations, and the insult of being offered *George Washington Slept Here*, now there was this final and most devastating blow. It took all of her steely strength and composure to order Joan up to the stage with freezing graciousness. Aherne nudged his wife, and at last the spell of terror was broken and Joan made her way awkwardly to the stage. She felt guilty about winning; given her lack of obsessive career drive, it seemed unfair that she should win when Olivia had worked so hard toward this moment and now for a second time had seen triumph snatched from her.

According to Joan, Aherne also had mixed feelings about the award. He had never made it to the front rank of stardom; he had never wanted Joan to be an actress in the first place, because that silly goose of a wife should not emerge too much; and now, she claims, he was more threatened than ever—especially since his career, such as it was, was slipping, and slipping badly. It was a painful evening on Rodeo Drive and Olivia could not bring herself to go through the pretense of giving long interviews to the press saying that all was forgiven and that she was thrilled by her sister's triumph.

In the wake of this crucifixion, Olivia found herself with little ahead of her except the constant pleas of Jack Warner that she change her mind about *George Washington Slept Here*. And, of course, there was the prospect of Joan's rapturous reception by both studio brass and critics for *The Constant Nymph*. Olivia's health worsened again and she was barely able to bring herself to make another comedy, *Princess O'Rourke*, that summer. She was much alone now, since John Huston had gone east to make films for the government.

Once again it was July, and once again the heat in the studio was severe. Her part as the bored and unhappy Princess Maria, exiled in a hotel suite in New York, obstinately refusing to marry a royal suitor, came from the bottom drawer of romantic comedy roles, a descendant of the sort of characters found in Molnar comedies of the Twenties and Thirties. The boredom and impatience of Princess O'Rourke were all too clearly mirrored in Olivia's feelings about losing the Oscar to Joan, and indeed her only consolation was that she very much liked Charles Coburn, the wonderful old character actor. Whenever he forgot his lines, which was often, she did her utmost to help him, and she even put up with the many breaks in the scenes due to his forgetfulness, and the numerous retakes.

She was less patient with her costar, Robert Cummings, who was making a picture at Universal, *Flesh and Fantasy*, and was frequently and unavoidably late on the set. His endless calls on the Universal lot would interrupt shooting on *Princess O'Rourke*, and Jack Warner complained incessantly about this. In many scenes, Olivia played to a double, which she always disliked since it was hard to give conviction to her acting in such circumstances.

Olivia herself was sometimes late on the set, and Hal Wallis, as always, was insisting she do retakes. On July 30, she came down with a bad cold—or said she did—and the following morning she called production manager Frank Heath saying she couldn't come to work, that her cold was worse, her throat was bothering her, and she had indications of a fever. She called that afternoon to say she wouldn't be in the next day either.

The director Norman Krasna shot around her for days, and finally assistant director Eric Stacey suggested to studio manager Tenny Wright that a studio doctor should go to Nella Vista and check on her condition. When this was suggested, she returned to work; but then she fell ill again, and this time a doctor did find her genuinely sick.

On August 2, Stacey begged Olivia to come in on the following day, a Monday, and succeeded in persuading her; but she was still fifteen minutes late reporting for work several days in a row and Wallis was endlessly retaking her scenes. On August 14, with the picture well over a week behind schedule, her behavior became increasingly eccentric. Robert Cummings, exhausted by his two schedules, came in an hour late and very sick and listlessly struggled through a scene with Olivia in the Lincoln Room of the White House. At lunch, she went to her dressing room and, suddenly feeling something snap, did the unheard of—she drove off the lot and went home for the rest of the day. Stacey wrote in a memorandum to Tenny Wright, "We have no accurate record on this production on the delays directly attributable to Miss de Havilland's non-cooperation, on no particular day has it been sufficiently long to make an official report, but it's always five minutes, ten minutes, fifteen minutes late from lunch, and it takes all day to get her out of her room and onto the set."

On August 16, she was absent from the lot for an hour without explanation; and Stacey, who felt that she had sneaked away in the hope her absence would not be noticed, wrote to Wright, "I felt that if I investigated too closely it might lead to an outburst of temperament and force further delays, so I felt the thing to do was to say nothing about it, and when Miss de Havilland returned . . . she acted in quite a guilty fashion, and it would appear that we did the right thing by not questioning it."

"Right thing" or not, Olivia remained temperamental and un-punctual for much of the rest of the shooting, and on August 30 she again went home without warning. A miserable ten days behind schedule, the comedy at last ground to a halt on September 9. Olivia was appeased by news that the studio was going to lend her to RKO for another picture set in Washington, *Government Girl*, which was certainly no improvement on the present movie, and which Barbara Stanwyck and Ginger Rogers had turned down.

Meanwhile, Joan—with a long and leisurely rest before her next picture, *Jane Eyre*, began on loanout at Twentieth Century-Fox—was having a wonderful time in New York City. She began to develop many society friends, relishing the long and—in those days—glam-orous train journey across the continent, with flat silver, crystal wine-glasses, and fine china in the dining car, protective and attentive red-uniformed porters, handsome staterooms and drawing rooms, eligible men, and many show-business friends aboard to join in card games, Monopoly, gossip, and the consuming of large quantities of scotch, gin, bourbon, and ice-cold martinis.

In the wake of her great success in *Suspicion* and *Rebecca*, and in the company of the rich and sophisticated, with the world at her feet, her personality was expanding joyously. The last vestiges of her youthful shyness, nervousness, and inferiority complex disappeared, and she daily became wittier and more amusing. She was at ease now with herself as a woman, no longer feeling inferior to Olivia and resentful of Olivia's repression of her over so many years. She took little non-sense from her mother and entered into a pattern of lighthearted, uncommitted, superficial affairs. One of these was with a White Russian who asked only that he be allowed to polish her shoes every night. She made arrangements with the desk clerks of her favorite hotels—the Hampshire House and the St. Regis—to satisfy his desire. She laughed charitably at his sad but funny obsession, but never let him know her amusement.

Back in Hollywood, Olivia could only grind her teeth with envy at reports in Winchell's column of Joan's social life in Manhattan. She was still suffering from headaches, exhaustion, temperamental attacks, and deep misery at her plight. Her temper wasn't improved later when Joan more or less remade *Princess O'Rourke* as *You Gotta Stay Happy*.

Surprisingly, Jack Warner thought *Princess O'Rourke* a good picture and cabled Krasna, now a lieutenant, in Miami to tell him so. He seemed to have overlooked the flaws in his own picture: the heavy-handed dialogue and situations, and the clumsinesses of continuity— such as the scene in which Olivia boarded a Douglas aircraft that somehow turned into a Boeing when it took off, and a shot of her in a black-curtained airplane sleeping compartment when in fact these were not used at the time.

Olivia had a slight break in her long ordeal when her cousin, the young British air ace and war hero Geoffrey de Havilland, arrived on a visit and stayed with Joan and Brian at Rodeo Drive. The sisters buried their rivalry for his benefit; and Geoffrey—young, dashing, uncomplicated, and reckless—followed the de Havilland tradition by flirting wildly with both of his famous cousins, drinking himself practically under the table, and brushing the Beverly Hills palm trees as he buzzed various famous people's homes with his plane. For once, hosts and hostesses like the mysterious fascist agent Dorothy di Frasso, British millionaire Sir Charles Mendl and his beloved wife Elsie de Wolfe, Barbara Hutton, and Cary Grant were able to invite Olivia and Joan to the same parties; with Brian and Geoffrey, they came as a foursome. When the handsome young man who was not overburdened with intelligence demonstrated his new plane to American personnel, Olivia and Joan were present. He left at last in the wake of gales of laughter and buckets of martinis at Rodeo Drive.

During Geoffrey's visit, Olivia began work on a new picture, *Devotion*, her second movie with director Curtis Bernhardt. It was a fantastical version of the lives of the Brontë sisters of Haworth Parsonage: Olivia was cast as Charlotte, Ida Lupino as Emily, and Nancy Coleman as Anne; their father was played by the admirable Montagu

Love. Something of the quality of the film may be judged by a passage from the synopsis issued by the studio:

> While Charlotte and Anne are suffering indignities as governesses and trying to write poems, Emily and Mr. Nicholls [a British curate played for some unknown reason by Paul Henried] become close and understanding friends. Emily trusts the friendly curate so completely that she tells him of her strange dream, the one about the cloaked horseman who gallops past her on the black horse, and in a tryst on the moors, shows him an old stone house that fascinates her. She calls it *Wuthering Heights*. . . . At the Heger Seminary in Belgium, Charlotte falls in love with the Headmaster . . . and callously reveals to Emily that the Reverend Nicholls kissed her. . . . Back at Haworth, Bramwell reads Charlotte's manuscript, *Jane Eyre*, and Emily's *Wuthering Heights* and announces that Emily and Charlotte are in love with the same man . . . William Makepeace Thackeray [Sydney Greenstreet!] squires Charlotte about in triumph . . . as Emily dies, Charlotte finally understands the integrity of her real greatness and the quiet strength of her love. Emily dies with the vision of the black horseman, not unwelcome now, in her eyes. . . .

In view of the above, it is not surprising that *Devotion* took a great deal of devotion to sit through. It is ironic that, at the same time, Joan was making *Jane Eyre*, based on the novel written by the author Olivia was playing.

There is no question that *Devotion* sounded the death knell of Olivia's career at Warners'. Making it was almost certainly the worst experience of her life and she never displayed such lack of control, such violent temperament, as she did on this production. On November 6, when she was supposed to do wardrobe and makeup tests, she did not report to the studio until after 1:00 P.M. She also was afflicted with an odd sickness in her legs, which broke out in large swellings that made it almost impossible for her to walk. The following day, Saturday, she was forty-five minutes late for makeup; and to make matters worse, Curtis Bernhardt was ill and did not come in until the afternoon. For the first time in her life, Olivia had serious problems in remembering lines. On November 16, she was exhausted by six o'clock at night, after hours of rehearsal and constant "going up" on her lines.

The tension went on and on. Olivia tried to break it with the entertaining visits of Geoffrey de Havilland and with the much publicized gags in which she had the Warners' lunchroom in an uproar with imitations of dogs, cats, cows, and bathing hippopotamuses. She chased about with her dog, a three-month-old airedale named Shadrach, a gift from John Huston; and she visited Ida Lupino on Sundays at a San Fernando Valley hog ranch, where she enjoyed feeding those cumbersome, grumpily snorting creatures.

But these were rare moments of lightheartedness in the protracted and grueling experience of making the film. By December 8, Eric Stacey reported that Olivia was showing "absolutely no regard for time" and she was late again and again. Both Olivia and Ida simply refused to play an elaborate sequence in Brussels the way it was written, and the great French star Victor Francen joined them in their disapproval. As Christmas approached, Ida broke all the rules by announcing that she wanted a week off to join her husband, Louis Hayward, during his army furlough, and Curtis Bernhardt was obliged to give it to her, since he was sure she would call in "sick" anyway if she didn't get it. This doubled Olivia's work, and on December 22 she again left the lot. When Stacey told her that as a result the whole company had to be dismissed, she laughed in his face and said she hadn't the slightest regret in the world.

Her illnesses, her tardiness, her outright refusals to rehearse caused bitter fights between producer Robert Buckner, who took her side, and Bernhardt, who hated her. Only Ida Lupino's professionalism saved the day; but it was not enough to save the picture, which floundered on the screen and was not released for three years. Worst of all, Olivia even fought with Ida, and the tension between the two women sometimes shows in the finished production.

By the time she finished *Devotion*, Olivia was once again a wreck. She flatly refused to make *The Animal Kingdom* and walked out on her contract. She had moved to 9560 Cedar Brook Road in Beverly Hills—at last living up to the standard called for by her star status—only to run into yet another problem. She had agreed to appear in the trashy picture *Government Girl* at RKO just to get away from Warners'; but almost as soon as she accepted, she wished she hadn't. Joseph Cotten was cast with her, and she felt neither one way nor the other about him; but he had heard about her behavior on *Devotion* and backed off, leaving her with the unfortunate replacement of Sonny Tufts. Charles Koerner, the nemesis of Orson Welles at the studio, liked Olivia very much and encouraged her, but he was hampered by the fact that she was now in an all-out battle with Warners' and was in default of her contract and indeed about to launch a lawsuit that would make legal history.

Olivia caused nothing but trouble on *Government Girl*, and seemed to be at sea playing the part of a Washington secretary who helped Tufts, as an airplane-manufacturing expert, to crash through red tape surrounding the building of bombers in World War II. Once again, she was saddled with a writer who was an inexperienced director, Dudley Nichols. His work was uninspired, he had a hot temper, and he and Olivia fought furiously day and night.

Joan and Brian, in the meantime, were still living together, although virtually estranged. Joan worked very hard indeed in the title role of *Jane Eyre*. Orson Welles—with his colossal ego, excessively heavy makeup, and false nose—overrode the director, Robert Stevenson, a charming, quizzical English gentleman who later made *Mary Poppins*. Arriving several hours later than Joan on the set every day, Welles shouted all his lines as though on the stage and took over the direction completely, turning Aldous Huxley's treatment of Charlotte Brontë's Gothic romance into a free-for-all of bizarre camera angles, murky effects (deeply shadowed interiors, storms, fog), and electric confrontations. Except in the early sequences, when the brooding atmospheric direction recalled Welles's best work in *The Magnificent Ambersons*, the picture began more and more to resemble a road-company melodrama.

Joan, of course, had a will of her own and became increasingly aggravated by the fact that she had to play scene after scene gazing transfixed with admiration at the vain and overweening star, who composed every shot to his own advantage. She was alone only in scenes where she dealt with the fragile housekeeper, played by Edith Barrett, and the insane wife's threatening custodian, played by Ethel Griffies; in every other sequence, she was swept off the screen. Nevertheless, her Jane had a touching combination of resolution and sweetness and an impeccable Victorianism of tone. Hers remains the best performance in the film—indeed, despite everything, she held the film together and gave it what little degree of conviction it had.

But even she could not give conviction to her next picture, *Frenchman's Creek*, which she made when Selznick loaned her out to Paramount, as he had done to Twentieth, for $2,500 a week when he was paying her only $1,200. It seemed cruel to her that Selznick, who had benefited so greatly from her performance in *Rebecca*, should be treating her so badly; and, in fact, when her agent, Jimmy Townsend, had moved from Myron Selznick to the Berg-Allenberg agency, she had happily gone with him. She came to Olivia's favorite, Mitchell Leisen, who was scheduled to direct, in a very bad temper (not eased by the fact that Leisen had helped earn Olivia the nomination in *Hold Back the Dawn*), and at one point rebelled and refused to play the part. Selznick besieged her with telegrams and urged Brian to bring pressure to bear on her. She stormed at Brian, but at last gave in out of exhaustion and returned to see Leisen a second time, trying to relate to him a little better. She told him as calmly as she could, "I'm going to give you twelve hundred dollars' worth of work a week and that's all." And then she laughed and they relaxed.

Leisen was obsessed with costumes of the utmost extravagance, and Raoul Pène duBois met with her and showed her a red wig and a dusty-pink and gray dress. All her attempted composure vanished; she said she couldn't possibly wear that combination under any circumstances, and once again she walked out. Selznick butted in, agreeing with Joan that red and pink would be hideous together, but finally Paramount boss Buddy De Silva had had enough and told Selznick to either take Joan back or shut up. Leisen was thrilled at the prospect of losing Joan; the greatest admirer of Olivia, he felt Joan was utterly without talent and even called Claudette Colbert to tell her she would have the part. But Selznick surprisingly backed down and abandoned Joan, who ultimately made herself accept the color tests of her costume. Her other clothes in the picture she grudgingly admitted were gorgeous; but from that moment on, she was in every way disaffected with Leisen.

Even more than Olivia, she suffered from the summer heat; she had to wear heavy and voluminous period costumes and she was almost suffocated in them. Nevertheless, she looked very beautiful in the picture, her first in color, and her hair, complexion, and delicate white skin were shown off to perfection. In spite of everything, *Frenchman's Creek* was a success at the box office, and, trapped in *Government Girl* with Sonny Tufts, Olivia once again could feel nothing but an agony of jealousy.

Not that Joan was happy either. She could no longer tolerate Brian's supercilious attitude toward her and his refusal to treat her as an independent star who in fact surpassed him in every possible way, since he had sunk to mediocre roles in films like *My Sister Eileen* and *First Comes Courage* ("Wrong," wrote one critic, "first comes a script"). One morning at their Thunderbird Ranch, she flatly told him there was no point in continuing. He replied coolly and indifferently behind the *Los Angeles Times* and told her that she should do what she thought best.

There is no question that Joan's marriage to Aherne was in every way a mistake. Neither of them had a strong emotional commitment to the relationship; they had entered into it superficially, without much thought and with very little feeling. Aherne, as his memoirs make clear, had very little respect for Joan as a woman; and she had very little respect for him as an actor or a human being. They were like the wax figures on top of a giant wedding cake: exquisitely groomed, beautiful, dressed in style, and yet expressionless, unfeeling, and facing straight ahead in the same direction. It was obvious that they could never have lived up to the public's fantasies of a fairy-tale relationship even if they had really and intensely loved each other; as it was, they could part without more than a shrug. They decided from the outset to make the divorce as simple and straightforward as possible.

Olivia, too, was involved in litigation, divorcing the Brothers Warner after her eleven years of peonage. She had been suspended six times, and each time her contract had been extended for aggregates of the layoff periods. She, of course, hated *Devotion* and regarded *Princess O'Rourke* as hopelessly trivial; she still was greatly irritated by losing *The Constant Nymph* to Joan, and she felt confident that Jack Warner would never give her the opportunities that Selznick had given her in *Gone with the Wind* and Paramount had given her in *Hold Back the Dawn*. She foresaw years of endless suspensions and extensions that would shackle her to Warners' for the rest of her life. Miserable, depressed, sick with anxiety, she went to see her famous attorney, Martin Gang, in August of 1943 and asked if there was anything she could do to break her contract and get out of Warners' for good.

Gang surprised her by saying he had done some research and found that indeed she could file suit against the studio, invoking California's ancient antipeonage law that limited to seven calendar years the time in which an employer could enforce a contract against an employee. Gang advised Olivia to file for declaratory relief in the California Superior Court.

This was a very daring suggestion of Gang's. He had many clients in the film industry whom he could not afford to provoke, despite his position and power, and for Olivia to embark on such a course could be exceedingly dangerous. It would in fact be a case that would throw open to question the very nature of the studio system, which depended on the long-term building up, glamorization, publicizing, and development of stars. It would also potentially play into the hands of the left-wing or Communistic elements in Hollywood, which questioned long-term contractual employment of various union and non-union employees; and it would throw into relief the constant nagging of the agents, who wanted to make independent deals for their clients.

It was a perpetual thorn in the side of the half-dozen men who ran Hollywood that certain stars—Charles Boyer perhaps the most notable of them—had never entered into contracts of any kind that would commit them to a single studio or independent producer, and as a result they had been paid at rates much higher than those accorded to the contract stars. Agents like Myron Selznick, Phil Berg, and Leland Hayward preferred such clients, of course, and were constantly twisting the arms of Mayer, the Warners, and Harry Cohn to pay inordinate sums to independent players when important roles came up that could not be filled by payroll players. The possibility that each star might eventually assume the position of a Boyer was a terrifying prospect to the Hollywood leaders. By going to court in this historic manner, Olivia would be imperiling her career and might even be blacklisted.

She filed for declaratory relief from her contract in the Superior Court of California in Los Angeles on November 5, 1943. She was strongly backed in her action by her friends Geraldine Fitzgerald and Edward Lindsay-Hogg; Geraldine's support was discovered at Warners', where she was under contract, and she fell rapidly into disfavor there. Bette Davis was cheering from the wings; even Joan told people privately that she respected Olivia's guts.

The reports on the Warner case in the Los Angeles press slanted the issue in the studio's favor. The papers had their advertising revenue to consider, and the studio was notorious for exerting excessive influence over the press in those days. The hearings were protracted and exhausting, dragging on for months and costing Olivia well over $13,000. A furious Jack Warner blacklisted her, threatening any producer who wanted to hire her with a lawsuit if they did so, effectively enjoining her from working in any film. Years later, when she attended a party at which Warner received the humanitarian award, she delivered herself of the line "I think humanitarianism should be encouraged . . . especially in Jack."

The case was watched at every step by the industry as a whole because of the concern at the ways in which its outcome would affect everyone's future. A curious element was introduced when Charles A. Loring, counsel for Warners', asked Olivia whether she had refused the part in *The Animal Kingdom* because of her love of an unnamed man who had gone to China. Through tears, Olivia said that the man had two or three weeks to go before he left for China and that she felt "with the interests of the country at heart I should spend as much time with him as possible. This boy might very well die." She was apparently referring to the young Major Joseph McKeon, with whom she had had a brief romance. When Martin Gang asked that the story be stricken from the record, Judge Charles S. Burnell said with a smile, "Well, it isn't pertinent, perhaps, but it's nice to have a little romance in the hearing, isn't it?"

In March 1944, Olivia was pleased to learn that the case had been decided in her favor. She was to all intents and purposes free, although Jack Warner immediately lodged an appeal against the decision. He also made it clear that she would be unable to work again for the indefinite future. Until the matter was resolved, she was still blacklisted.

The Aherne divorce case was heard in the Superior Court in June 1944, with, oddly enough, Martin Gang also representing Joan. At the hearing, Joan spoke of the mysterious influence of Aherne's butler, who had run the household over her head, refusing to change the ways that he had established under Aherne before the marriage and giving her orders in her own household. She talked of Aherne's coldness and indifference to her and said that she felt like a guest in the house; that she wasn't allowed into the library or even to receive her friends, whom she had to see at the studio. She also said that she was unhappy because the desert climate was a problem to her. Her secretary, Veada Cleveland, confirmed her statements and described Joan's miserable headaches and streaming nose at the ranch. Aherne scarcely bothered to put up a struggle.

Husband and wife agreed to relinquish all claims on each other's earnings and that Joan would release right, title, interest, and claim to their community property. She made no claim on the Thunderbird Ranch(!) or on the war bonds, even those taken out in her own name, and she also surrendered the 1941 Buick convertible. Each agreed not to hold the other liable for any debts, and that all money earned from the studio contracts would be his/her own. Joan kept only the house in Hollywood; and it was agreed that if, due to ill health, her income should fall below $25,000 per annum, Aherne would be responsible for augmenting it to the point of a suitable level of financial stability.

It is clear from the entire arrangement that Joan was anxious to avoid a protracted legal struggle; by not making demands on Aherne, she would make it easier for him to accept the charges of extreme cruelty and grievous mental suffering that were widely used to secure divorces in those days. The marriage had lasted four years, seven months, and six days—and on June 5, 1944, Joan was a free woman.

That year she was busy with an amusing film, *The Affairs of Susan*, in which she expertly played a girl who assumed entirely different characters for each of her lovers. Meanwhile, Olivia, out of work and restless, assumed the new role of real-life war heroine, emulating her cousin Geoffrey, the British air ace. She flew to the Aleutians to entertain the troops with recitations and some flirtatious gags; since she could neither sing nor dance, she offered the boys little more than some much-needed feminine attractiveness. These appearances infuriated Jack Warner, who objected violently and with legal threats, especially when she broadcast from Alaska on a "Hollywood Victory Program" linkup.

While she was on line at a local canteen, she heard she had won her case against Warner in the appeals court. She was jubilant, but the severe weather conditions, with sudden storms and choppy seas, made her trip something of an ordeal, and the constant word from her agents, Phil Berg and Bert Allenberg, that there would be no work on her return made her fret that spring. Still, she enjoyed meeting the soldiers at the camp shows, and the entire experience gave her embattled ego a considerable boost. She hadn't faced a live audience since the Hollywood Bowl, Berkeley, and Chicago audiences for *A Midsummer Night's Dream*, and she especially enjoyed being queen of a sports carnival at an Alaskan outpost. She was grateful that Brian Donlevy had fallen ill, though sorry for him, thus clearing the way for her invitation from the War Department.

Jack Warner's annoyance at Olivia's appearances was heightened by the fact that her tour was arranged by the very same Marco Wolfe who had proved such a nuisance to him in the matter of the *Midsummer Night's Dream* tour. Warner was a great friend of General H. H. ("Hap") Arnold of the U.S. Army Air Force and tried to pull strings with him to get Olivia out of the tour, but his shortsighted attitude in time of conflict was especially unattractive to the War Department, which needed as many entertainers as possible to raise the morale of the troops. Indeed, Olivia earned great admiration in Washington and her efforts were not forgotten.

In October, she set off on another war-camp tour with the personal approval of President Roosevelt. In full uniform, she headed for New

Caledonia in the South Pacific, where there was a large U.S. Army, Air Force, and Navy base. She stopped off in Honolulu for a quick meal at a service mess and was joined by a flight nurse for the next leg of the trip.

There was a very peculiar aspect to her wardrobe on the journey: She was wearing Joan's clothes. The reason was that she had been hesitating over the trip because of exhaustion following the court case and the Alaska-Aleutians journey; and when she finally made up her mind to go, she suddenly realized that all her summer clothes suitable for a tropical climate were in Hollywood. But Joan was in New York, and in desperation Olivia turned to her. Joan graciously lent her her wardrobe, and the two sisters became friendly again for the first time in years. It would be fair to assume that Olivia was actually more concerned with patching up their differences than with solving a clothing problem, as it would have been a simple matter for her to have stopped off in Los Angeles to pick up some dresses.

She was a great success talking to the boys, 3,000 of them, at local bases; but the combination of tropical rain and suffocating heat weakened her already shaky health and she collapsed with viral pneumonia. She found herself in a tiny room in a hospital in the crowded tropical port of Suva, surrounded by a mosquito net, and haunted by the sounds of bullocks, harbor noises, and the pervasive scent of copra. The humidity was so intense it mildewed her shoes, and there was no air conditioning in the primitive hospital. Large and creaky ceiling fans scarcely relieved the humidity, and Olivia tossed and turned miserably. She had chest pains and coughed up blood; her temperature hovered around 104°. Sleep was almost impossible due to the severe paroxysms of coughing that shook her and the fact that the nurses had to constantly change the sweat-soaked linens. When she finally got weakly to her feet after some six weeks of suffering, she weighed barely ninety pounds, but she was able to take nourishment and walks. On doctor's orders, the rest of her tour was canceled and she returned to the United States.

At the same time, her legal triumph against Warners' literally rewrote motion-picture history, just as she had hoped it would. There is no question that the great power today of the stars and their agents and the collapse of the old studio system is in part due to her action. By the early 1950s—with the advent of television, the separation of the theater chains from their owners by the Department of Justice, and the new picture-to-picture deals—the old San Quentin governorship of the Mayer-Warner-Cohn world was doomed. There is no doubt that the ruthless and brutal exploitation of stars had to cease, and Olivia can only be applauded for taking the landmark action that she did.

Free now to work where and when she pleased, Olivia moved into a new phase of her career. Like many stars, she very much enjoyed doing radio, and had fought many bitter battles with Warners' because they hated loaning her out even for a week to do such important series as the "Lux Radio Theater." In January 1945, she appeared in Lux's production of *Tender Comrade* in the part created by Ginger Rogers on the screen, and her performance was widely praised; unfortunately, though, she made a hasty and unwise decision in replacing Paulette Goddard in an impossible comedy called *The Well-Groomed Bride*, again with Sonny Tufts.

Back at North Rodeo Drive, Joan had removed all mementos of Brian and was back under contract at RKO, the studio that had so coolly disposed of her several years before. Once there, however, little work could be found for her. The studio's witty and attractive chief executive, William Dozier, was fascinated by her and undoubtedly wanted her to work for him to be closer to her. A lean, very intelligent, dynamic and outgoing man, Dozier was attracted to Joan from the beginning, yet he seemed to have very little idea of preparing vehicles suitable for her talent. In January 1945, he offered her a worthless script, of B-picture quality, entitled *The Strange Woman*, based on a novel by Ben Ames Williams about a scheming hoyden in nineteenth-century Bangor, Maine. She turned this down, yielding the part to a blank-faced Hedy Lamarr; and instead of finding her a good play or novel, Dozier then offered her to the resident king of the horror B's, Val Lewton, most famous for such underground curios as *The Curse of the Cat People* and *Leopard Man*.

In urging her on Lewton, Dozier sent a letter to that producer on February 7 that scarcely suggested his attraction to her was matched by any more respect for her talents than Aherne had. Lewton wasn't interested.

In an even less flattering note on February 9, Dozier suggested Joan for a part in *None So Blind*; and soon after, he recommended her for the lead in *Ondine*, based on the play by Jean Giraudoux, in which she would play a water sprite who fell in love with a knight.

Fortunately, Joan was not privy to this correspondence, and the upshot of it was that she made only one picture of a five-picture deal, a very modest programmer called *From This Day Forward*, in which she played a struggling working-class girl. Although she thought little of the project, she had warmed to Dozier by the time she made it, as a note in the studio files attests. Topped by an elaborate personal crest made out of her initials as a de Havilland, the note is addressed to "Bill, darling," and thanks him for "the largest collection of red roses ever assembled . . . in the history of the genus. . . . I think we're awfully smart—roses without the bed of thorns." She apologizes for her nervousness, which has delayed shooting, and concludes with, "Dear Bill, you have my devotion, my respect, and if this keeps up, my running shoes!" She was referring to the fact that much as she liked Dozier, she wanted to run away from the picture.

She was distracted also by a curious, brief affair with the forty-year-old producer and writer John Houseman that began while she was waiting to start work on the film. She had met Houseman socially on several occasions and was drawn to his considerable and rather weighty charm, his imposing self-confidence, his keen intelligence, and his knowledge of several literatures. He was already almost bald, with a chubby face and a stocky, somewhat overweight figure; but he exuded virility, energy, magnetism, and drive, and was a great conversationalist on any occasion. Although Joan may have been aware that Dozier was attracted to her, she was irritated by what she felt to be his misuse of her and she was also eager to get over the memory of Aherne's condescension toward her. The fact that Houseman took her seriously and understood her finely tuned, delicately subtle mind and brittle sense of humor appealed to her enormously. He was one of the few men she had ever met who gave her the time of day in terms of conversation. While she was with him, he made her feel the most important person in the world—an infallible technique for winning a woman in those days, when women were treated as inferiors.

Houseman wrote very frankly to his friend Mina Curtiss:

> An actress brings to her copulation some of the warmth and energy or anger or sadness that she has carried over, physically and emotionally, from her performance. . . . Not so the movie star. At a certain level of stardom she is transformed into a Goddess—with Divinity's capacity to change her identity and to be in a thousand places at once. . . . At the same moment that I am making love to [Joan] in my own private and personal way on a large bed in a dark room in Beverly Hills she is appearing . . . to millions of others, for each of whom she is a legitimate object of artfully simulated lust. . . . What to do

about all this? Suffer pangs of cosmic jealousy? Or be content to swim around in the warm flood of desire that surrounds her?*

According to Houseman's account, he slept with Joan three or four nights a week, went for weekend visits with her, and enjoyed parties with her. He describes her as adorable, childish, sweet-smelling, elegant, calculating, sophisticated, lecherous, and innocent, following that adjectival barrage with one puncturing word, "faithless." This last word undoubtedly refers to Dozier. Houseman states categorically that the affair was entered into by Joan in order to exasperate Olivia, a great friend of Houseman's, who would meet her frequently at Edward and Geraldine Fitzgerald Lindsay-Hogg's house. Oddly, Joan today cannot recall the correct facts of Houseman's birth, describing him in her memoirs as half French, half English, when in fact he was Rumanian.

In the spring of 1945, Houseman, forty-one, and Joan, almost twenty-nine, wandered about exploring mountains and woods in New York State, looking for a site on which they could build a house, as they planned to marry. Their accounts of the reasons for their breakup differ in their memoirs. Houseman simply records that two weeks after their arrival in New City, New York, Joan, after constant telephone-calling to the Coast, suddenly decided to go back to California. He makes the decision seem meaningless, ruthless, and arbitrary; but Joan mentions that his mother and aunt frequently joined them in New City, a fact that he omits. One evening in New City, Houseman's mother and the architect Henry Varnum Poore were going over the blueprints of the new house when suddenly Houseman's mother informed the company at large that she would be living in the house with John and Joan, and had made a change in the designs so she would be closer to the children. Joan decided on the spot that she would not marry a man whose mother would live with them, and she returned to California to make *From This Day Forward*, using the film as an excuse.

In all events, Joan was in a depressed mood when she made the glum working-class story Dozier had ready for her; and perhaps the strain of wondering how much she had lost by not marrying Houseman, and her unease with *From This Day Forward*'s script, brought on a mysterious ailment that made her eyes and body swell between the morning and the evening. Her dresses in the film had to be altered and realtered, and by the end of the shooting she had to make arrangements to go into the hospital. To make matters worse, no sooner had she recovered than she experienced another major setback.

*John Houseman, *Front and Center* (N.Y: Simon and Schuster, 1979.)

# *Eight*

 In those days, Joan used to go riding with her great friend Charles Bennett. She and Charles would trot their mounts across the trails of the Santa Monica mountains, which were not then built up or intersected by freeways. One day, they cantered across the Will Rogers estate to a bridle path on a high ridge that was very narrow and was known as the Camel's Back. They rode into a puzzle of strange paths; Bennett was one of the few people who knew the terrain. Joan was riding ahead when something frightened her horse and she backed it into bramble bushes. The bushes pricked the mare, which reared suddenly and sent Joan tumbling down the side of the cliff.

She hung there on the edge of the abyss like the heroine of *The Perils of Pauline*. Charles crawled down and pulled her out of the bushes; he even managed to raise her up on her horse. She was in great pain, but there was no other way to get her home. Bennett managed to calm the horse and lead Joan back to the stables. From there, Joan was admitted to the hospital with broken ribs. Hedda and Louella both reported that Joan had been attacked by a rattlesnake. Olivia's comment has not been recorded.

While Joan was recovering from the fall, Olivia moved ahead to a triumph. Paramount sent her the script of *To Each His Own*, an entertaining soap opera in which she would play the part of Josephine "Jody" Norris, who at the opening of the film is discovered in wartime London on air-raid-warden duty with the sophisticated Lord Desham, played by Roland Culver. In a flashback that takes up the bulk of the film, she reminisces about her life. The flashback begins in World War I, when Jody Norris, working in a drugstore, meets a war hero, played by John Lund. They have a brief affair and Jody becomes pregnant, but the hero is killed in action and she has to raise the illegitimate child. Through a series of complications, a friend of hers, played by Mary Anderson, raises the child instead, and the soap-opera complications grow from there.

The story was a stock Hollywood melodrama, made persuasive and interesting by the clever writing of Charles Brackett. It provided a field day for an actress, however, offering the opportunity to run the gamut from youth to middle age; through comedy, tragedy, melodrama, and soft-edged sentiment. Despite Olivia's weakened condition, not only from the pneumonia but from some mysterious tropical ailment that hung on, causing her a form of dysentery and night sweats, she was overjoyed when she received the script—a great relief after the silliness of *The Well-Groomed Bride*. Her main concern was the choice of director. The studio urged her to accept the British Lewis Allen, who had just made the successful ghost movie *The Uninvited*. Olivia, with her customary steely will, was unconvinced but did agree to watch Allen's pictures. After seeing several of them, she realized that his style was too diffuse and lacking in firmness to save the story of *To Each His Own* from bogging down. She dismayed the studio executives by refusing to work with Allen, demanding Mitchell Leisen instead.

The studio sent Leisen the script in New York and he turned it down at once, hating soap opera more than any other genre. Olivia used all of her powers of persuasion on him until at last he yielded and, together with Brackett and Olivia herself, expertly reworked the script. Once again, the indispensable Phyllis Laughton, now Mrs. George Seaton, came in to guide Olivia through her lines, and Olivia and John Lund would talk out the emotions of the scene in their dressing rooms while Leisen laid out the shots. As the shooting went on, Leisen grew more and more enthusiastic, reworking the script more tightly and with more realism. Olivia worked out the smallest details of her performance with Leisen; he would say to her, "All right, relax," and she would reply, "Now tell me what I'm thinking in the scene," and he would add, "You're thinking of [so-and-so]," and then she would say, "Now give me my pitch."

Fortunately, the movie was shot in sequence, so that Olivia looked convincingly thin, young, and frail in the early scenes; then, as she became pregnant, Leisen had her stuff herself with cakes and chocolates and pies until her cheeks filled out and she got a double chin and she put on about fifteen pounds. Her stomach was padded to add even more size, and as a final touch she wore a "frankly forty" foundation garment filled with cotton. In later scenes, she was aged according to photographs in a *Life* magazine history of Winston Churchill, showing his upper lip thinning with time and lines developing around his eyes. She discussed the prospect of whitening her hair, like that of Ray Milland's wife, but in the end both she and Leisen decided that a woman like Josephine Norris would dye her hair in middle age. This kind of attention to detail made Olivia admire Leisen forever. And the fact that she could rehearse to perfection and then not struggle through endless takes put her totally at his feet.

There were many moments of laughter on the set. In one sequence, set in the 1920s, Olivia had to wear a chinchilla-trimmed gown in studio temperatures of over 100° and Leisen called out to her, "Don't you *dare* perspire!" He also taught her how to flourish a cigarette holder as her character grew more "sophisticated" and, in order to make her feel completely part of the scene, encouraged her to wear a different perfume for each successive era in the story. She went to her mother, who still hovered behind the scenes, and asked her what she had worn in the 1920s, when she and Joan were children. "Chypre," Lilian replied without hesitation. Olivia searched through many stores before she could find any; for a later sequence, she wore Chanel No.5, because that was the most popular perfume of World War II.

Yet there were problems during the shooting. Toward the end of the picture, there was a scene in which John Lund was to get married in London and Olivia had to tell him before the wedding that he was her son. It was an outrageous sequence by any standards, and when it came to shooting it, Leisen threw up his hands in despair and told Olivia and Charles Brackett, who was also the producer, that he simply couldn't direct it as it stood. Before everyone, Brackett ordered Leisen to continue. Leisen stormed off the set, drove to the studio gate, changed his mind, drove back, charged into Brackett's office, and offered to help do a rewrite. Olivia dropped in to offer her own suggestions, and in the end the speech of self-revelation was cut, much to Olivia's relief, and replaced with a scene in which the young man recognizes his mother at the close, after the wedding is over.

Olivia's carefully modulated, firm, and tactful performance earned her excellent reviews, very strong preview responses, and an Oscar nomination. One sequence was added after the previews: Brackett felt that Olivia should cry helplessly when she took her child to Mary Anderson for guardianship; he was convinced the scene was too flat as it stood. Leisen was very upset and Olivia was dubious, but Brackett insisted. The entire set of a house had to be reconstructed and John Lund brought back from another picture; and Olivia dutifully cried and cried until everyone started to laugh. But after spending $70,000 on the additional scene, it was badly received in New York City and had to be cut out, proving that Leisen's and Olivia's judgment had been right all along.

The picture was a big commercial success, grossing close to twice its production cost by late 1946. Almost in an act of malice, Warners' released the poor film *Devotion*, which it had held up for three years, immediately on top of the excellent *To Each His Own*, but even this ill-advised decision could not affect Olivia's remarkable comeback.

There was little consolation for Joan, immersed in the dreary *From This Day Forward*. Moreover, she grew notably cantankerous and difficult on her promotional tour to New York City for that film. She complained bitterly that the publicity department simply sent her flowers and failed to meet her or make her welcome in her suite at the Hampshire House; and she said that the same publicity department insulted her by sending around an obscure girl underling to take her to a store and pose her with inexpensive dresses for an unknown magazine called *Fascination*, with a circulation of a mere 3,000. When she gave an MCA broadcast, there was no one from the publicity department present, and promised interviews never materialized. She was shocked because she was given a second-rate suite and no one made sure she was comfortable in it or took care of her personal arrangements.

At the end of 1945, Joan was sicker than ever. Laid up in the hospital, where Dozier visited her with arms full of roses, she canceled her next picture (*Christabel Caine*, later retitled *Born to be Bad*). Then she moved into the convent of the Sacred Heart at Menlo Park for a complete recovery from her illness.

She entered into the relationship with Dozier with the same casualness, pliancy, and apparent lack of emotional commitment with which she had entered into her marriage to Aherne. Perhaps because of her early suffering, she now became, more than ever, flippant, cool, tough, and somewhat offhand. She was even further removed now from the intense, driven, overserious, dedicated, and impassioned Olivia.

Joan, as always, was fast-moving, walking with the peculiar stoop-shouldered stride that was reminiscent of her spinal problems in adolescence. Even during the dull shooting of *From This Day Forward*, she had bustled about with remarkable energy between bouts of sickness, and if she flew into a temper, nobody forgot it. Despite her slenderness and near frailty, she still ate heavy food, and Dozier begged her in vain to diet.

Joan's relationship with Dozier gradually deepened, and yet the differences between them became rapidly clear. They had in common a sharp wit, keen judgment, sophistication, and the joint experience of picture-making. But they also looked at life very differently in many ways. Dozier certainly was disillusioned, but he was relaxed, genial, and fond of living, never cynical. For all her antic humor, Joan had an inescapable severity inherited from her father. She was altogether too hard on herself and others, a kind of mirror of Olivia in that respect. Although she had more "give" than Olivia, and was more capable of enjoying herself, she was like the scorpion in the ancient legend. The story had it that a man was crossing a river on foot, barely able to keep his head above water, with a scorpion, which could not swim, perched on his shoulder. Halfway across the river, the scorpion stung him and he drowned, carrying the scorpion with him. The moral was that the scorpion could not help itself: It was its destiny to sting, even if that meant its own death.

Joan simply could not help herself, any more than Olivia could. Dozier says, "Joan would be smiling and charming and then there would be a barb. Finally, she lost one friend after another. She's the kind of woman who inevitably winds up alone."

Olivia was busy making *Dark Mirror* at Universal, a strange melodrama about twins, one good, one evil, in which she was costarred with Lew Ayres, whom publicity reports had had her dating several years earlier. The director, Robert Siodmak, irritated her by driving her to give an exceptionally cruel and harsh edge to the evil twin, which, protective of her image, she tried to soften; and he sought to remove the excessive sweetness she brought to the role of the good twin. She had little or no rapport with Siodmak, who directed with matter-of-fact detachment. Her arguments with him were frequent, and she was unhappy with the results: She acted both parts mechanically, with technical skill but with none of the emotional commitment she had brought to *To Each His Own*.

While Joan began seriously dating Dozier in the spring of 1946, and he obtained a divorce from his wife, Olivia boarded the train to New

York with Phyllis Loughton Seaton. During the journey, Phyllis said that she thought Olivia should settle down with one man now that she was almost thirty years old, and Phyllis knew the perfect choice for her: the novelist Marcus Goodrich. As it happened, Olivia remembered Goodrich—she had met him in 1942, at a dinner party at the home of the M-G-M producer Arthur Hornblow, Jr. Goodrich had said that he was tired of American women and their aggressive behavior and that he wanted to go to Sweden, marry a simple farm girl, and raise children. Olivia had said coyly, "Why go to Sweden?"

Goodrich had made his name overnight at the beginning of 1941 with his novel *Delilah*, based on his own experiences on a destroyer in World War I. It was a highly wrought and intensely personal story, written with flair, about the aforementioned vessel in the South Pacific in the six months preceding World War I. It dealt with a tense relationship among three men: Warrington, the sensitive, able-bodied seaman based on the author; the crazy Irishman O'Connel, a figure reminiscent of the characters to be found in Jack London; and the elevated, almost spiritual Lieutenant Fitzpatrick. Apart from Jack London, the influences of Conrad and Maugham were clear; the action was harsh, brutal, and candid, and there was a strong tug in the narrative between the navy men and the political authorities occupying desk jobs at home.

A man's book for men, *Delilah* was steeped in authentic experience and rugged and vital in its narrative drive. It owed much not only to the author's maritime experience but to his years as a newspaperman, writing for the *New York Tribune* and *Times*, drinking himself traditionally in and out of the world's gutters, mingling with the Hemingway set, and working as a journeyman Hollywood scriptwriter (*Night Waitress*, *Navy Born*, and *The Trumpet Blows*).

Married and divorced from Caroline Sleeth, Goodrich had a daughter whom he never let interfere with his romantic life. Broad-shouldered, muscular, with close-cropped hair, jug ears, ruminative eyes, a large nose, and a firm, determined mouth, Goodrich lived the role of Hemingway-ish author to the hilt. A kind of precursor of Herman Wouk, he was seldom without a large pipe stuck in his mouth at a rakish angle, and sported the obligatory range of tweed jackets and brogue shoes. He spoke with a Texas accent, which many women found appealing: his great-grandfather, Benjamin Briggs Goodrich, had signed the Texas Declaration of Independence and helped draft the Texas Constitution, and one of his uncles had been killed at the Alamo.

As Phyllis Seaton described this paragon on the seemingly interminable train journey, Olivia could not help but be impressed; and
the fact that his full name was Marcus Aurelius Goodrich and he had
been extravagantly praised by Clifton Fadiman in *The New Yorker* and
Otis Ferguson in the *New Republic* went to her head completely. She
probably had visions of somebody with the southern virility of a Rhett
Butler and the writing talent of a Louis Bromfield.

When Olivia and Phyllis arrived in New York City, Phyllis wasted
no time: She instantly encouraged Goodrich to call, and he took the
two women out to dinner. On the third date, Phyllis discreetly withdrew with an imaginary headache.

Olivia was strongly attracted to Goodrich. She was always drawn
to rugged, intelligent men, and it had been some years since her affairs
with Howard Hughes, James Stewart, and John Huston. The last had
a disconcerting tendency to turn up in her life even at this stage,
presuming to take up his affair where it had left off. Goodrich had a
greater strength of will than all of the men she had dated except
Huston.

When she began rehearsals for appearances in New England in the
play *What Every Woman Knows* by J. M. Barrie, Goodrich was with
her constantly, finding little time to work on his new novel about
Mexico. They talked constantly, sometimes until 4:00 A.M., leaving
her exhausted for the next day's rehearsals; but she couldn't resist
such topics as Jungian philosophy, the atom bomb, J. M. Barrie, and
her cooking specialty that Goodrich liked—kidneys cooked in red
wine.

At the end of rehearsals in New York City, they were very much in
love. Given Olivia's nature, it can be said that her feelings ran deeper
and more intensely than Joan's, and she flung herself fully into the
relationship.

Joan, at that time, was in the midst of several meetings with William Dozier to discuss reviving the film *Christabel Caine*, and was
surprised to hear him propose marriage. He had just divorced his wife
of seventeen years, and Joan, totally fascinated by him, was unable to
resist his offer. They decided to elope to Mexico, where Joan's friends
the George Conways were living. They flew by American World
Airways transport from Lockheed Airport to Mexico City, along with
Dozier's old friend Colonel Max Felix. Mrs. Conway acted as Joan's
attendant and Felix was best man. The wedding was held in the
Conways' living room. Joan wore a shantung suit with a hat trimmed

in brown and green orchids; a dark green handbag filled with brown and green orchids swung on her right arm. The wedding ring had a barber-pole pattern of tiny diamonds, it was a prop for *Christabel Caine* bought by Dozier from his own wardrobe department.

The couple honeymooned at the La Borda Hotel in Taxco during the Cinco de Maya festival, the whole town resplendent with fireworks, burning effigies, streamers, mariachis, and wild crowds. Neither would forget that night. They proceeded to Acapulco for three days, staying at the rose-pink Las Flamingas Hotel overlooking the harbor. Dozier went deep-sea fishing, thrilling Joan with his macho expertise when he came back with a one-hundred-and-fifty-pound marlin. In Mexico City, the couple went to Ciro's to see the famous A. C. Blumenthal, and they bought presents for Joan's secretary, Mary; her cook, Augustine; and her maid, Mona.

When they flew to New York, Olivia, who had decided to try to patch up the differences, got up at dawn to meet them at the airport. They rushed off to see all the plays on Broadway, and Joan brought her hat collection up to eighty-five. According to publicity, they discovered they had two extra tickets for the successful *State of the Union* and gave them to two twelve and ten-year-old fans in the hotel lobby.

Back in Los Angeles, they moved into a charming house on Fordyce Road in Brentwood. It was built of redwood and flagstone, set among three and a half acres of trees, and there was an orchard and a pool. The couple tried to make the living room as informal as possible with pottery and plants, grass-mat carpeting, card tables, and a built-in Capehart. But the honeymoon was short-lived. They moved into the house on a Saturday morning, and on Saturday night Joan took off for Canada to make *The Emperor Waltz*, a period comedy for Billy Wilder.

Dozier went with Joan to Jasper, where the scenery of the Canadian Duchies capped with snow was magnificent. The national park filled with tourists to see Joan, dazzling in the period wardrobe, moving against a background of mountain peaks. Joan was desperate to have a child, Dozier recalls. "We did everything except hang from the chandeliers so Joan could conceive." But it was not long before she was grumbling at being pregnant.

Back in Hollywood there were many problems with Robert Dozier, Bill's teen-age son by a previous marriage. Robert had first met Joan during one of her hospital stays, but the ice hadn't really broken and there was considerable mutual hostility between them. The boy was living with his mother, and Dozier arranged for him to meet Joan again. Dozier says, "Joan walked into the room the usual several minutes late, which stars always employ as an effect. Stretching out her hand royally, she said to Robert, 'It's lovely to see you again. And don't you *dare* call me mother!' Robert was furious. He said sharply, 'I'm not going to call you mother, because you *aren't* my mother!' End of conversation!"

At Westport, Connecticut, where Olivia was appearing in *What Every Woman Knows*, Goodrich installed her and Phyllis in a local inn and rented a cottage nearby for a week. So strong was his desire that, back in New York at the Hammer Galleries, he bought an antique engagement ring made of two gold bands beautifully set with heart-shaped Siberian amethysts framed in diamonds. He also began immediately laying plans for the marriage and the honeymoon as soon as the run of the play was over. Olivia, who was accustomed to taking the upper hand in everything, rather enjoyed being swept off her feet in this manner; Goodrich brought out the suppressed romantic streak in her, a certain giddiness and recklessness that were not usually her style.

Once Olivia decided she was going to marry Goodrich, she couldn't wait to brag to Joan. Joan had been first in marrying, and in winning an Oscar, but at least Olivia wasn't going to be an old maid. She called her sister and said excitedly, "I've got the most thrilling news—I'm going to marry Marcus Goodrich!" Joan said coldly, "*Who?*" Olivia turned to ice as she reminded Joan that he was the well-known author of *Delilah* and that Joan knew him. "Oh, yes. I think I was introduced to him on the set one day," Joan said. Olivia was furious. Joan was totally unimpressed and certainly had neither read *Delilah* nor had any desire to read it. When Hedda and Louella called Joan for a comment, all she could say was "It's a pity Marcus Goodrich married four times but only wrote one novel!" Olivia became savagely angry when she read the item in a column.

After discussing California as the setting for their wedding, the director George Seaton, Phyllis's husband, suggested Westport, Connecticut, as the perfect place, and Olivia and Marcus agreed. Lawrence Langner, producer of *What Every Woman Knows* and director of the Theatre Guild, agreed to give the bride away; his wife, the lovable Armina Marshall, would be the bridesmaid, Phyllis would be matron of honor, and her husband George Seaton would be best man, with Irene Selznick in attendance. There was no sign of Lilian Fontaine, who, with characteristic eccentricity, was as absent from this occasion as she had been from Joan's marriage to Dozier.

On a Sunday night, Olivia and Goodrich took the necessary blood tests and on Monday morning they went to Weston to obtain the marriage license. At eleven o'clock that same morning, August 26, 1946, they returned to the Westport Inn to meet the Reverend Fredric L. Lorentzan, who performed the ceremony at noon on an ornamental island in a garden pool of the Langner house in Weston where the Chinese goddess of happiness stood with a miniature pagoda.

Olivia was traditional in wearing something old (pearls given her long ago by Joan); something new (a handkerchief presented by Irene Selznick); gloves she had borrowed from Phyllis Seaton; a blue hat; and a Roosevelt dime, in place of a sixpence, in her shoe. Just before the ceremony began, she had a sudden impulse and called her mother in California, saying, "Be thinking of me during the next twenty minutes!" At Olivia's characteristic insistence, the word *obey* was omitted from the ceremony.

The Doziers sent flowers; the wedding luncheon was held on the terrace surrounded by banks of snow-white gladioli and clusters of asters. At the end of the lunch, everybody laughed as Olivia read out a cable from her dear friend Nunnally Johnson, saying, "What a wonderful idea!"

Throughout the occasion, Olivia had extreme stage fright. She had held off from marrying anyone for so long and now she felt a threat to her independence. She almost called the whole thing off, but Marcus Goodrich knew what he was doing. He said, "Don't think too far ahead. Just pretend this is a one-act play. Don't worry about the other two acts!" She said later, "If Marc hadn't kept me from thinking too far ahead, I doubt if I would have gone through with it!" And then of course there was the thought that she was marrying a famous author, a man of the world of the romantic age of forty-eight, with a lifetime of maritime and literary experience behind him. She buried her doubts and sailed forward bravely as she always did. Little did she know what agonies lay ahead.

The honeymoon was long and drawn out. The couple drove south from New York to Williamsburg, Virginia, a city with many echoes of the early days of the Goodrich clan. Marcus told Olivia of the journeys of his forebears from Williamsburg to homestead in the wilderness. The couple followed the Wilderness Trail to Eufaula, Alabama, Goodrich filling Olivia's ears with fascinating historical information, and then she suggested they proceed to Atlanta, with all its echoes of *Gone with the Wind*.

They continued almost three thousand miles across the continent. Olivia wired ahead, asking the Doziers if she could stay with them.

Joan was very nervous about this. What was Olivia up to? She wasn't impressed with what she had heard about Goodrich. He sounded eccentric and unkempt. However, she reluctantly agreed.

When Olivia and Marcus arrived after hours of extricating themselves from the intricacies of Glendale, they buzzed the doorbell; but then it took them some forty minutes to get sufficiently organized to enter the house. Later, Olivia complained that she and Marcus had been left standing at the door. Dinner was cold, and Joan was upset. And when Olivia asked the Doziers that night to support her in her campaign for James Roosevelt, son of Franklin D., as head of a new Democratic party group, they (Dozier recalls) flatly refused.

In Hollywood, Olivia and Goodrich moved into a rather ordinary two-bedroom apartment in west Hollywood in a building owned by Mitchell Leisen. One of the problems from the beginning was the disparity between the two incomes. Although Goodrich was not poor, and *Delilah* had made its way into the lower rungs of the best-seller list, paperbacks were not common in those days and the picture was not sold to the movies. Goodrich was a very macho male who probably was affected by the fact that while he was struggling to write a new novel set in Mexico and had to protect his income very carefully, Olivia was among the highest-paid stars in the world, earning well over $200,000 a year. Their desire not to live in a large house in Beverly Hills was probably influenced by his circumstances and by Olivia's desire not to make him feel inferior. But there was a savage streak in her, and her powerful ego may have been somewhat threatening to him. Their quarrels were lethal in the confined space they lived in.

William Dozier gave a party for 250 people at Romanoff's to celebrate Joan's birthday, and he and Joan decided to invite Olivia and Goodrich. They accepted—but just one hour before the party, Olivia called and said, too sweetly, "I'm so sorry. We can't come. Marcus has a cold." Dozier said, "There are two seats saved for you. The press will make hell if you don't appear. Leave him at home!" And Olivia answered, even more sweetly, "Oh, no! I couldn't *possibly* leave Marcus at home with a cold!"

The eternally contentious Olivia was fighting in that autumn of 1946 with her agents Berg-Allenberg, and specifically with her old friend and representative Jimmy Townsend. When Myron Selznick died prematurely as a result of alcoholism, Townsend consolidated his position with Phil Berg and continued to work for Olivia. For most of he year, he had tried to persuade Olivia to play the leading role in a film called *Ivy*, based on a novel by Mrs. Belloc-Lowndes about an Edwardian murderess in the early days of telephones and airplanes who poisons her husband and tries to send her lover to the gallows for his murder in order to clear the way for her marriage to a wealthy businessman. Olivia, however, had hated the ordeal of playing the bad twin in *Dark Mirror* (quite apart from the nightmarish technicalities of matching shots when she was doubling in the two parts), and she did not want to play a woman of all-out calculating evil. She correctly saw that whereas in *Dark Mirror* there was one twin with whom the audience could identify, in *Ivy* there would be nobody in the picture for the public to hang on to, and thus, she felt, the movie would be a commercial failure.

She was even more aggravated by her discovery that Berg-Allenberg had interests in the Dorsey Corporation, later known as Inter-Wood Productions, Inc., which was partly made up of the company of *Ivy*'s director, Sam Wood. She felt very strongly that she was being forced into the part only to earn her agents an additional percentage, which would in fact be a breach of the Sherman Act, which dealt with the issue of monopolism. In mid-November 1946, when Olivia finally learned the truth about her agents' involvement in Inter-Wood Productions, she exploded with rage and refused to sign the contract just four days before she was due to go in for costume tests with her old friend Orry-Kelly (later replaced by Travis Banton). She claimed later that Townsend and Phil Berg tried to force her to play the part and prevented her from playing others by announcing that she was committed to *Ivy*, and indeed it is true that she was out of work for six months, at an approximate cost to her of well over $100,000.

She sued Berg-Allenberg for loss of income and for suborning her, and she charged that they had been in breach of normal agent's etiquette and procedure. In retaliation, the tough Phil Berg immediately offered the part in *Ivy* to Joan, who gleefully seized upon it and rushed into Olivia's costumes. The clothes were gorgeous—lacy, elegant, intricate—and Joan looked ravishing in them, carrying a fine array of white silk parasols. She was fascinated by the handsome, Germanic paintings of every setup by William Cameron Menzies, a designer and graphic artist of formidable skill.

Joan disliked working with Sam Wood as much as Olivia had when he had taken over *Gone with the Wind* and had made *Raffles*. The work was taxing: Joan became part of the decor, an exquisite face and figure woven into the texture with little opportunity to develop a complex characterization. Ivy Lexton was motivated by a greedy desire to marry riches, and by the frustration of an impoverished marriage; it was made clear from the beginning that she had ruined her weak and charming husband by squandering his savings on an elaborate wardrobe. She was sly, subtle, and devious, and Joan effectively conveyed her duplicity. But she could not manage to suggest the determination that Olivia would have brought to the part; she was too casual, relaxed, and genuinely charming; her villainy seemed frivolous and her ultimate fear of discovery too assumed. The performance remained external, and the movie suffered from it. But there were splendid moments—especially the opening, when Ivy ascends the staircase to the parlor of the clairvoyant whose prophecies are accompanied by the clanging tones of a spinet; and the trial scene in which it is clear that Ivy intends to send her lover to the scaffold. Lilian Fontaine appeared in the film as a titled woman whose daughter was engaged to Herbert Marshall. She made a very ordinary impression.

Yet, as Olivia had foreseen, *Ivy* was not a great success at the box office; it was too literary, too severe; and as Olivia knew, nobody could identify with the heroine. The picture proved a setback to Joan's career. But then, she had a compensation—she was pregnant at last. Lilian's only remark to Joan was "Now you can put the child on the mantelshelf along with your Oscar!"

Meanwhile, Olivia joined the Kurt Frings Agency; this was somehow appropriate, since *Hold Back the Dawn* had been based in part on the Kurt and Ketti Frings story. She was quite happy with the agency, and her only sadness that fall of 1946 was that Geoffrey de Havilland was killed in a crash in the Thames Estuary, flying a new jet plane designed by his father, the girls' uncle. It seemed horribly unfair that the handsome, dashing blade who had been so full of joy in his visit to Hollywood some years before had been cut down in his prime.

One of Kurt Frings's friends was the sophisticated and sharp-witted director and ladies' man Anatole Litvak, the White Russian whom Olivia had dated briefly at the beginning of the 1940s. Like Olivia, Litvak had broken with Warner Brothers, where she had often run into him during the war years. He was now under contract to Twentieth Century-Fox. Using most of his $75,000 capital, he had obtained the rights to a novel, *The Snake Pit*, written by the young Mary Jane Ward, wife of the writer Edward Quayle. It was the story of a girl stricken with severe depression and mental disorders who is admitted to an institution for the insane, finds the conditions there atrocious, violent patients housed together with those only slightly ill, a chilling detachment of doctors and nurses toward patients looking desperately for mental and moral support and reassurance.

Olivia very much wanted to play the heroine of the story—a simple housewife whose ordeal threatens to destroy her, but who finally emerges through the love of her husband. Characteristically, Olivia asked that the husband be played by Joan's leading man in *From This Day Forward*, Mark Stevens.

While she was preparing for the part, and Frings was negotiating the contract with Darryl F. Zanuck at Twentieth, the 1947 Academy Awards took place. As so often before, there was considerable excitement and tension in the air when Olivia and Joan arrived with their husbands. When Olivia won for *To Each His Own*, a great cheer went up from the crowd. Photographers, led by the famous Hymie Fink, rushed up with flashbulbs to snap the sisters together; but as Joan reached out, smiling in congratulation, Olivia turned coldly on her heel and walked away—thus providing one of the most memorable photographs in Hollywood history.

It was a very serious mistake on Olivia's part. It gave the impression she was a poor sport, vindictive, and inconsiderate; but Joan emerged very well, looking as she had intended to, thoughtful and forgiving. Olivia could not forgive. She was maddened by Joan's crack about Goodrich. She was under great tension at home, and under strain as she weighed the emotional and physical demands of her part in *The Snake Pit*. And there was the wearing business of the depositions, charges, complications, and costs of the suit against her agents. She was very far from being happy, even with her gold statuette and the unmitigated approval of the industry.

As for Joan, she hid in seclusion until the ceremony was over; and Lilian, uncharacteristically attending it, and taking Joan's side now, was forbidden by Olivia to go backstage and give her congratulations.

Joan decided to make the best of a bad job. She completed arrangements to form Rampart Productions with Dozier, hoping to deepen and cement their marriage with this imposing corporate name that suggested great strength and something solid for the future. Her arrangement was that she would make two pictures a year, one for Rampart and one for an outside company, and for a time the relationship was indeed improved because she and Dozier were working on a common plan. But unfortunately the picture she embarked on, *Letter from an Unknown Woman*, proved to be as much of a frost at the box office as *Ivy*. Directed by Max Ophuls, an Austrian director of great talent, this version of a Stefan Zweig novella about a deceived mistress was hampered by the fact that the heroine died of typhus in the final scene, a sure guaranty that the public would stay away. Ravishingly staged in a re-created nineteenth-century Vienna and Linz, and played by Joan with the greatest delicacy and adeptly simulated tenderness of feeling, the movie remains a classic among specialists, and is virtually forgotten by everybody else.

Universal-International's *Kiss the Blood off My Hands*, in which Joan played the unhappy wife of a low-class British criminal improbably played by Burt Lancaster, was equally grim and cheerless in mood. Directed by Norman Foster and set in gloomy, dank, cheap rooms and yards in rain and fog, it left the viewer in a state of acute depression, and not even Joan's skillful performance could save it.

The difficulty of shooting these pictures was exacerbated by Joan's pregnancy. Although she had wanted a child, she almost instantly resented her condition, and when she made an insignificant comedy, *You Gotta Stay Happy*, she was rendered miserable by the physical activity called for on the set.

Joan also made a very serious mistake: She decided that they needed a larger house with more room for the child and the nurse. On Sundays, she and Dozier toured endless homes for sale, exhausting herself in her condition by climbing stairs or stumbling through dark cellars. When nothing would quite do, she decided to build a house and hired an architect, but when she received the estimate, she realized the costs were far too high.

In the end, she and Dozier decided to build a new wing onto the existing house, with a guest suite for Dozier's son, a large glass-walled room for parties, and two more bedrooms. Joan worked day and night with the architect and engineers, moving out almost all the furniture and storing it so there would be room for the workmen to trail in and out on newspaper-covered floors. From her vantage point at a kitchen table in the living room, she ran a complex operation involving plumbers, carpenters, electricians, and painters. Walls had to be ripped out, pipes added, and wires replaced, hence for long periods during her pregnancy there was no water supply and no illumination. The water heater failed to fit, the furnace ducts were too small, the electrical cables were unsatisfactory, but Joan, overwhelmed with bills, struggled on. The Doziers had made a second serious mistake in not hiring a contractor, who would have given them a guaranteed price for the entire job. By doing the work piecemeal, the cost escalated ruinously.

Moreover, the noise was so intense that the couple had to move into the Bel Air Hotel.

Olivia's simultaneous work in *The Snake Pit* was hard, harrowing, and rewarding. With typical enthusiasm, she had visited and studied numerous mental institutions watching shock treatments; the inhabitants gazed transfixed as the famous star wandered about, conferring with doctors and nurses. She steeped herself so completely in the part that her nerves became frayed once again and life at the Goodriches' was increasingly tormenting.

To make matters worse, she was terrorized by a bizarre Chicago painter named Paul Randall, a disturbed fan who was constantly sending her letters inscribed with mystic symbols and filled with outpourings of a would-be lover's affection. Jittery, fearing possible murder, Olivia reported Randall to the police when he followed up a threat by flying to Los Angeles in May and insisting that he would see her at once or else. The police advised her to promise to go to his apartment on North Las Palmas Avenue in Hollywood. He waited, pacing anxiously, hoping to take his idol in his arms, but instead the police arrived and arrested him. Under interrogation, Randall insisted that Olivia had made romantic overtures to him. He was held in custody.

Olivia was very unsettled by this incident. She was also irritated by the sudden reappearance in the press of the long-lost Walter de Havilland, now living on Victoria Island in British Columbia, Canada, who made a statement for no particular reason to the Associated Press that he wanted to see his daughters reconciled.

Then two strangers besieged her, copying Randall's tactics. One man sent her a five-hundred word telegram from La Guardia Airport in New York City. The long, rambling wire ordered her to contact the sender or regret it to the end of her days. The sender went on to state that he knew he was talking to a famous star but that he himself would be running for vice president next year. Kurt Frings turned the telegram over to the FBI. The other man, in his sixties, appeared at Frings's office and said he would kill him if Olivia didn't return the money he had lent her.

When further investigation revealed that Paul Randall believed he was Saint Paul, Olivia felt she was living the plot of *The Snake Pit* in real life. She was emotionally drained by the time the shooting of the film ended, and not consoled by further battles with her husband. Nevertheless, she correctly saw her performance in *The Snake Pit* as her best to date. She was sensitive and convincing, playing with an intelligent grasp of character. Resisting the temptation to ham up the scenes with excessive eye-rollings, she quietly conveyed a feeling of mental disintegration, daringly looking ungroomed, even unattractive, in many sequences. She was particularly powerful in the horrifying episode of the hydrotherapy shock-bath treatment, written and directed without compromise. She was also very effective in the sequence in which a portly institution doctor prods her with a plump finger and she bites it. She succeeded in overcoming the weaknesses of Leo Genn's excessively smarmy performance as another psychiatrist in her confrontations with him.

She received the best reviews of her career. *Time* said she had at last emerged as an actress. *Redbook* said that seldom was a performance "so carefully wrought, so beautifully sustained and so artfully executed."

Joan had her first serious labor pains in November 1947, and on November 4 she gave birth. She told Gladys Hall of *Photoplay*:

> Childbirth is pain and frenzy. It is worse than I thought it
> would be. With a spinal, it might be bearable in a baleful sort of
> way. But I turned out to be allergic to all known ways of
> deadening labor pains, with the result that for ten and a half
> hours, I was in pain. I remembered them tying me
> down . . . even so, two hours after Deborah was born, Bill
> leaned over to me and whispered, "Do you still mean it?" and I,
> knowing he meant did I still want four children, said, "Yes I
> do." And I do.

Becoming a mother at St. John's Hospital in Santa Monica was, she wrote later, "an entirely humiliating, embarrassing, degrading experience." She wrote also that her child—a daughter, Deborah Leslie—refused her mother's breasts and would accept only bottled milk and water.

The Doziers sent Olivia a telegram reading, "You are the aunt of an eight and a half pound baby girl named Deborah Leslie Dozier. She and mother are very well." Olivia did not reply; Joan was furious.

The ever-perverse Lilian, when Joan called her with the news, was very upset that she was now a grandmother. She made no attempt to come to see the child. Olivia, of course, was in every possible way indifferent.

William Dozier says, "The baptism presented a problem. Hedda and Louella had to be involved. If they hadn't been, or if one had been there and not the other, watch out! Joan was very clever with the press, and especially with the two queens of gossip. So Hedda was asked for her grandmother's antique lace baptismal gown; and Louella was allowed to hold the baby before Debbie was dipped in the font. If Louella had known that Debbie was wearing that gown, she'd have dropped her right on the floor!"

Recovering from childbirth, and trying rather awkwardly to relate to her baby, Joan was also greatly troubled by the house in Brentwood, which was far too elaborate and pretentious for her. Dozier liked to have a constant flow of people coming and going, and Joan was irritated by that, as well as by the lavishness of the entertainment and the constant expenditures of herself, her husband, and ill-fated Rampart Productions on extravagances on and off the set. Only by the strongest will was Joan able to stop the endless outlays on caviar and champagne; she began making the most severe economies, learning what was to become a lifelong grasp of accounting and investments.

She was drifting further and further apart from Dozier. Instead of binding them together, Debbie drove them away from each other; and Joan was very severe with the child.

There were many frustrations. The Doziers had given up their bedroom to turn it into a nursery, and built a new room for themselves in the courtyard of the house. Next to the nursery, they installed a record player and a library of classical music so that Debbie would hear nothing but "great works" from the beginning of her life, but the idea failed because Debbie's nurse refused to play the music and instead played soap operas on the radio through the night and "The Crime of Mary Smith" every morning, and Joan could not bring herself to fire her.

Debbie was baptized a Catholic like her father, and according to many press reports Joan laid out an elaborate plan for the child's education: She was to see all Joan's pictures being made, from scripts to final cut, and attend every television and radio program Joan was to make; she was to be trundled around orphan homes, prisons, hospitals, and law courts to be exposed to the physically, mentally, and morally sick; and was to visit factories and coal mines as well as country clubs and luxury hotels so she could see how both halves lived and how lucky she was to be rich. Fortunately, nothing came of this plan.

# 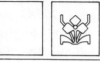 *Nine*

Early in 1948, Olivia, nominated for another Oscar for *The Snake Pit* and voted one of the most popular stars in the nation, embarked on an even more important project: the screen version of *The Heiress*, which had been adapted from Henry James's *Washington Square* by Ruth and Augustus Goetz and presented on the stage in New York City by the legendary Jed Harris. Ralph Richardson was to create a new version of his brilliant theatrical performance as Dr. Sloper, and Olivia would take the part created by Peggy Ashcroft in London and Wendy Hiller in New York as Catherine, the unhappy daughter of the stern Victorian pater-familias. The unhappy Montgomery Clift was cast as the fortune hunter Morris Townsend, who seeks to marry the plain and un-wanted Catherine.

At first, Olivia was excited that she would be directed by the fa-mous William Wyler, who had guided her great friend Bette Davis through the stormy seas of *Jezebel*, *The Letter*, and *The Little Foxes*. Born in Germany forty-six years earlier, Wyler was, on the surface, a small, pixieish, jug-eared charmer with a knotty physique like a light-weight boxer's; a quick, impish smile; and a soft, ingratiating voice. Underneath, however, he was a firebrand with a fierce drive and a cutting edge made even sharper by the irritability resulting from partial deafness caused by an injury sustained while making a documentary in World War II. Since he had just triumphed in making his masterpiece, *The Best Years of Our lives*, a brilliantly sustained portrait of men returning from war, he was at his yeastiest and most confident when he embarked on *The Heiress*. And he was also very far from happy with the casting of Olivia.

Wyler told me that he felt Olivia was far too beautiful for the part of Catherine Townsend. Moreover, he found her inflexible, intractable; she refused to wear shabby clothes, drab mittens, or to allow herself to look really ugly, and she also resented his endless takes and retakes. At last he became so maddened by her that he gave all of his instructions to her through the assistant director. It was, he told me, the most unhappy working relationship he had ever had with a star, and he took great pains never to work with Olivia again.

It is unfortunate that Olivia also had little time for Wyler, much as she respected his talent. Her favorite director remained Mitchell Leisen, who was, of course, not nearly in the same class. But Leisen would consult with her; he would discuss scenes; he would rehearse everything in full and then shoot on the first take. Wyler, on the other hand, refused to rehearse and did those countless takes, which rendered her fretful and irritable. He was also a stickler for punctuality, and she hated to be punctual; he ignored her, never discussing interpretation with her, simply asking her to "Do it once more." Ralph Richardson also offered her little comfort, since that charming man had completely worked out his performance years before and was letter-perfect, simply expecting Olivia to be the same.

In short, she felt no pleasure and no succor, and perhaps that was why her performance had a restless, nervous edge and a tremendous power of anger when she burst out at her father, talking of the cruelty she had acquired, "I have been taught by masters!" She had indeed: George Fontaine, John Huston, and William Wyler had that much in common.

But despite all the problems of shooting, *The Heiress* remains a very powerful motion picture. Under Wyler's instruction, the cameraman, Leo Tover, explored with great fluency the house at 16 Washington Square. The interior sets—heavy, opulent but oppressive—mirror the mood of Catherine Sloper; as doors constantly slide shut, they emphasize her exclusion from life and from passion. The camera dips low behind a tall chair as Dr. Sloper looms over the pathetic girl; when he goes off to die, we see a labyrinth of mirrors, cold, formal, and recessive, while her face remains fixed with disdain.

Wyler's direction of Olivia and Ralph Richardson was at its best in the definitive touch with which Catherine decisively snips the thread from the last letter of her embroidered alphabet, symbolically cutting off Morris Townsend as he rattles the door knocker. In another fine touch, while Catherine and her father are sitting in a sidewalk café in Paris, Dr. Sloper taps his spoon very hard on the teacup, the sound artificially augmented to indicate a note of finality.

The dialogue, much as Olivia may have resented Wyler's control of it, is masterfully orchestrated, particularly when Dr. Sloper says, looking at his wife's portrait and comparing her to his ugly-duckling offspring, "She dominated the color," and Townsend's singing of "Chagrin d'Amour" to Catherine's quickly suppressed outbreak of delight.

For all her physical miscasting, Olivia's performance in *The Heiress* stands beside her playing in *Gone with the Wind* and *The Snake Pit*, rich in its range of detail, marred only by the excessive strength the actress could not quite conceal. She was nominated again for the Academy Award, and won it for the part in March 1950.

Perhaps because she was accustomed to the somewhat orotund language of the play, a watered-down version of Henry James, Olivia became excessively pedantic, measured, and musical in her private utterances at the time, and not infrequently after that; indeed, in the film itself, her line about Townsend to her aunt Lavinia (Miriam Hopkins)—"He came back with the same lies!"—was too rounded in tone. She sometimes seemed to address her friends from an invisible pulpit, and when the frivolous Joan got wind of this she would throw back her head and laugh uproariously.

Olivia became pregnant during the shooting; again some of her dresses had to be let out, and she became quite ill, seemingly no more comfortable with her condition than Joan had been with hers. It was not untypical of actresses of prominence to almost instinctively resent what many women would have welcomed. This was partly because pregnancy was highly inconvenient to a career, particularly when that career was at its height, and also because in those days doctors often advised comparative and sometimes complete inactivity.

As the months dragged on, Olivia, in bed all the time, was in very poor physical and psychological condition. She was arguing constantly with Goodrich; and at the same time she gave out interminable interviews to the dragon army of columnists, led by the inescapable Hedda and Louella. These two insisted on being present at the crib, like witches in the fairy tale, to cast their baleful eyes on the newborn.

Like Joan, Olivia had a sharp sense of the necessity to humor these harpies without seeming to be favoring one over the other. As it happened, Joan was a close friend of Hedda's, probably for convenience rather than anything else, and thus Olivia gave her "exclusives" to Louella. The two women came to see her in relays, their visits carefully timed by Olivia's press agent so they would not run into each other in the entrance hall. Oddly, Olivia and Goodrich moved to Brentwood, not far away from Joan, but not until Joan had left for Europe to make *September Affair* for Olivia's former producer, Hal Wallis.

In the meantime, Joan had returned to RKO, at last to make the picture *Born to Be Bad*, a title that proved to be all too accurately descriptive of both film and performance. Joan mechanically walked through the story of a destructive woman, behaving more like her character off the camera than on as she battled with the pretentious director Nicholas Ray, who had already become something of a cult figure in Europe. During the shooting, Howard Hughes suddenly reemerged on the scene, buying RKO—for a variety of motives, one of which may have been that he wanted to acquire control over Joan's career. He had always regretted his failure to include her in his list of women, and that she had refused him so abruptly when he was having his curious, unsatisfactory relationship with Olivia.

She found him changed, but not for the better. He had been in a plane crash, which had affected not only his looks but also his mind, and his eccentricity was already deepening into outright weirdness. Over the years he had become even more deaf and he still spoke in that disconcerting high-pitched voice. The only food he would eat was one butterfly steak a day, with exactly twelve peas, no more and no less, on the plate beside it. He was afraid of germs and sometimes wore gloves in high summer.

All this was unsettling; and so, too, was the news that he had fired the attractive Barbara Bel Geddes, daughter of the famous stage designer Norman Bel Geddes (and 1980s star of *Dallas*) from *Born to Be Bad*. Worse, Joan learned from studio boss Dore Schary that Schary had decided to leave the studio when Barbara Bel Geddes was dismissed. Indeed, Schary resigned or was fired for his intransigence.

Hughes wanted the studio for a tax deduction and he paved the way for the destruction of RKO through catastrophic and clumsy management. As studio chief, he embarked on a dreary flight picture, *Jet Pilot*, begun by Josef von Sternberg, directing sequences himself. He also got involved with a third-rate western called *Rancho Notorious*, directed by another over-the-hill German craftsman, Fritz Lang.

In view of the fact that Joan was still married and the mother of a small baby, and also since even a hint of adultery could be severely injurious to a career in the puritanical Forties, it seems almost incredible that Joan would have dated Hughes at the time.

William Dozier told me, "Joan has always tried to give the impression that Hughes chased her, but this is completely wrong. Joan was in competition with Olivia once again. She remembered how his affair with Olivia hadn't worked out and now she wanted him to marry her and give her all his millions. I never saw anything like the determination with which she chased her objective."

According to Joan's memoirs, she was greatly offended when Hughes showed her a hideaway house that he had bought in which they could meet clandestinely—she was afraid of losing her daughter in a custody suit. She came back to earth when Hughes suggested renting a ranch for her in Nevada or Arizona while she waited for her divorce. This was too much for her to contemplate and she told him point-blank that she couldn't go ahead.

At this unpleasant moment, Joan was given a reprieve when she was offered *September Affair*. The bedridden Olivia can only have felt envy as she read that Joan, costarred with Joseph Cotten, would work in Rome, Venice, Florence, and the gorgeous island of Capri. Joan was to play a beautiful woman who meets a married man in Italy. The plane on which both were scheduled to fly home crashes and they are presumed dead. While the man's tortured wife (the admirable Jessica Tandy) broods in New York, the couple enter into an adulterous liaison, knowing all along that when the truth of their existence is disclosed, they will not able to continue.

Joan agonized over the possibility that leaving her tiny baby for months might jeopardize her rights in a future custody battle. When the time came, she simply gave Debbie to her husband and took off. Hedda Hopper aggressively insisted on going to Italy as Joan's companion, and Joan decided that it might be a shrewd move to encourage her. Louella, of course, was furious about this and as a result practically lived at Olivia's house, protectively clucking over Olivia's pregnant condition.

A triumphant Hedda met with Joan at the Los Angeles Airport. She was a remarkable woman, pretty as a fox and just as sly, with aquiline features; high, photogenic cheekbones; and an almost emaciated body achieved by relentless dieting. Her living room on Tropical

Avenue in Beverly Hills, where Joan and Olivia were often entertained, boasted a blown-up *Time* magazine cover of her with a typewriter on her head in the form of a hat, the photo framed in gilt like a Rembrandt, and flanked by votive candles. She also had a cocktail bar so crowded with glasses it looked like the glassware department in a store.

She was consistently and relentlessly vulgar, and the summit of her ambition was going to the racetrack with Bob Hope. Her favorite anecdote concerned the flights of doves released at singer Lawrence Tibbett's funeral, which defecated on the congregation to her braying amusement. She belted scotches and defied her liver to complain. But although she was loud, pushy, and bossy, people seemed to warm to her more often than to Louella. She was far more physically attractive and she could sometimes be witty in her coarse way, but with a skillful veneer of sophistication.

She always was regal and she couldn't resist trying to upstage Joan from the moment they got on the plane. Fellow passengers recalled that she did nothing but talk about how Joan must be missing her baby, while at the same time she was far too shrewd not to know that Joan could hardly wait to get away.

In Paris, Joan abandoned all pretense of sophistication and took off to see the sights. Tourists were amazed to observe her ostentatiously and eagerly chatting away on the Eiffel Tower's high, windswept platform, trudging through the Louvre to stare dutifully at the *Mona Lisa*, or keeping the Ritz Bar in an uproar with her dirty stories.

She flew on with Hedda to Italy. Hedda's office had cabled ahead to make sure that Hal Wallis had a red carpet rolled out for Joan's arrival in Rome. A large crowd of paparazzi was at the airport, headed by the handsome and athletic young *Time-Life* cameraman George ("Slim") Aarons. A dashing man of the world, Aarons had a widespread reputation as a romantic stud and he exuded a powerful sex appeal. Joan immediately cottoned to him and according to Hal Wallis she astonished everyone by simply getting into a car with him with her many suitcases and driving off. Hedda's rage was volcanic, and it was compounded when Joan, who was booked to share a suite with her, moved into another that was even more opulent—and then moved Slim Aarons into it. Joan attempted to quell Hedda's anger with gifts of champagne and flowers, but she would not apologize, and took off with Aarons again.

Hedda's fury increased still further when she set up various parties in Joan's honor and Joan was far more interested in continuing her liaison with Aarons. She ran around with him everywhere, returning to script conferences looking very much like the cat that swallowed the canary.

The weather was perfect that summer of 1949, and although Italy was ravaged by war, and by the scandal of the Rossellini-Bergman romance, it was a glorious country to be visiting at the time. Capri was particularly charming, with its aerial tramway that ran high to the ruined castle at the top of Anacapri; passengers felt like birds as their feet dangled over the olive trees. And the Blue Lagoon provided an exquisite adventure, with its rippling reflected light and its echoing rocky recesses.

Florence, too, was a joy. Joan had the rare pleasure of afternoon tea with the celebrated aesthete Bernard Berenson, who found her charming and intelligent and wrote to friends about the meeting. But Joan, according to Wallis, was capricious and unreliable and disappeared from the set and the hotel with Aarons for days. Wallis, no less disciplined than he had been at Warner Brothers, was furious. He told me:

> The next day Joan sailed cheerfully onto the set as if nothing had happened. With someone as cool and superficial as that, I knew anger would be futile, though I was, nevertheless, angry. Without a serious apology or a tremor, Joan went straight into a love scene with Joe Cotten, who played it with anger in his heart and a seraphic smile on his face, the face of a man in love. I never admired his acting more.

During the shooting in Venice, Cotten, an old friend of Orson Welles, was delighted to find Welles making an eccentric version of *Othello* there. Orson had just fired his Desdemona, Betsy Blair, who had appeared with Olivia in *The Snake Pit*, and had replaced her with the unknown Suzanne Cloutier—later the wife of Peter Ustinov. Cotten appeared in *Othello* as a senator in a bit part to help Orson out, and Joan proved how good her figure still was at the age of thirty-one by dressing up as a page boy. She looked marvelous in the film.

Joan's happiness during *September Affair*, the fulfillment of her nights with Slim Aarons, and her love of the romantic scenery—seeing Michelangelo's *David* was especially thrilling—was reflected in her acting and in her appearance. She never looked more beautiful in any picture. Directed by the imposing William Dieterle, who had guided Olivia through the pleasures and torments of *A Midsummer*

*Night's Dream*, the movie was beautiful in terms of photography and sound recording, evoking a romantic sojourn in an elaborate reworking of its immediate predecessor, David Lean's *Brief Encounter*. It offered the bonus of the great Françoise Rosay, whose imperious presence fascinated Joan, and of Walter Huston's irresistible croaking rendition of "September Song," first recorded in Kurt Weill's *Knickerbocker Holiday* and redone specially in Hollywood for the new picture.

Once the shooting was over, Joan proceeded to London—and ran immediately into a problem. Because of her allergies, her delicate skin could not accept anything but prescription cold cream, skin foundation, powder, and shampoos. Indeed, the wool blankets in her bed in Florence had caused her eyelids to swell so much that she could hardly see; and when she found there was a feather pillow in her hotel room in Venice, she had to put a rubber pillowcase over it. Now, the airline had lost her makeup box and she was unable to face the press in London for several days; she had to hide, blushing behind her freckles, until the box arrived.

Oddly, she had never been to England before. And as always, she was a keen tourist, leaving the Savoy every morning to see the sights of London, and descending on the de Havilland family with great enthusiasm. She went to see her famous uncle Sir Geoffrey, in his great house at Hatfield, sharing with him memories of his son, killed three years earlier. Brilliant and genial, Sir Geoffrey had recently become even more famous for his development of the Comet aircraft, which Howard Hughes had tried to buy. "He's always trying to buy the de Havillands," Joan quipped to her uncle.

She also went to see her three-year-old goddaughter, Sarah Hough. Joan had met Sarah's father, Richard Hough, during World War II when he was an RAF pilot in training in California.

Joan's allergies worsened in England, where summer flowers bloomed in profusion, and pollen, blown about by the ceaseless English breezes, was prevalent. By late September, she was seized by paroxysms of coughing. Bronchitis followed, and in order to avoid pneumonia, she went into the London Clinic, the best hospital in the city, where she was taken care of far more expertly than she would have been in Los Angeles.

The day before Joan took sick, Olivia, still very weak, went through a childbirth no less agonizing that Joan's. She gave birth to a son, Benjamin, who, surprisingly in the circumstances, looked healthy and bouncing. But when she went home with Ben to the house in Brentwood, her life became a nightmare. She said later in a courtroom:

> During the first five and a half weeks of the baby's life I took care of him all by myself. I wanted to take care of him all by myself and I did. During that period of time, well, the baby was four weeks old and I was caring for him in the bedroom of the house, my husband became upset over something—I cannot recall what it was—it was unimportant—and he became extremely violent and abusive in his manner and he struck me. . . . I had to turn my body so that the baby would not be injured because I was holding Benjamin in my arms at the time.

This streak of violence in Goodrich terrified Olivia, who was fragile and sickly following Ben's birth. According to her statements under oath, another shocking incident followed not long afterward. She was driving with Goodrich in Bel Air, trying to make conversation to overcome his thunderous silence, when he became so maddened by her personal mannerisms that he—according to her testimony later in court—literally pounded her left arm with his fist and caused it to become black and blue. When they reached their home, he told her that he would kill her.

She ran out of the car, down the driveway and onto the road, and clambered rather awkwardly through the shrubbery, hiding, trembling with fear. Goodrich, she said, charged in after her. She barely escaped, stumbling down the road in her high heels to the safety of a neighbor's house. She said her bruises were so bad that she had to wear long-sleeved dresses for days, but she dared not sue Goodrich for injury lest he really did kill her.

Thus, not long after Joan had felt her marriage slip away, Olivia knew hers was doomed.

There is a curious conflict among the various accounts of Joan's return to the United States. According to Hal Wallis, Joan called him (he had been working on another picture in London) and insisted she go on the same ship with him back to the United States, as she was being called by Howard Hughes for retakes on *Born to Be Bad*. He told me:

> The French Line told her there were no cabins, but Joan refused to take no for an answer. Fortunately, I had influence

with the line and they managed to squeeze her into a stateroom. I went on board, firmly expecting to find a bottle of champagne in my suite with a thank-you note. Nothing. I didn't see her in the dining salon that night and wondered if after all her desperate efforts she'd missed the boat. Then I ran into her playing backgammon with a group of friends. Instead of embracing me and thanking me for my efforts on her behalf, she nodded coolly and went on with the game, not even bothering to introduce me to her friends.

According to other versions, Joan lay ill for a long time in the London Clinic after Wallis left for New York. She slept or read in a pleasant pastel-decorated room on the clinic's fourth floor, looking down on Harley Street, the famous doctors' thoroughfare. Roses, carnations, and chrysanthemums meant for her filled the rooms of other patients since she could not receive them due to her condition. Meanwhile, she was greatly disappointed that she could not attend the glamorous opening of Sir Geoffrey's exhibition of photographs of African wild game at the Ilford Gallery.

Simultaneously, Olivia was offered the part of Blanche opposite Marlon Brando in *A Streetcar Named Desire*, and Joan was offered the part of the "other sister"—a fantastic concept of Charles Feldman, the famous agent turned producer of the film. Both stars were actually seriously considering this possibility, but fortunately this horrible idea fell through and Vivien Leigh and Kim Hunter were chosen instead. Joan had to accept a very uninteresting part in a picture entitled *Darling, How Could You?* based on a play by James Barrie, *Alice-Sit-by-the-Fire*, which had been a great success with Helen Hayes and Mary MacArthur. The film had originally been intended as a screen comeback for Mary Martin. Gloria Swanson had also been mentioned for the part, but had refused to test in the wake of her great success in *Sunset Boulevard*. *Darling, How Could You?* was the story of a couple in the Edwardian era who come back to America after a long absence and try to bring about a reconciliation with their children.

It was a pleasant, unimportant picture, but it did achieve one thing—a reconciliation between Joan and the director Mitchell Leisen, after the ordeal of *Frenchman's Creek* and his intense dislike of her. Leisen told his biographer, David Chierichetti:

I dreaded working with Joan Fontaine again, but the first day, she came up to me during a break and she said she was just doing it for the money, she wasn't out to prove anything any more, and she would act it whatever way I told her. And that's just what she did: she couldn't have been more delightful to work with. It's the most complete reformation I've ever seen. We had a ball doing the picture.

It is clear that Joan's mood had been improved by her trip to Europe, and the relaxing romance with Slim Aarons; and when she filed for divorce from Dozier it was with a strong sense of pleasure at the thought of being free. She had enough sense to avoid the March 1950 Academy Awards, at which Olivia again triumphed.

Inspired by this new success, Olivia made a radical decision to pose for photographs, disguising the misery of her marriage. Sleepless after only three hours in bed, she came down the stairs to the press in her dining room the following morning and by prearrangement Goodrich, in husbandly fashion, offered her a glass of orange juice. Very few people were fooled.

Already, Olivia had plans to return to the stage. She talked with producers about coming to Broadway in, of all things, *Romeo and Juliet*, for which she had neither the stage experience nor the correct age. It was a vanity trip for many actresses to attempt Juliet, who is, of course, supposed to be played only by a very young girl.

In the summer of 1949, shortly after her return from England, Joan had again left Debbie, this time at the invitation of Conrad Hilton to go fishing at a hunting lodge in British Columbia. One of the other guests was a pleasant, relaxing, witty southerner named Collier Young, who produced and wrote motion pictures and television series and had just divorced Ida Lupino. Their marriage had involved making movies together, with Young writing and producing and Ida directing. It was a relationship fraught with peril. On one occasion, Young, in his capacity as producer, had complained to his wife that she had gone over budget. By way of reply, press reports alleged, she hurled a siphon bottle at his head. At that point, he decided to divorce her. But they went on working together, even after she married actor Howard Duff.

Young had an almost childish sense of humor and an open charm that was very rare in Hollywood. Oddly formal, he usually wore a suit and tie, even in sunny California. During a conversation with Collier one day, Joan suddenly recalled that her long-lost father, from whom she had not heard in well over a decade, was living on the island of Victoria, not far from Vancouver, and that it was almost his seventy-seventh birthday. With Collier, she went to see him at his favorite haunt, the Victoria Chess Club, and was dismayed to find that, apart from his physical decline in his late seventies, he was still the same autocrat—cold, haughty, and filled with loathing for Lilian—he had been all along. It was a painful meeting, which had the effect of making Joan feel better about her mother than she had in some time. When she and Young returned to Hollywood, they were happy to see a great deal of Lilian, who very much approved of Collier.

In October 1950, Olivia was in negotiations with Kermit Bloom-garden in New York for *Romeo and Juliet*, and her agent Kurt Frings was demanding that she receive fifteen percent of the gross profits plus fifty percent of the net, with a $3,000 guaranty per week. This was an extravagant demand in view of the fact that two very big stars of the legitimate stage, Gertrude Lawrence and Tallulah Bankhead, asked for only twenty-five percent of the net profits along with fifteen percent of the gross. Even Katharine Cornell, who was involved in the production of her shows with her husband, Guthrie McClintic, received just ten percent of the gross plus fifty percent of the net. No other stage actress had demanded as much, and Olivia had to step down and accept much more modified terms.

Irritated, she pressed ahead with the production anyway. Unfortunately, rehearsals did not go very well, despite the patient and careful guidance of Peter Glenville. Oliver Messel's sets were elegant, and Jack Hawkins made a powerful and humorous Mercutio, but the little-known Douglas Watson, who had played with Katharine Cornell, was, for all his good looks, disappointing as Romeo, and Olivia was severely handicapped by her years in pictures. She had become used to the protection of the studio, where lights could be constantly rearranged to flatter her face now that she was no longer very young; and where her odd shifts of mood, latenesses, procrastinations, and difficulties with lines could be hidden from the press. A further problem was that the much-liked producer, Dwight Deere Wiman, died suddenly in the early weeks of preparation and this cast a pall over the company. Worse, Olivia had grown cold and hard in the wake of her suffering with Goodrich, and she told friends that her husband had a maddening tendency to appear at rehearsals and either criticize her or go to the other extreme and absurdly ask certain actors to turn their backs on the audience in her big scenes. This, she said, was greatly aggravating to her and to the director.

On the credit side, she respected Peter Glenville, who strove to give the story the pace, excitement, and "traffic" that Shakespeare wanted. He sought a headstrong approach, filled—in Brooks Atkinson's words—with "not only romantic love but carnival, feuds, slaying, intrigue, mystery, catastrophe and suicide." He also strove to direct Olivia beyond the limits set by such notables as Katharine Cornell, Jane Cowl, Eva Le Gallienne, and Vivien Leigh. The problem was that Olivia lacked the warmth, vibrancy, and sheer lovingness necessary for the part of Juliet. She could (with a supreme effort) manage at times to look fourteen; and she was very strong where steely strength was called for, particularly in the potion scene with Friar Lawrence. But she was, by all accounts, too passive, supine and detached.

While Olivia was still in rehearsal, in the early months of 1951, Joan obtained her divorce from William Dozier. The agreement between plaintiff and defendant provided that Dozier would pay Joan a mere $100 a month toward Debbie's support, maintenance, and upbringing.

The arrangements were not dissimilar to those she had made with Brian Aherne, showing Joan to be the least greedy and acquisitive of wives. She could easily have claimed half of Dozier's company, properties, and investments under the community-property law, but instead husband and wife relinquished and renounced all claims on each other and Joan did not even ask for alimony. It was agreed that their property would be separate and that neither would make a claim on any future income or financial acquisitions of the other. Dozier held Joan harmless from all liabilities, and she held him harmless, and neither would make any claim on the other's separate estate. Joan agreed to pay federal income tax assessed on both their incomes for 1949—a remarkable act of generosity on her part. Dozier agreed to pay one-quarter of her state taxes. Both agreed to cooperate in further tax filings before the decree was made final.

In addition, Dozier gave up to Joan the house (her identical arrangement with Aherne), the furniture, the 1946 Lincoln convertible coupé and the 1949 Ford station wagon, her own bank accounts, and her stocks and bonds, which were surprisingly insubstantial and included $17,000 in Los Angeles City School District bonds and $5,288 in U.S. savings bonds. She also got full possession of her clothing, jewelry, furs, and other personal effects. Dozier retained the 1949 Cadillac convertible, a block of land, and some furnishings—including the Duncan Phyfe mahogany drop-leaf table, a pie crust table, and such odd items as a ceramic whiskey-keg lamp and an ottoman.

In the question of Debbie's custody, Joan was accorded the rights, with reasonable rights of visitation to Dozier. There was no limitation on the number of days he could visit Debbie. Joan agreed to consult with him on all decisions relating to Debbie's upbringing. Joan agreed to join with Dozier in paying for the child's education, the amount to be determined from her net taxable income. Any rulings would have to be brought before the superior court.

The details were ironed out at a meeting in January. The meeting was tiring, and Joan became annoyed with her lawyer, Martin Gang, despite his most skillful assistance, and instead hired Stanley Aaron to handle the matter for her. Collier Young relieved the pressure with his humor and charm; but Joan seems to have been irritated at times by his almost juvenile behavior, and she cuttingly remarked that when one-and-a-half-year-old Debbie treated Young as someone of her own age, she was right to do that.

With the divorce firmly under way—it would be declared final a year later—Joan set off on a goodwill mission and publicity junket to South America. She hobnobbed with Evita Peron in Buenos Aires and thought of playing the dictator's wife in a motion picture. While visiting Peru, she was attracted to a rich importer, the wealthy Gustavo Berckemeyer. According to Dozier, she thought of marrying Berckemeyer when her divorce became final.

She traveled to Cuzco with Berckemeyer and then to Machu Picchu, on the tortuous mule ride up to the mountain ruins of the Incas. While she and Berckemeyer were touring the ruins, she noticed a child sitting on a rock next to a stone hut. The child, in her little plaid dress, her limbs covered with lesions, slipped down from her position and showed Joan her stone hut and the ruins. She introduced Joan to her family in a mixture of Spanish and Cuechua, the local Indian tongue. Her father was the caretaker of the Machu Picchu ruins.

That night, Joan tossed and turned, unable to sleep in the pale moonlight that streamed through the windows of her hotel room. She kept seeing Martita gazing up at her trustingly, unaware of her fame. She had to adopt Martita. Debbie needed a sister, and there was no way Joan would face the ordeal of giving birth again.

The next morning, accompanied by interpreters, she made her way to the Pareja house and talked to Martita's parents, mentioning the life that would open up for the child if they handed her over. After a family conference, they agreed that adoption by Joan would mean a far better life for Martita. The decision did not come easily. Joan promised faithfully to bring the child up as a Roman Catholic and she made a financial arrangement with the Parejas.

She immediately whisked Martita through all the red tape—no time must be wasted in this, a very remarkable adventure in unofficial adoption; Peruvian law allowed adoption only when a parent was over fifty.

Thus, Joan did not adopt Martita formally. According to one source, Joan went ahead of her to prepare the house and also tell Debbie about her. Martita boarded the plane to America in the care of a stewardess. The child was filled with anger that her parents had let her go, even to a better world, and she was terrified of the plane—it was so totally alien. She was too inexperienced to understand why she was going or where. The green scarf she wore that Joan had given her felt to her unnecessary.

She arrived in Miami—in those days a traditional stopping point on the roundabout journey to Los Angeles—with no immigration documents. Joan met her at the airport and found her curious and scared. She remained silent because nobody spoke Spanish. Joan had prepared a dialogue sheet in Spanish and English so that she could ask the child questions like "Do you need a drink?" "Are you hungry?" "Are you happy?" "Do you need to go to the bathroom?" And Joan had learned "I love you" in Spanish.

Joan's impulsiveness had landed her with a sweet, lovable, but utterly alien creature who was bewildered by the glitter of a world far removed from that of her family in Peru. She was confused by the smart shops, the luxury, the cleanliness of everything, and fundamental things like doorknobs, mirrors, bathrooms, ice cream, candy, and the beach. They traveled together to Los Angeles, where Joan, with her usual very "British" formality, introduced her to Debbie. The two girls embraced each other.

According to William Dozier, there was considerable sibling rivalry between the children. "Debbie attacked Martita," Dozier recalls, "and sank her teeth into her forehead!" (Neither daughter remembers this.) Says Debbie:

> Father, of course, would tell the truth. It's true I did resent Martita at first. Of course, when I first saw her—I remember it as though it were yesterday—I was fascinated and I held her close. But it was strange to find an elder sister—Martita was older than I—from nowhere! We fought as all siblings do. And at that time I wanted Mother to myself.

It was not until later that things grew bad between me and my mother. At that time she was fun to be with, and I was fascinated by her. I didn't even want to go to my father—I wanted *only* to be with my mother. And here was this stranger! But later, as time went on, Martita and I became very, very close. We still are.

Joan had a great struggle trying to help Martita. Dozier recalls the sheer determination of Joan's efforts to make Martita a normal American child. He says that she was not content simply with having skin specialists heal the sores on Martita's legs, and physicians straighten her little legs with braces, but had to teach Martita to wash herself, comb her hair, and gradually assume a well-groomed appearance. This took many weeks of hard work.

While Joan was in England on a visit, Martita was left in the hands of teachers who instructed her in English. Later, she learned more at school. On her return, Joan took her through the pages of English classic novels that she had enjoyed as a child, and Martita—resistant at first—gradually learned to love being read to in Joan's musical voice. In the early stages, Martita was hard to teach because she was stubborn; but once she became aware of the pleasure of literature, reading became as obsessive as it had been for Joan as a child, and she read in closets, under covers, even by moonlight, until Joan told her this would ruin her eyes. However, despite Joan's success in getting her to enjoy reading, Martita refused to be the gay, enchanting, extroverted creature Joan fancied she would become. Driven on the one hand by resentment and on the other by an intense curiosity about Joan, whom she found awesome and powerful and frightening, Martita offered silence and thunderous stares. She was particularly silent when she was with William Dozier and his wife, Ann Rutherford, later on, because she felt Joan disapproved of them and she didn't know what to say to them.

Undaunted in public as always, Joan quickly began giving interviews and posing for photographs with both Debbie and Martita, boldly projecting her most audacious scenario: that she had achieved a melding of these two very different children; that Martita was a happy, well-adjusted young American enjoying the benefits of the Great Society. It says much for her acting prowess that she was able to carry off this fantasy, and it says a great deal about the press of that time that it accepted her version of the facts.

While Joan worked grimly in the house at Brentwood, striving to have Martita learn English, Olivia was having her unfortunate experience with *Romeo and Juliet* extended throughout a patchy tour. The strain of performing on stage night after night wore her down, and she began to show signs of near-breakdown once more. Apparently, stories of her difficult behavior resulted in very few, if any, offers for movies at the time, and she rashly decided to set about another stage venture, *Candida*, for which she was singularly ill prepared.

It was not until later in the year that she read an interesting script. Based by her old friend Nunnally Johnson on Daphne du Maurier's novel *My Cousin Rachel*, it was a teasing, maddening, but entertaining melodrama set in nineteenth-century Cornwall, about a woman of mystery who may or may not have been a murderess. Originally, George Cukor got hold of the property and spoke to Garbo about making a comeback in it; but Garbo was reluctant to let her public see that she had grown older, and she objected to playing the part of a woman who might have committed murder. Cukor gave up on Garbo, but decided to go ahead with the film anyway and traveled to Britain to confer with Daphne du Maurier. He realized how important the wild and haunted landscape of Cornwall was to the story, and realized also how much better the excellent *Rebecca* and the indifferent *Frenchman's Creek* would have been if they had been made in that British county. But he was unable to persuade Darryl Zanuck at Twentieth Century-Fox to shoot the picture on location; and when Vivien Leigh also rejected the part, and when he saw the designs Zanuck wanted—far too American, far removed from Miss du Maurier's concept—he gave up.

Zanuck asked Mitchell Leisen to take over, and Olivia instantly agreed to proceed. At Cukor's suggestion, the very young and romantic Richard Burton was hired to costar with her. But at the last minute, Paramount forbade Leisen to make the picture; instead, they wanted him to do a musical based on the career of the Duncan sisters, with Betty Hutton. As it turned out, that film was never made.

The delays went on and on, and in the meantime Olivia, disappointed at losing the chance to make a new film with her beloved Leisen, went ahead with her *Candida* tour in Canada. Her costar, Terry Kilburn, recalls that she was totally incapable of "carrying" the part, and indeed the reviews following her opening on Broadway late in 1951 were quite unfavorable. While struggling with the problems of her impending divorce, she also had to endure an attack on her by the dean of New York critics, George Jean Nathan, who said the following of her Candida:

Last year, it will be recalled, the lady came on from Hollywood to display herself in *Romeo and Juliet*. The result was not to be mentioned in theatrical society. As the Bard's romantic heroine she indicated to even the most hospitable critics a flawless lack of talent for the dramatic medium. Determined as she was to prove herself, it was immediately evident that she had none of the necessary qualifications of an actress ambitious to succeed in the classic drama or, for that matter, in any kind of drama; and her failure was predestined.

Nathan went on to say that though the Shaw role imposed lesser demands than the Shakespeare, Olivia was no better in it; that she still read lines mechanically as if being instructed by a coach signaling to her from the wings, and that her few gestures resembled those of a child brought into the room to entertain family friends with a school recitation! He said that the role of Candida would have been better read by the stage manager over a public-address system. The rest of the cast, he observed, performed as if they thought Shaw was the bandleader of the same name (Artie Shaw).

It was typical of the contrasting lives of Olivia and Joan that Joan once again took off on a joyful spree to Europe while Olivia was going through various forms of agony. Following her caprice in adopting Martita, and after considerable work futilely trying to bring the two children together, Joan suddenly flew off to France, leaving both children behind in the care of Collier Young. She wanted to enjoy the summer social season of the racetrack crowd, and she was not allowed to take Debbie abroad. She met Prince Aly Khan and they entered into a romance that was the talk of Paris. They first met at a party at Sir Charles Mendl's; the next night, they danced cheek-to-cheek at the Chez Florence nightclub; and they spent much of the weekend together, hurtling about in Aly Khan's dangerously fast Ferrari. Joan always opened up in Europe, and this was the best time she had had since Italy two years earlier and the wild romance with Slim Aarons. On Monday, she and Aly created a sensation as they kissed openly on the dance floor at a party given by the wealthy New York builder Norman Winston. There was nothing to this; it was simply a sexy interlude. Aly showered Joan with gifts—including an exquisite desk clock—and overwhelmed her with roses.

Joan was fascinated by Aly Khan. The heir to a vast fortune and son of the spiritual leader of fifteen million Muslims, Aly devoted his whole life to women. A classic stud—relaxed, sensual, fearless—he made women feel more intensely feminine than they felt with anyone else. His dark, muscular body was irresistible, and when he was with a woman he used the infallible technique of making her feel she was the only one in the world for him. He talked to Joan like an eager child, hanging on her opinions. He danced with her, as Elsa Maxwell wrote, "slowly and rapturously, as though it was the last time he would ever hold her in his arms." Three months a year, he visited his father's followers all over the world, pursued everywhere by crowds of Muslims.

He told Joan of his admiration for her talent, her beauty, and her intelligence—it was the latter praise that, of course, meant most. He talked cheerfully about his racing stable, his nine stud farms, and his English Derby winner, Tulyar, sold to the Irish National Stud for $750,000. At forty-six, he had boundless energy and loved to take wild chances. Like Joan, he had a streak of recklessness; he would drive eighty miles an hour through Paris, or on two wheels along the Grand Corniche of the Riviera.

At the time Joan met Aly and became involved with him, he was still married to Rita Hayworth, whose Riviera wedding to him had been one of the most spectacular events of recent years. Rita was bitterly jealous of Joan.

After only two weeks of the romance, however, Joan took off for London somewhat soured on Aly Khan. Once his romantic accomplishments began to lose their novelty, she became aware that he was difficult, tight with his money, and sometimes badly groomed in public. His habit of constantly going over his restaurant checks and never tipping a centime over the minimum put a considerable dent in his romantic image. He also had the irritating habit of the very rich of refusing to spend money on trivial purchases. There was no question that Joan had far too much sense to consider for a moment a serious relationship with Aly Khan.

In London, she proceeded to make a version of Sir Walter Scott's novel of the Crusades era, *Ivanhoe*. The movie evoked ancestral memories of the de Havillands; and the producer, Pandro S. Berman, had always been thoughtful to her during her embarrassing early days at RKO. She moved into an expensive apartment in Grosvenor Square, the most popular address for visiting American stars; the service was excellent and the furnishings opulent to a degree. Once again, she discovered that at a certain level London was the most comfortable city in the world; she was entirely at home, and her days were made all the more pleasant by the presence of the young and charming

Yugoslavian princes Nicholas and Alexander. Sometimes, all three would fly in Aly Khan's private plane for visits to the south of France.

Despite the tedium of making *Ivanhoe*, Joan continued to have a very good time, and only an accident on the Riviera on Aly Khan's hundred foot slide, which caused a disk fracture in her spine, served to slow her down—for about five minutes.

Back in Hollywood, Martita remembers that Joan would try to train her faulty memory in a most determined manner. She would often send her to the store with verbal instructions to buy certain items—bread, coffee, tea, fruit, various vegetables, cereal—but without giving her a written list. She was expected to bring back everything exactly as ordered on Joan's account. Naturally, the shy and awkward child would become so tense that she froze completely on arrival at the store and could remember almost nothing. She bought what she thought was correct and returned to Joan in fear; Joan would then send her back to the store again and again, until she had more or less filled the order.

It wasn't that Martita was being picked on—Debbie came in for her share, too. When Debbie expressed a dislike of doing flower arrangements, at which Martita was adept, Joan would have her do them all day long, all over the house. The "battle of the flowers" was exacerbated by the fact that Debbie felt inferior to Martita in this area. Debbie, however, was very good at remembering things, at shopping, and in mathematics, and Martita suffered from the contrast in those areas.

Again and again, as she grew older, Martita asked herself why Joan had "adopted" her. She concluded that it was as much to show the world that she was a kind of Pygmalion or female Professor Higgins, who could take a waif and turn her into a lady, as it was to give Debbie a companion.

# *Ten*

 Much to her relief, Joan's divorce from William Dozier became final in February 1952. But almost immediately she ran into a problem. She had been offered the opportunity to make a picture in Spain, *Decameron Nights*, and once again she looked forward to the opportunity of going to Europe. But she wanted to take her seldom-seen four-and-a-half-year-old Debbie with her, along with Martita, and was dismayed when Dozier flatly refused to allow her to do anything of the sort.

Dozier, in fact, brought action against her, claiming that Debbie's health was not up to such a journey and that she would be completely deprived of the care and visitation of her father. He stated in the custody "Show Cause" that the unsettled military and political situation of the world, the armament races and threats of strife, and the shortages of food and medical supplies in certain Latin countries could jeopardize the welfare of a child. He was also concerned that the necessary inoculations and vaccinations for Spain, all of which would have to be done in a very short space of time, would cause the child extreme distress and endanger her health. He further pointed out that Joan's work hours in Spain would be long and arduous, leaving her little time to attend to her offspring, and he charged that her social life (there was a direct reference to Aly Khan in his court desposition) would also prove detrimental.

In April, Joan was faced with a brutal fight. She found great support in Collier Young and in her friends the illustrator John Falter and the actress Maureen O'Sullivan, mother of Mia Farrow. At the hearing, however, Dozier proved adamant; he was narrowly restrained from introducing Joan's affair with Aly Khan into the proceedings. Frances Ruegg, housekeeper and nurse to Joan's children, shocked Joan by turning against her and testifying that it would be a serious mistake if the "sickly" Debbie went to Europe and that it was shocking Collier Young was living with Joan. The upshot of it was that Joan lost.

It was the same month that Olivia suffered from the hatchets of the New York critics in *Candida*. It was a very bad month for both sisters.

Forced to return to Europe once again without Debbie, Joan flew to Spain with Martita. For once, Martita enjoyed herself, even appearing in a tiny part in *Decameron Nights*. But a ghastly incident took place in Spain. Somebody had given Martita an exquisite doll—a flamenco dancer, complete with real black hair, a mantilla, a high comb, a shawl of the finest brocade, a rich traditional dress, and a fan clasped in the hand. For the first time in her life, Martita discovered something to love. She hated baby dolls, but loved the idea of a doll in the form of an adult. She was partly of Spanish blood, and perhaps her ancestry stirred in her veins. In any event, she clutched the doll to her and hated even setting it down.

Joan, on the other hand, loathed the Spanish doll from the beginning. She told Martita that the fact that it had real hair was disgusting and horrifying and awakened creepy, nauseous feelings in her. Without warning, one day Joan destroyed it. Martita was inconsolable. Joan tried to make it up to her with a Kewpie doll, large and blonde and rather like Joan herself, with eyes that opened and shut and a voice that squeaked a welcome to mother when pressed in the navel. Martita was curious about the mechanics of the doll's eyes and the noise the doll made, so she operated on it surgically to find out how it worked. But she hated the doll.

In Spain, Joan was "linked" with King Umberto of Italy, despite the fact that her only meeting with him involved his elderly winks at Martita in the dining room of the Palace Hotel in Madrid, which caused the child to blush and hide her face in a napkin.

The making of *Decameron Nights* was distinctly ragged. The director, Hugo Fregonese, and his wife, Faith Domergue, led the troupe across Spain by caravan of limousines, trucks, and buses, with Faith acting as interpreter. Each afternoon, to the astonishment of the Spanish crew, crumpets and tea were served for the benefit of Joan and the British-born actress Binnie Barnes; white-coated waiters set up tables with sterling silver, Crown Derby plates, and white tablecloths. Joan typically filled every instant of her spare time with activity. She visited a monastery at Guadaloupe, went to one bullfight after another, and allegedly had a romance with the bullfighter Jose Maria Martorell, who created a sensation at the Segovia Corrida when he dedicated a bull to her. She joyously flung a flower at his feet.

She traveled on to Paris with Martita, taking her on a tour of the children's shops. Then she left for Venice for the special showing of *Ivanhoe*, came back to Spain, and from there returned to Hollywood where she agreed after much discussion to wed Collier Young in November.

A return to Peru with Martita, long promised, or threatened—depending on whether it was spoken of as a reward for good behavior or as a punishment for malfeasance—finally took place. It was perhaps the most serious mistake Joan ever made. Martita had finally accepted the idea that her parents had handed her over only because they wanted to help her, and she was excited at the prospect of seeing them again.

Accompanied by Mrs. Connie Wolf, Joan and Martita arrived in Lima in severe heat, stepping out into a filthy, overcrowded airport where dust blew in on the harsh Peruvian wind. Martita stood awkwardly in her expensive, hand-tailored outfit—neat white straw hat, beautifully cut white dress, and matching white shoes and gloves—looking as though she stepped out of a bandbox, while her parents, and seemingly half the population of Peru, gathered around her smiling and greeting her. She was utterly remote from them now. They were in depressing clothes, none too clean, and surrounded by buzzing, insistent flies. There was a heavy odor of sweat, dust, and garlicky food.

It was with a sense of shock and determined pride that Martita realized her roots. She felt painfully out of place, gazing into her parents' eyes as though from the wrong end of a well. She could not relate to them in the least and felt not the slightest tug of filial affection, much as she wanted to. She was swept off to their home, which was no longer in Machu Picchu but several miles away. It was made out of dirt and had flies. She stood in the middle of the floor, her white dress standing out against the dun brown of her surroundings, staring and unable to speak Spanish—and Indian dialect would have been well beyond her. She wanted to help her mother—it was her natural instinct—but could do nothing.

She hated the fact that Joan left her alone there; she was embarrassed because she was wearing such elegant clothes. She knew now the burden she must carry for the rest of her life as a child: that she did not belong to either her real or her surrogate parents; that she was a stranger everywhere.

Yet another problem arose when Joan sent Martita to various Catholic schools (as she had promised the child's parents she would). Not only did Martita have to leave the schools after brief enrollment and after beginning to make new friends, because of Joan's constant travels and her insistence on taking Martita with her, but Joan also undermined Martita's religious teaching. For a child of Martita's origins, the Catholic church provided consolation. Moreover, it was, quite simply, the most interesting religion anyone could belong to, since the mass was almost the equivalent of a weekly motion picture, filled with the odor of incense, the stir of voluptuous costumes, and the rich beauty of incantation. Joan, an agnostic like George Fontaine, believed in nothing except pragmatic reality; her fantasies and dreams colored her daily events (despite many rude shocks) but did not extend to the romantic visions of the Catholic religion. As a result, Martita was bewildered and confused, having to adjust from the teachings of the Orders of Sisters to the down-to-earth questionings of Joan.

As she grew older, she was more painfully conscious of the differences between herself and Joan's image of what she could be. When she misbehaved, she felt threatened with deportation back to Peru—a thought that filled Martita with dread after her glimpse of Peruvian reality. Even today, she does not know how many boys and girls there are in the count of her six siblings.

In the meantime, Olivia was delighted with Benjamin. He could, she claimed, pronounce such words as Mesopotamia and Popocatepetl. She had been consoled for the New York reviews by a successful tour, in which she broke records largely on her name alone; and her 323 performances put her ahead of Katharine Cornell (though not in quality) in the record books.

In June, Olivia began shooting *My Cousin Rachel* in Hollywood under the sympathetic direction of Henry Koster. She followed Joan—this was a Daphne du Maurier novel. Richard Burton was a surly but talented foil to her ambiguous, aggravatingly ambivalent heroine; the teasing elements in the story were well reflected in Olivia's elusive, disconcerting, and hard-to-pin-down personality, and she played the romantic sequences with great concentration. When I asked her years later whether the central figure of the story was guilty or innocent, she smiled and declined to answer. The probability is that neither the director nor star ever knew, and that this was the problem with the picture, explaining to some extent why intriguing though it was, it was not in the first class and did not reach a very wide public.

At last, Olivia faced up to the ordeal of the divorce hearing against Marcus Goodrich. Through floods of tears, she described his terrifying outbursts of temper; the attempts on her life; her fear for her son's safety; the attack on her on Sunset Boulevard and her subsequent flight through the Bel Air underbrush. She said she couldn't bear the idea of divorce, she talked of trying to avoid it; but then Goodrich had indulged in such slapstick melodrama as throwing a beefsteak at her because it didn't have kidneys in it. All of this was, of course, in direct contradiction to the image of marital bliss that she had so carefully built up. It was as difficult for her to face public disclosure as an embittered and beaten wife as it was to face the fact that her romantic relationship was over.

With her usual passion, seriousness, and dedication, Olivia turned to her three-year-old son, Ben, concentrating a staggering amount of love and energy on him, along with discipline. She noticed his remarkable technical leanings—his ability to take apart anything from a music box to a mechanic set and put the pieces back together again—and dreamed that one day he would be an engineer or a scientist. She thought she would move to Connecticut, glowingly described to her by Bette Davis, where there would be boating in the summer and sledding in the winter; or she might buy Havilland Hall in St. Peter Port, Guernsey, and return to the world of her ancestors. In a curious mood of nostalgia she even encouraged her father to come to Hollywood at the end of 1952, and met him at the train with seeming affection, exchanging reminiscences with him that entirely excluded any mention of his behavior long ago.

While Walter de Havilland was in Los Angeles, visiting with Olivia, Joan was married to Collier Young—without her father or Olivia being present.

She and Collier were married at Saratoga on November 12, 1952. They had been together for three years. Past miseries were forgotten as George and Lilian Fontaine appeared as the only witnesses to the ceremony. Everything went wrong at the wedding. When the couple arrived from Hollywood, they found that the airline had lost their luggage, including Joan's trousseau and going-away clothes, Young's formal wedding suit, and even the marriage license. Joan and Lilian screamed through the phone and the airline officials at last traced some of the luggage, which was sped by taxi to Lilian's house; the bride's hat and the wedding license did not turn up until later. Everybody was in an uproar; Martita, who was at school in Paris, barely made it to the ceremony by plane.

At last, in midafternoon, the wedding took place—in the library of the Villa Montalvo, the estate of the late Senator James D. Phelan. The Reverend Gordon L. King of the Saratoga Federated Protestant Church presided. Joan wore a navy blue taffeta cocktail suit by Hattie Carnegie and a Lily Daché beret trimmed with opalescent sequins.

The moment the wedding was over, the couple sped to the airport to fly to Chicago to attend the wedding of Collier's brother, Air Force General William D. Young. But Lilian's elaborate wedding reception at the villa held them up and they missed the plane and had to lay over in San Francisco overnight. For the second time in her life, Joan spent her wedding night on the window ledge, in the grip of an allergy, yet again reliving the experience of the fogbound balcony scene in *Rebecca*.

Suddenly, Joan's and Olivia's roles were reversed. Olivia emulated her sister by taking off for Europe. She had briefly become entangled again with John Huston, who had followed his great triumph of *Moulin Rouge*, the film biography of the painter Toulouse Lautrec, with a rather strained résumé of their earlier romance. She had heard much about Paris from Huston and had been fascinated by the film.

She was invited to go to the Cannes Film Festival and accepted at once, but insisted on an extra ticket for Ben. He was exceptionally animated on the journey, and fascinated by the workings of the airplane. She was met at the airport by her agent, Kurt Frings, who was accompanied by a good-looking, very serious man, Pierre Galante, author, former wartime secret agent for the OSS, and editor of *Paris Match*, the famous French illustrated magazine. She met him again at Cannes, at the Carleton Hotel; he had been very attracted to her from the first moment he met her and arranged with the Festival Committee to be placed next to her at all screenings. She quickly became aware of his interest, but did not respond at once. The divorce from Goodrich had left her, in her late thirties, deeply wounded and she wasn't particularly anxious to enter into any situation that might prove to be a problem.

From Cannes, she and Ben went to England to see Sir Geoffrey de Havilland and her cousin Peter, descending on them without warning and presenting them with considerable problems in the matter of avoiding any mention of Joan, whom they had been recently and joyously seeing. Ben was given his own suite at the Savoy. Apparently, Olivia had not known that Joan had stayed in the same suite she was in, or she would have asked for another.

Pursued by Pierre Galante via phone calls and letters, Olivia returned to the United States with Ben and started rehearsals in Dallas for a misnamed play entitled *The Dazzling Hour*. Due to a change of plans, the play was presented in La Jolla, California, instead; and although Olivia enjoyed her starring with José Ferrer, star of the admired *Moulin Rouge* and great friend of John Huston, she found little sustenance in the play itself.

She was distracted by the fact that Galante arrived on the scene, full of charm and persuasion, and offering her extraordinary considerations for her future, including a handsome house in Paris and the opportunity to be a queen of French society. With great skill, despite his limited English, he poured sweet nothings into Olivia's ear, and she agreed to marry him. But she held back until her decree was final; she dared not risk losing Ben in a custody battle, and she wanted to be free to travel with the boy wherever she chose.

Meanwhile, Joan made a film, *The Bigamist*, oddly enough under the direction of Ida Lupino, Olivia's costar in *Devotion* and Collier Young's former wife. It was an entertaining picture, directed with great shrewdness, but when Joan saw it she was horrified. Whereas Ida, who was no beauty, was photographed as sexily as possible in scene after scene, Joan was made to look dowdy and unattractive. She always felt that it was Ida's joke against her for having taken over Collier Young.

Olivia was involved in major problems in 1952. First, she engaged in a fight with the Bureau of Internal Revenue over $48,000 that the bureau said she owed in back taxes. The bureau claimed that she had paid George Fontaine (still her manager) too much money for his services in 1945 and 1946, and that she must pay taxes on the excessive payments. The bureau also said that she had improperly claimed deductions for gifts to Kurt Frings, Phyllis Seaton and Edith Head. Judge Eugene Black allowed the deductions because they were given in recognition of professional services, and he also made allowances for the extra payments to George Fontaine. She won the case hands down—only to run into another legal problem in France.

Whereas she was free in the United States following her divorce decree, the French government demanded a nine-month wait before she could remarry. After a futile struggle with the French courts, she sensibly gave up. Instead, she accepted an offer from the celebrated director Stanley Kramer to return to the United States and make *Not as a Stranger*, from the best-selling novel by Morton Thompson. The story was set in a hospital in a large American city, and Olivia was to play a Scandinavian nurse.

She threw herself into the work with her usual intensity from the beginning. Stanley Kramer was a stickler for accuracy and so was she, and so, too, was her seemingly laconic and impervious costar, Robert Mitchum. From the first meetings with Kramer in Hollywood, Olivia understood what he wanted: nothing less than the most authentic hospital picture ever made.

She toured hospitals and carefully watched operations, rising at 6:00 A.M. and spending between six and nine hours a day in the operating theaters. Made of steel, she never flinched for an instant, and those nurses and doctors who thought she might faint at the sight of blood or entrails soon learned what a formidable woman they had on their hands. She worked very closely with the technical adviser, Dr. Maxwell, and his assistants in passing instruments with perfect precision; indeed, Maxwell jokingly told her that such perfection in a scrub nurse went beyond realism and that she must occasionally fumble or break the rhythm. But both she and Kramer agreed that the slightest mistake, although possibly accurate, would disturb the audience and that in this one instance realism need not prevail.

She worked with the charming Virginia Christine, wife of the German character actor Fritz Feld and later Mrs. Olsen on the Folger coffee commercials, on her Swedish accent until it was so ideal that Ingrid Bergman and even Garbo were drawn to comment favorably on it. The trick was to use the odd, almost singsong rise and fall of Swedish speech patterns without seeming strange or laughable—or, more important, incomprehensible—to the mass audience.

Olivia talked in great detail to the writers, Edward and Edna Anhalt; pored over books on nursing; and studied every piece of equipment and all medical terminology. After seeing tumor surgeries, open-heart operations, and an appendectomy, she was virtually a trained nurse. The most fascinating operation she saw involved an eight-year-old boy whose right thumb was distorted. Through the attaching of a tendon, the thumb was restored to use again.

Mitchum was equally dedicated. Although his performance was criticized, he was in fact very assured in the part and struck exactly the right note of cool efficiency as he tied sutures, took blood-pressure readings, and percussed chests. He even did something few other actors had done in the part of a surgeon: He learned how to hold his hands away from his body, his elbows akimbo, as Olivia put on his rubber gloves.

Hard-edged, cool, and cutting as a scalpel, *Not as a Stranger* was in many ways an intelligent and accurate portrait of hospital life. It showed how doctors and nurses were mostly hardworking laborers in the vineyard, neither angels nor devils, their motives mixed like everyone else's; they were concerned with the sick, but they were also humanly selfish and self-protective in a world that tended to blame them for everything. Olivia's performance was exactly on target, the result of her careful preparation and meticulous attention to detail. She struck just the right note of hardworking efficiency without seeming excessively bossy. She was in a good mood during the picture, pushing Marcus Goodrich from her mind and concentrating hard on the second author in her life—Pierre Galante.

In early 1954, Joan took over from Deborah Kerr in *Tea and Sympathy* on Broadway. She was rehearsed by Karl Malden and directed by Elia Kazan in the part of a schoolteacher's wife who makes a student realize he is not homosexual.

Joan was so difficult at the time that she refused to rehearse in New York and insisted Malden prepare her for the part in Hollywood. He was a dedicated actor in the realistic school of the Group Theatre and had little patience with movie stars of the Joan Fontaine caliber. He believed in characterization in acting and was dismayed when Joan resisted every attempt to make her play the part as someone other than herself; she insisted on interpreting every line as she would have said it. Since she was totally miscast as the warm, sweet, and tender woman who gives the boy confidence in his heterosexuality, the problem became quite severe: A matronly, gentle woman was rapidly being turned into a cool, hard sophisticate, and it became obvious to Malden that he could not work with her.

He tried to improve Joan on the train trip to New York City, and at least on Broadway she melded better with the company, including Anthony Perkins. But she never really got a grip on the part and clearly knew her limitations by the time she was ready to work with Kazan.

The high-minded tone of *Tea and Sympathy* was ideal for the whistle-clean Fifties, although dated by today's different standards, Robert Anderson's drama at least offered a carefully modulated portrait of a compassionate middle-class woman, which Joan could enjoy. But her old inferiority complex, buried in her successful social career, flared up again and she was paralyzed with fear every night at facing a live audience. She also knew that there could really be no understudy for a star of her magnitude; that if some unknown took over on the night of a performance, the audience might demand its money back. Indeed, the entire show rested on her, since Perkins was not then the big star he was to become with *Psycho*. She became excessively nervous about her recurring sinus problems and about the possibility that, despite her extreme care, she might forget her lines.

Her spirits weren't improved by the arrival of Olivia, who intently watched the performance and came backstage to shake everyone's hand as though she were the queen of England. According to Joan, Olivia's only comment, spoken in a cool condescending voice, was a meaningless "Isn't it something!" There was certainly no word of praise for Joan. Fortunately, Joan's spirits were raised again by the sudden appearance of Aly Khan on the scene, and their romance, according to the gossip columnists, resumed.

Olivia was on her way to Paris, and to Spain, where she worked on the same location as Joan had during *Decameron Nights*. The film was *That Lady*, based on a Katharine Cornell stage vehicle. She was to play Princess Ana de Mendoza, who had only one eye; Ana was the mistress of Philip II and was romantically involved with the Spanish minister Antonio Perez. Paul Scofield, the most gifted star of the British stage, was cast as Philip; and Gilbert Roland, a revenant from the silent era, was Perez.

The director was Terence Young, a sophisticated, well-traveled, urbane man of the world and a former British Army Guards officer. Young recalls that while in London waiting for Olivia's arrival, he had lunch with William Wyler at the Les Ambassadeurs Club in Mayfair. "You won't enjoy working with Miss de Havilland," Wyler said with a sharp twinkle in his eye. "I suppose you tried to get Vivien Leigh after failing to get Garbo!"

Wyler was correct. Young had tried to interest Garbo without success, and although Vivien Leigh was interested, her deteriorating physical condition due to tuberculosis made her impossible to insure. Olivia was third choice.

Wyler told Young of the struggle of making *The Heiress* and the fact that he was reduced to giving Olivia instructions through the assistant director. Young, however, in his meetings with Olivia, who always appreciated suave Englishmen, found her somewhat mellowed and visibly in love. He didn't expect much trouble from her, especially since he knew her limitations: She was, he felt correctly, a technical, almost scientific actress, and at the same time suffered from the insecurity and fear of failure shared by almost all performers, calling for constant reassurance, flattery, and ego support. Fortunately, Galante was around as much as possible.

Young was fascinated by Olivia. He sensed more than anyone else at a first meeting the banked fires of rage and passion that existed behind the almost Germanic precision of her style. He was surprised to find also that she had odd lapses as a supposed woman of the world. When he took her to Kornilov's in Paris, one of the finest Russian restaurants in Europe, he was astonished when she confessed she had never eaten caviar.

They arrived in Spain, moving into Segovia where many scenes were shot. Young checked Olivia into the best suite of the best hotel, but when she walked in, the manager made the mistake of telling her that Joan had lived in the suite and, of course, had slept in the bed. Olivia turned to Young, her cool demeanor swallowed up in anger, and said, "I will *not* move in there! Get me another suite!" Young explained to her that this was the Royal Suite, the best in the house, but Olivia was adamant, saying, "Exchange mine with Scofield's." Young went to see Scofield, whose face broke into an unaccustomed smile. "Smashing!" he said as he immediately started packing his clothes.

During the shooting, Young sometimes quarreled with Olivia, who was stern and steely to a degree still remembered by such fellow players as the young Christopher Lee, also a famous screen Dracula. Lee found her formidable; but Young, by loosening the reins, by removing from her the most severe constraints, allowed her to act in a relaxed manner. She found it difficult to wear the eye patch because it produced considerable eyestrain and it was hard to adjust her vision when she removed the patch. Also, people constantly aggravated her by reminding her of Joan's local sojourn. On the whole, she wasn't sorry when *That Lady* finished shooting. Young's only regret was that he could not show her extreme sexiness, her voluptuousness, far more obvious off screen than on; but the rules of censorship, particularly in Great Britain, were excessively strict in those days.

Olivia and Pierre Galante were married in a village near Paris on April 2, 1955, the same date as the wedding of Napoleon to Josephine.

At a party shortly before the wedding, Olivia met a prominent attorney and member of the government who told her that if Galante betrayed her with another woman, she "could kill him with complete impunity since no court in France would send her to the guillotine." She seemed greatly reassured.

Olivia's move to Europe was, as Terence Young says, a very serious mistake, since it took her out of the mainstream of the English-speaking film world and people tended to think of her only in terms of runaway productions. Generally, Hollywood producers preferred performers to be locally available for meetings and discussions and removal to Europe suggested semiretirement or a declining career to many people. Moreover, Olivia gave up her spacious and airy Brentwood home for a series of cramped apartments and later a *hôtel particulière*, or town house, at 3 rue de Benouville, where she lived with Galante. Although the street was pleasant and fashionable and the continuous din of Klaxons and screaming tires was subdued there, the house was quite claustrophobic. It was twenty feet across, four floors high, and Olivia made it seem even smaller by stuffing it with furniture and bric-a-brac. It was typical of houses built in the era of the Second Empire—the plumbing was in poor shape and there were few of the domestic conveniences that were available in America. Olivia soon found she was paying a high price for being so chic and socially well placed.

She had always dreamed of a home on the sunny side of the street, with a spreading tree in front, and a gas lamp; but the rue de Benouville establishment was on the shady side, had no tree, and Paris hadn't been lit by gas in almost half a century. There were problems of how to cope with the French domestics. She had to have a nurse for Ben, and a cook and a maid. In order to keep the nurse separated from the cook and thus avoid arguments, she put the nurse and Ben on one floor and installed a dumbwaiter so that meals could be sent up to his own tiny dining room, which was outfitted with its own silver and china. The nurse did her own and Ben's washing up, sent the service platters back down on the dumbwaiter, and she and the cook never had occasion to meet except in passing on the stairs. The nurse slept with the Ben on the third floor, and the maid and cook slept on the top floor, with their own bathroom, so there was no fighting over whose turn it was to use the tub.

There were two principal rooms on the ground floor: an intimate salon and a dining room. The salon she decorated with the gifted designer Gerard Mille and with Victor Grandpierre. She spent much of her savings achieving a re-creation of a small town house of the period of Marie Antoinette and Louis XVI. There were Italian paintings with Venetian frames by Marieschi, a student of Canaletto. On the mantelpiece were two Chinese ornamental trees that had belonged to the British poet Siegfried Sassoon; Olivia had found them in an antique shop on the Faubourg St. Honoré. The mirrors were English, and struck a slightly incongruous note; the bronze doré candelabra and chairs were Louis XVI. The settees were of a slightly later period, but blended in well; the Meissen plates Olivia had found in British Columbia on a visit to her father. The mirrors in gold frames were Chinese Chippendale; Olivia had picked them up at an auction in London when the British playwright Christopher Fry had closed his big estate in Wales.

In the formal dining room, Olivia installed wax-pine paneling, flanking the walls with huge mirrors in ornate Venetian sconces that gave an illusion of great width and depth. Dinner parties were always held by candlelight. The dining-room table and six chairs were British pre-Chippendale, matched with four other chairs that were actually Chippendale. The dining-room carpet was an Aubusson.

Olivia kept her Oscars in the boudoir of her bedroom. The bedroom was directly over the salon; the boudoir over the dining room. Among her souvenirs were a picture of the house in Japan, a photograph of herself in *Alice in Wonderland* as a child, a photograph of Sir Geoffrey de Havilland, and pictures of her great-grandfather and great-great-grandfather in Guernsey.

The bedroom was romantic and subdued. There was an enormous off-white bed with a quilted headboard facing a mirrored marble fireplace and bookshelves. There were a commode brought from California, antique-framed scenes of flowers, and a bouquet made of shells under a glass dome flanked by two antique candlesticks. There was a small doll at the bottom of the bouquet. Pale green scenes of Apollo, Zeus, and Mercury printed on off-white silk from an eighteenth-century French master decorated the walls. For some reason, Olivia's pet bulldog, Bolboule, kept wanting to attack the commode, and Olivia had to go to extraordinary lengths to protect it and the bed. The overall effect in the house of French, English, Italian, and Asian was very striking.

In the kitchen, however, what she strove for most of all was American efficiency. Determined to make the tiny space workable, she struggled with inept French electrical and gas "experts" and was, like most Americans, reduced to utter exasperation by them. Although she spoke later with humor of her experiences, it is clear that she maddened French craftsmen with her imperious demands for the kind of technical expertise to be found in America.

She even overrode her husband and redesigned the front of the house in white and gray in a perhaps unconscious echo of Nella Vista Drive. Indeed, she found that the original stone was cream-colored, and merely by restoring it she achieved the effect she wanted.

Olivia continued to be very high-handed. She admired her maid, Françoise, but was not content that Françoise wore simple black; she tried to put her into cap and uniform like a maid in a British household. She obviously had seen too many films in which the French maids of movie stars always wore frilly caps, aprons, and white cuffs. Like so many actresses, she seemed to be living out a fantasy life as lady of the manor and French society queen (she would have been better off with the publisher instead of an editor of *Paris Match*). She gave exquisite dinner parties in her tiny dining room and bought her clothes at Dior. Once again, however, she was earning far more money than her husband, and although he was more sophisticated about it than his predecessor, the resulting strain was inevitable.

One night in New York, Lilian went with Connie Wolf to see Maxwell Anderson's *The Bad Seed* on Broadway. It was a play about an evil child. In the middle of the first act, when the packed house was completely silent, held in the grip of the drama, Lilian suddenly exclaimed, very loudly, "That's Debbie! That's really Debbie!" Everyone looked around in dismay, and several people recognized her. The next day, this ugly libel was the talk of New York.

Joan fretted constantly about the restraints of her life in Hollywood; about her children; about Collier Young's now somewhat wearing, monotonous humor; and about making the dreary *Serenade*, a travesty of James M. Cain's celebrated novel of homosexuality, with a portly, childish, and wildly insecure Mario Lanza endlessly booming away at her on the sound stage. She could think only of escaping back to Europe and New York; Olivia's life must have seemed glamorous to her now that their social and geographical positions were so drastically reversed.

To keep her hand in, Olivia made an innocuous comedy, *The Ambassador's Daughter*, in which she played a Paris resident who pretends to be a Dior model, involved in a superficial affair with a GI while engaged to marry a prince. It was a reworking of the type of empty comedy Olivia had done a decade earlier, and it is significant that

Norman Krasna, who had guided her more or less through the torments of making *Princess O'Rourke*, directed this equally innocuous new effort, which was at once far pleasanter to make and even less important. The cast was good: Adolphe Menjou was admirable as always as a U.S. senator; Edward Arnold was wonderfully reliable and charmingly obese as the U.S. ambassador; and the veteran Francis Lederer made a distinguished prince. The chief problem was that Olivia was outclassed by the effortlessly sophisticated Myrna Loy as the senator's wife. Another problem was that she was playing a girl in her twenties when she was pushing forty. It is surprising that she was given the much-cherished Prix Femina for her part by the Belgian film critics.

The movie made little impression; what did make news was that that same year Olivia became pregnant for the second time. On July 18, 1956, she gave birth to a daughter, Gisele. At Olivia's age, forty years old, childbirth was a problem, but she was given very good care at the American Hospital at Neuilly and the French doctors, about whom she was a little nervous at first, were excellent. Throughout the pregnancy, she was advised to watch her weight carefully. She went on a diet, had regular massages, and exercised regularly from four months into pregnancy up to delivery. Christian Dior designed exquisite maternity clothes and she felt better for wearing them. Moreover, she was able to relax until she felt like getting up. Most pleasing of all, for the first month after she returned home, the American Hospital provided her with a special nurse who was also an infant nurse. The nurse she was given, an Italian named Tina, turned out to be a treasure.

Olivia nourished Gisele on powdered milk and mashed carrots; the child had a healthy, loud voice. As for Ben, at first he worried Olivia because he said he wanted a little brother; but just hours before Gisele was born, he decided he wanted a sister. Olivia was determined to avoid the sibling struggles that had marked her own childhood and the grim atmosphere of the house in Saratoga. Indeed, George Fontaine's death shortly before Gisele was born seemed to firmly slam a door on the past.

## Eleven

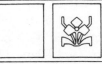 
 Early in 1957, Joan ran into problems. She was charged by William Dozier with being in contempt of court in Los Angeles for willfully disobeying the custody orders laid down in March 1953 regarding Deborah. The agreement still called for the parents to divide care, custody, maintenance, and support of their daughter, allowing each of them six months of the year with the child. This was dependent on their both residing in California; if both of the parties were absent from the state, Joan would be entitled to sole custody for nine months with visiting rights.

The complaint stated that Dozier had redecorated rooms in his house on Greenway Drive in Beverly Hills specifically for Debbie; that he had advised Joan of the commencement of the six-month custody period on March 1, 1957; and that she had refused to supply Debbie accordingly. According to Joan's attorney, Marvin B. Meyer, Joan had not acted improperly and Dozier was not entitled to custody on that date. Meyer stated under oath that he had tried to seek an amicable disposition of the matter with Dozier without success.

Joan was busy making a film about World War II New Zealand, *Until They Sail*, for the director Robert Wise, and she was very distracted throughout the shooting by the struggle in the courtroom. A temporary compromise was finally reached, running to some seven pages and signed by both Joan and Dozier. The court order was modified to allow Joan to take Debbie with her to Europe in the summer of 1957; Dozier's custody period would be adjusted accordingly. Some flexibility was allowed in mutually convenient terms, provided that Debbie continue to be raised as a Roman Catholic. The child would be shared between the parents on birthdays, at Christmas, and Easter, and all arrangements would be made upon special notice.

But Joan was faced with another problem. She had earlier completed *Island in the Sun* in the Caribbean, and had played many love scenes with Harry Belafonte. As a result, she was attacked with poison-pen mail, some of which emanated from the Ku Klux Klan. The Klan threatened her in letters that, in Joan's words, looked as though they had been written "by somebody's feet." She handed them over to the FBI and took off to Cannes for the premiere that spring.

Matters worsened when she was charged with not merely appearing with Harry Belafonte but sleeping with him on location. He himself was also attacked for his alleged affair with Joan. The matter dragged on into August of 1957, until at last it became yesterday's news. Joan's state was not helped by the fact that she hurt her foot in a fall and was stricken with severe Asian flu when she got to London.

Olivia ran into a storm of her own at the time. She was accused point-blank of overstaying her residence abroad, and at a hearing in Washington she was subjected to a cross-examination by Un-American Activities Committee counsel Frank Tavenner, vis-à-vis charges that she was involved with the Hollywood Independent Citizen's Committee, which was being investigated for Communist activities. She was very annoyed when she was reminded of this. She had taken an active part in the committee, denouncing Nazism in California, and had been particularly forceful in criticizing the extremely right-wing Gerald L. K. Smith of Arkansas, but she had gradually realized that the committee was very left of center and was not a genuinely democratic institution. She told the Washington hearing board:

> I had been told that the idea of this committee was to examine any issue independently and come to an independent decision about it, but I noticed that automatically any matter that related to labor, the position was that labor was right.
>
> I am a good union member, but I cannot always believe that unions are always right. This was a matter of policy. This was not independent.

The next thing I noticed was that whenever there was conflict between Russia and the United States, Russia was always assumed to be right and I thought, "I can't understand this. If we reserve the right to criticize what the United States' policies are, why don't we reserve the right to criticize Russia?" But nobody criticizes Russia in this organization.

This is a completely inexperienced person beginning to learn. I thought, "All right, this organization is not independent. It has two policies. One is prolabor and the other is automatically pro-Russian. It is not what it says it is. It is not independent.

"Who, what group, would be most interested in endorsing these two policies at the same time?" And I thought that there can be only one and that is the Communists. Communists are the only ones who would automatically endorse flatly, without question, these two points of view, and I got rather upset.

When evidence was introduced showing that Olivia had resigned from the committee once she determined its political orientation, she immediately was cleared. In fact, Congress passed a special bill, introduced by Democratic Congressman Francis Walter of Pennsylvania, waiving in her behalf the special McCarran-Walter immigration requirement that she return to the United States or lose her citizenship. In introducing the private bill, Walter referred directly to Olivia's patriotic work in World War II. The bill also allowed her to remain in France for an indefinite period with her husband. She was greatly relieved; she had actually been threatened with losing her passport unless she returned for eighteen consecutive months at the end of the five-year period. Had she stayed in France, she would have become stateless, with two children who were American citizens. Her relief was enhanced by the fact that, cleared by the Department of Labor, she could now comfortably proceed to make her next movie, *The Proud Rebel*, in Utah.

*The Proud Rebel* reunited Olivia with Michael Curtiz, who had asked for her for this Western drama, sensitively written and intelligently put together by Paramount. Olivia was very distressed to find a severe decline in Curtiz's condition; he was already suffering from cancer, which was to kill him. She also had a ghastly experience at a party. Someone touched her on the shoulder, saying her name, and she spun around, expecting to see an old friend, and saw instead a fat, bloated, horribly depraved-looking man with liquor on his breath, bloodshot eyes, and a double chin. She froze, and the man walked off, looking dejected. Only later did Olivia discover that the man was Errol Flynn. She started to cry when she was told.

On location in Utah, Olivia found she very much liked her costar, Alan Ladd, who surprised her by being exceedingly sensitive and talked to her with great affection of his family, including his charming wife, Sue Carol, who had been a former musical actress and had launched his career as an agent. His son, David, played the part of a boy stricken dumb with shock at the sight of a murder.

*The Proud Rebel* was a touching and beautiful movie. Olivia was in every way admirable as a frontier woman cut off from the world in the period after the Civil War. Olivia managed to completely deglamorize herself for the role, and she found herself strongly drawn to the child David Ladd, who recalls that he was fascinated with her and worked well with her.

While Olivia worked through the uncomfortable summer of 1957 in Utah, Joan was off to Europe again with Debbie and Martita. During this vacation, she met the handsome and talented Peter Viertel, author of several outstanding screenplays, including *The African Queen*, written for Katharine Hepburn and Humphrey Bogart. John Huston, who excellently directed *The African Queen*, was one of Viertel's closest friends. It was typical of Joan that she should take up with Viertel, thus emulating Olivia's passion for John Huston.

Viertel's mother, the famous Salka, widow of the director Berthold Viertel (whose personality had formed the basis for Christopher Isherwood's novel *Prater Violet*), had been among the most distinguished Hollywood screenwriters. Her World War II Santa Monica weekend parties for such great European émigrés as Stravinsky, Thomas and Heinrich Mann, Bruno Walter, and Franz Werfel had earned her extraordinary acclaim. She was the most intimate friend of Garbo, who frequently stayed with her in her elegant house in Klosters, Switzerland, where Salka held court with all of her old dazzle and assurance.

Peter had inherited his mother's charm, skill, and warmth; he was an irresistible example of the artist as athlete, a former marine and OSS man like Galante, well practiced in a variety of sports. At the time he met Joan, he was married to a very remarkable woman. Virginia Viertel—known to all her friends, the great and famous of the world, as Gige—was adored by Ernest Hemingway and had formerly been married to the writer Budd Schulberg. She was in every way intelligent, beautiful and desirable; her marriage to Viertel was long considered ideal. The couple doted on their daughter, Christine, who was born in 1952. But Viertel had experienced a gradual souring of the marriage; his wife was jealous because he was so attractive to women, and she became increasingly moody and suspicious in the mid-Fifties when he took up with the French model Bettina.

He also became involved with Ava Gardner, who was then at the height of her beauty. It was in many ways an improbable match because Ava, for all her effort to reach the level called for by the international literary and artistic set, was distinguished only by her looks and presence; born in poverty in the tobacco fields of North Carolina, she had risen rapidly, but had never really succeeded in acquiring an intellect. The virile Peter Viertel undoubtedly took great pleasure in this sensuous and voluptuous woman, but they had little else in common. Ava had affairs with bullfighters and the relationship disintegrated in the hothouse atmosphere of her torrid life in Madrid.

Peter had far more in common with Joan. Joan was well read; she had a high IQ; she understood art and had a good collection of paintings in her home in Brentwood, including a Utrillo. Moreover, she had known many of the distinguished literary figures whom Salka had entertained at her Saturday afternoons, and she had seen and admired and understood the movies that Peter had written.

Theirs was an immediately dynamic relationship. There is no question that Joan was more profoundly moved by Viertel than by any man with whom she had been in love. Come hell or high water, she would marry him. Of course, not only did Collier Young stand in the way, faithful and reliable man that he was, but so did Gige and her circle of influential friends, headed by Christopher Isherwood. And there was the question of her own children and Viertel's daughter.

The romance was carried on all over Europe. Even at this stage, however, a relationship with a married man when she also was married could have done severe harm to Joan's career, and it says much for the power of the studios over the press that there was little hint of it in print. Nevertheless, the danger of public exposure remained great, and Collier Young was sent for, to join Joan and the children in the south of France to still the wagging tongues. The whole thing was a severe blow for Gige Viertel. She turned to her friends for support, but found little in any of them except Christopher Isherwood, who stood firm. Gige rapidly began to go to pieces.

Still facing a storm of criticism over her imaginary affair with Harry Belafonte, and anxious to see Peter again, Joan had a very strained meeting with Darryl Zanuck, who insisted she go to London for the royal command performance of *Island in the Sun*. He put so much pressure on her that she finally yielded and in a fury took off for London, dazzling her way through one interview after another at the Savoy, talking about nothing in particular and privately wishing she were somewhere else. Like some other stars, including Marlene Dietrich, she was a far better actress off screen.

Restless, always looking for new thrills, Joan, in love with Viertel, went off with him to Ireland in the fall of 1957 and trained for the hunting season at Kilcock. Although she was an excellent horsewoman, she had never had jumping lessons and she reduced the locals to paroxysms of laughter as she kept falling off her mount. She plunged into a twelve-lesson course at Colonel Hume Dudgeon's Stillorgan Riding Stables near Dublin, where she was taught such basics as how to sit forward on the jumps and how to hold the reins.

She roamed around Viertel's rented thirty-room mansion in a great mood. She loved the soft Irish rain, the green of the grass, and the horses of every description; a great thrill was being "blooded" at a hunt—the blood of the fox being placed on her forehead. She set off for Martita's thirteenth birthday party in Paris in November in a very good humor, taking great care to avoid seeing Olivia while in the city.

Olivia was still enjoying the romantic fantasy of being the lady of her rather cramped town house. She still dressed at Dior, and her hair was done in the French manner; but she wasn't entirely at ease in Paris, and refused to drive in the dangerous and hectic traffic. Each morning, she stood on her head for five minutes in a yoga position, then walked for half an hour along the avenue Foch, with its sandy sidewalk and rich plantings of trees, almost as far as the Arc de Triomphe and back. She answered letters with amazing promptness, often spending three hours at her desk typing or dictating into a Dictaphone. She worked on a leisurely nonbook, *Every Frenchman Has One*—a lighthearted and superficial account of her four years in Paris, avoiding her emotional conflicts with Galante. At lunch, when Gisele and Benjamin were home, only English was spoken. After lunch, Olivia would go to her boudoir and have her afternoon coffee. She worked at her desk from her half-hour siesta to four o'clock tea. Once or twice a week, there was a dinner party at which she was likely to be seated next to an ambassador.

Despite all of her problems, she was still in love with Galante, but there is no question that the tensions in their relationship were beginning to tell.

Joan's and Viertel's endless travels created a problem in their relationship. Joan, eager for Viertel, was restless and nervous, and knowing that he was on location with *The Sun Also Rises* in Spain, kept announcing that the infestation of mosquitoes in part of her country house in France, where she lived with Debbie and Martita, was unbearable and that she would have to leave for a time. William Dozier says, "Mosquitoes do not favor particular parts of houses; but Joan was anxious to find an excuse and she would complain of the mosquitoes, then fly to Madrid to be with Viertel."

Viertel was taking a substantial part in the production of the film. There was great tension in the air when Joan arrived, since Ava Gardner was believed to have resumed her affair with Viertel. Henry King recalled later how dramatic the atmosphere became, with the two screen beauties ignoring each other and Viertel caught in the middle. Joan, however, was clearly the victor.

As restless and transitory as ever, Joan, in high spirits, took off with Peter to Switzerland in the winter of 1957 for a skiing holiday at Klosters. She visited with Peter's mother, Salka, and Salka's circle of friends. Everything seemed to be fine, but then while skiing she felt suddenly dizzy and sick. She was seized by an acute fever and a headache. Feeling increasingly ill, she went for tests, which showed that she was a victim of infectious mononucleosis. Unfortunately, the doctors initially misdiagnosed the illness and as a result did not order bed rest during the feverish period. Joan's only consolation was that she could laugh at the idea that the disease was caused by kissing. The question was, whom? Neither Martita nor Debbie nor any of the Viertels had had the illness.

Just before leaving for Hollywood, Joan accepted an offer to make the film *A Certain Smile*, based on the novel by Françoise Sagan and directed by her old friend Jean Negulesco. Due to her illness, she had great difficulty in making the film.

A curious situation developed in 1958. Whereas Joan had replaced Deborah Kerr in *Tea and Sympathy*, Deborah replaced Joan in Peter Viertel's sympathies.

Joan had once again been separated from Viertel by travels and working schedules. This time, Viertel was in Vienna making a movie entitled *The Journey*, with Yul Brynner and Deborah Kerr. Joan had decided finally to part from Collier Young and had made up her mind to marry Viertel. Collier, amenable as ever, seemed prepared to accept divorce and Joan firmly expected Viertel to obtain a divorce from

Gige. Impetuously, since he had not asked her, she decided to fly to Vienna and pop the question herself.

Unbeknown to her, however, Viertel had become irresistibly attracted to the leading lady of *The Journey*.

Deborah Kerr had made her reputation early as a beautiful, gifted actress who played with great sensitivity, tact, and delicacy. She had a beautiful speaking voice and a sense of smoldering sensuality under her cool ultra-British exterior that fascinated male audiences. She had married young—to the British air ace and war hero Anthony Bartley, a handsome and athletic man of great charm who had come to Hollywood with her. They were married on November 28, 1945, with Bartley's RAF squadron in attendance at St. George's Church in London, and they had two children—Melanie Jane and Francesca Anne—at the time Deborah met Viertel.

One of the problems was that Bartley had become known as "Mr. Kerr." Because of immigration problems, he was unable to work, and anyway had no skill except flying. With no particular occupation, he felt very much out of place in Hollywood. Although magazine articles described their marital bliss, the fact is that the marriage was merely a facade; much of the year, Deborah was away on location while Bartley stayed at home in Los Angeles with their children.

However, Bartley had a British stubborn streak and refused to contemplate a divorce. When he heard that Deborah had fallen in love with Viertel, he was enraged and charged Viertel with enticement. There was an ugly, drawn-out court battle over this.

Gradually, Deborah and Peter were drawn more closely together. Under her ladylike exterior, Deborah had a strong sensuality and warmth. Their romance began in the glowing *Letter from an Unknown Woman* atmosphere of Vienna, a perfect city for a love affair with its carriages, classic old hotels, its waltzes and parks and gardens and palaces.

When Joan flew to Vienna to see Peter, she was annoyed to find that he was not at the airport to meet her. Unable to reach him by telephone, she went out with an escort to dinner—and was appalled to see Peter across the room at a banquette with Deborah. She stormed out. The setting of *Letter from an Unknown Woman* had become a real-life nightmare.

Joan flew to Hollywood, desperate, furious, and ill with despair. When Viertel and Deborah arrived, the situation became insufferable, even for outsiders; hosts like Jean Negulesco and Lenore Coffee were in an impossible situation, not knowing whom to invite and when.

According to William Dozier, Joan was so distraught that she decided to go to Lake Arrowhead with the children. Dozier took exception to this move, claiming that Joan had acted in outright contempt of court in breaking the custody arrangements laid down in 1957 when she took Debbie to Lake Arrowhead and withdrew her from the St. Martin of Tours school to enroll her in a school in the mountains. Dozier claimed that "the acts of the said Joan Young . . . were wilfully and knowingly done and made for the purpose of making ineffectual the visitation rights afforded him under the provisions . . . of the stipulation order."

In response, in the Superior Court of Los Angeles, Joan's doctor, Henry J. Rubin, stated:

> Mrs. Young has suffered for as long as I have known her from recurrent acute sinusitis, manifesting itself in left-sided headaches and nasal discharge. It has been my observation over the years that the episode occurs most frequently during residence in the Los Angeles area. For this reason I have suggested in the past and again now that she reside elsewhere, preferably in a drier climate. Lake Arrowhead has been mentioned as a possibility and I feel that she would be better there than here. Mrs. Young presently suffers from infectious mononucleosis, a disease which she has had for at least several months. This has aggravated her nasal difficulties and I have reiterated my recommendation that she would be benefitted by a drier climate.

On the advice of her attorney, Joan refused to testify at the Los Angeles hearing. She could be in contempt of court if she did not agree to the conditions that she must return Debbie immediately. If she didn't agree, she might well face a possible jail sentence. The public was denied the thrill of seeing a prominent star behind bars: Debbie went back to Dozier. Joan was furious, of course. She alleged (Dozier and Debbie deny it still) that Debbie herself had symptoms of the same sickness and had benefited greatly from the climate at the lake. The child's Thanksgiving vacation had been totally disrupted and Joan's blinding headaches, listlessness and fatigue had made life miserable for both mother and daughter. The Lake Arrowhead Elementary School was excellent and Debbie hated leaving it. All told, November 1958 was a ghastly month and Joan never forgave Dozier for what he had done to her and the unhappy Debbie.

According to Dozier, when Joan handed over the eleven-year-old, she said coldly that she never wanted to see the child again. Debbie never got over the rejection. It seemed that Joan was so bitter about losing that she wanted to cut the harness completely. Dozier says, "Joan exercised her rights two years later and brought Debbie to New York. But Joan soon tired of her, and when Debbie returned to the West Coast, Joan decided that she didn't want to see her any more."

Typically, Joan picked up the pieces—after all, there was always the reliable Collier Young (who came back to her like the sweet man that he was). Meanwhile, Gige Viertel sued Peter for divorce, charging extreme cruelty, while Deborah's husband, Anthony Bartley, was still suing Viertel for enticing Deborah from him. When Deborah divorced Bartley, Gige began her own proceedings. Isherwood testified in her behalf that Peter had left her for another woman, not named.

Gige went from bad to worse. In February 1960, only a few months after Peter's engagement to Deborah, she dropped a lighted match on her flammable nylon nightgown in her Pacific Palisades, California, house and died as a result of burns over sixty percent of her body.

The year of 1959 was uneventful for both Joan and Olivia. Olivia's life was running in a fairly steady groove, watching her children develop; Joan recovered with painful slowness from her sickness, lacking in energy, and reluctantly coming to the conclusion that there was no point whatever in continuing to be married to Collier Young— their marriage had reached the point at which even in their best moods they grated on each other's nerves. In 1960 they at last decided to call it quits.

Joan more or less walked through an uninteresting play called *Hilary* on a nationwide tour. She was troubled through most of it by continuing problems with Martita, distracting herself only with sailing into the sky in a balloon in Holland as a member of the winning team in the International Balloon Race.

The disastrous forest fire of 1960 swept through Beverly Hills and Bel Air, consuming many of the stars' homes and leaving an unparalleled wake of destruction. The fire leaped from hill to hill until at last it reached the home Joan had lived in for over a decade in Brentwood. Her paintings, her furniture, her books, and numerous letters, scrapbooks, and documents of every description were destroyed. Joan received word of the tragedy in New York; appropriately, she was at dinner that night with Charles Addams. She was dating the famous

*New Yorker* cartoonist, whose amusing, charming and attractive nature totally belied the creepily sinister world of his drawings. He was also an expert on the crossbow, like so many of Joan's ancestors, and had a collection of them in his apartment in New York.

Joan took the news of the fire with remarkable composure, perhaps because she was in a strange sense relieved that this further link with California had finally snapped. There had been much pain in that house: the pain of her disastrous marriage to Dozier and the years of struggle over Debbie; the painful knowledge that her own inescapable dominance had helped to wreck her personal happiness; and the realization, acquired during her long illness, that most of her friends were of the fair-weather variety—once she was sick and no longer amusing, everyone had disappeared.

As for Olivia, she achieved an ambition: to act a lady of leisure. She played Lady Maggie Loddon in a movie called *Libel,* a turkey resurrected from the 1935 Broadway stage, costarring Dirk Bogarde. In this film, Olivia unfortunately adopted a style that was to become the mark of her later career: She became excessively haughty and dignified, reading her lines with a pause between her words, her vowels excessively orotund; the *New York Times* remarked that she played the wife "as if she were balancing Big Ben on her hat."

She was very busy in 1960 correcting the proofs of *Every Frenchman Has One,* which was published the following year with some success and to very mixed reviews.

Early in 1962, Olivia was crossing the Atlantic to New York on the S.S. *Queen Elizabeth.* There was a violent storm, and sturdy Olivia was one of the few passengers not devastated by seasickness. Among the few survivors in the Grand Salon was Edward Heath, future prime minister of Great Britain, who asked her for several dances. They had quite a struggle keeping their feet on the dance floor, and she was very impressed with his coolness in difficult circumstances. She told a reporter:

> I saw him persisting in games of squash, with the ship at all sorts of angles. And then I saw what a sensitive man he is. We had an S.O.S. message from a freighter after two men had been badly injured in a boiler room explosion. They had no doctor on board. The *Queen* located the ship but was unable to lower a doctor because the seas were too mountainous. The Captain had

to tell us that it would be a case of losing nine lives in a bid to save two. I remember the shadow that came over Edward's face as he heard that we had to turn away and leave these two injured men to their fates.

Nine years later, Olivia was to meet Heath again and provoke much foolish speculation of a possible love relationship.

In 1962, Olivia made a film called *Light in the Piazza*, a story with odd parallels to the life of her friend Bette Davis. Bette had adopted a little girl, who turned out to be mentally retarded, and in *Light in the Piazza* Olivia's character had a twenty-six-year-old daughter with the mind of a ten-year-old. The drama arose from the painful situation that occurred when the young girl, played by Yvette Mimieux, fell in love with a handsome Italian and the mother failed to inform the prospective husband's family of her daughter's problem.

*Variety* called Olivia's performance excellent, remarking that she played "with great consistency and subtle projection," while *Time* said that she played with "dignity and restraint." Indeed, her performance was very good, only occasionally marred by excessive touches of haughtiness.

At the beginning of 1962, Olivia had daringly decided to make a third stab at the Broadway stage. She appeared in Garson Kanin's play *A Gift of Time* with Henry Fonda; she played a wife whose husband was dying of cancer. The heavy melodrama opened at the Ethel Barrymore Theater on February 22 and caused the audience acute distress; one male spectator was so horrified by the play's medical detail that he vomited in the aisle. The reviews were excellent and Olivia was exceptionally powerful in the final scene in which the man, about to die, asks his wife to slit his wrists. She strops the razor and holds him as she hands him the instrument, saying, "I love you. I love you. Please die."

Euthanasia was not a popular theme, and, despite good reviews, the play barely struggled through ninety-one performances. It was typical of Olivia's strength that the play's content never disturbed her, made her tense, or cost her any sleep. However, there is no doubt that the separation from her husband and children worried her—and indeed it did help to break up the marriage finally. When she returned to Paris later that year, she began divorce proceedings and then suddenly suspended them, obviously unable to face the anguish of litigation for the second time in her life.

Although Olivia said in many interviews that she was raising her children far less strictly than she herself had been raised, the fact was that she raised her children with a strong hand: She insisted they be perfect. The tiny house in Paris resembled a set for *Craig's Wife*, the famous old melodrama about a woman so meticulous that every inch of every room was immaculate and symmetrically arranged down to the last stick of furniture. Benjamin had orders that if his mother entered his room, it must be neat as a pin.

The pressure in the house was almost unimaginable. Because Ben was the less orderly of the two children, he suffered more than the neat Gisele. The natural athleticism of a young boy was undercut by sensitivity and the constant strain of trying to live up to his mother's standards. But Olivia loved the children deeply.

Joan, as always, lived a life that was the exact opposite of Olivia's cramped, grim, and disciplined existence. She shot a version of *Tender Is the Night*, from the novel by F. Scott Fitzgerald, forming a close friendship with Lauren Bacall, who was then involved with Jason Robards, Joan's fellow actor in the picture. She was also friendly with Jennifer Jones, who was so paralyzed with shyness and unease that she developed a nervous tic of the head. She would call her husband, David O Selznick, endlessly seeking reassurance and support for her fragile ego, and at times she would break into tears. The director Henry King told me:

> It was difficult working with Jennifer. But Joan was great fun to work with—provided you realized she was a movie queen and didn't expect her to get involved in "interpretation." She worked out her performance as a reflection of her carefully built-up public self: extrovert, superworldly, ultra-sophisticated, amusing and brittle. She brandished a cigarette holder with all of the aplomb of an Elinor Glyn. She was ideal in every way.

Joan also appeared on television in a version of *The Closed Set*, based on a story by Gavin Lambert included in his collection *The Slide Area*. She played Julie Forbes, a granite-hard movie star of the Joan Crawford mold who imperiously runs the set, terrorizes her lovers, and defies nature by wearing fishnet stockings and risking a high kick. Lambert wrote the script with enjoyably acid wit, but the problem was that Joan wouldn't play the crushing *monstre sacré* she was called upon to do on camera; Lambert recalls that she was "Julie Forbes to perfection—off camera!" Like most movie stars, she was afraid that if she was less than noble and sweet and considerate, her public might lose faith in her. Thus, she deliberately worked against the grain of the character and greatly annoyed everyone.

She was, in fact, becoming increasingly difficult to work with. Like Olivia, she was now moving into the autumn of success, in which actual performance was replaced by the determined sustenance of an image. All this reached an apotheosis when she took off for Japan to open the new American School in Tokyo: Lady Bountiful from Hollywood, she glittered through embassy parties; and when she returned, she emerged at a White House dinner with the Kennedys and the Radziwills looking like a radiant empress. She spent much of the evening telling the president about Joe Kennedy's dating her. It was typical of her that she would talk about herself even in the presence of the chief executive.

She also talked incessantly about her own affairs while sailing on the presidential yacht with Charles Addams. She and Addams finally tired of each other, and she took up with the intellectual, balding, clever, and decent Adlai Stevenson, then ambassador to the United Nations. Once again, the affair was never more than superficial, simply that of two high-powered individualists who talked of possible marriage the way many people would talk of a possible vacation in the Bahamas. Joan's pattern was always a dangerous one: of getting involved in situations that were socially appealing and offered an extension of an already crowded social life, but left little room for emotion or profound feeling. Her delicate health may have been part of the problem; like so many with recurring chronic illnesses, she apparently had a fear of committing herself to feelings that could exhaust her and bring down her fragile defenses.

While Joan was whirling through lunches, cocktail parties, and dinners, Olivia was running her Paris establishment with discipline. In the mid-1960s, Benjamin started to grow into a handsome boy with small, regular features; a slender, delicate build; and a remarkable mind for mathematics and science. A typical scene would have Olivia enjoying lunch in the elegant courtyard restaurant at the Ritz, with a fountain splashing nearby; she would seem to be completely at ease and then without warning she would turn her large, seemingly soft eyes on her agent or business contact and say, "Be sure to call Benjie and warn him that his room had better be tidy before his mother returns!"

Once again, in a condition of great strain, Olivia accepted an invitation to come to Hollywood, this time to make a controversial thriller, *Lady in a Cage*, based on a true incident. She was to play Mrs. Hilyard, a wealthy woman recovering from a broken hip who has to use a special elevator to go from floor to floor in her mansion. The elevator gets stuck when she is alone in the house over the Fourth of July weekend, and she is entrapped by several criminals, including the gross, greedy Sade, played by Ann Sothern, and the very young James Caan, making his screen debut. The film was put together by the writer and producer Luther Davis, a handsome, extremely virile and robust man who, she told her friend and agent Roy Moseley, attracted her more violently than anybody since Marcus Goodrich. Like Huston, Flynn, and Goodrich, and quite unlike the charming Pierre Galante, Davis was dominating, forceful, able to give as good as he got in an argument.

Although part of Olivia wanted to overrule men, another part of her wanted to be controlled by a will that was stronger than her own. Roy Moseley says flatly that she fell madly in love with Davis, even though she knew that this might finally end her marriage and place her children in the intolerable position in which Joan's found themselves. She had now reached an era in which adultery was no longer a scandal, and in this more sophisticated climate she was not hesitant to tell Mosely of her passion for Davis. Inspired by her feelings for him, she went to extraordinary lengths to give him the best performance she was capable of, playing with all-out emphasis that stopped just short of hamminess. Of course, there could be no hope for her marriage now.

Olivia was more involved in *Lady in a Cage* than in any other film she had made since *The Heiress*. She was fascinated by the theme. She told a reporter from *Films and Filming* in London:

> There is the isolation of the individual living in a city where there are millions of people . . it is a characteristic of modern life, this strange indifference of one human being toward another in distress in a city. It's a strange phenomenon which certainly wasn't the case thirty years ago because then people reacted much more instinctively, and if somebody was in distress they wouldn't have been able to think, their spontaneous reaction would be to go to somebody's rescue. But that doesn't happen anymore—it seems to be absent now in the urban personality and really bears a lot of thinking and talking about. I think a film like this can be extremely thought-provoking and valuable.

The director, Walter Grauman, a charmer and a talented man, liked to rehearse the players in full around a table and then on a set; and Olivia of course responded warmly to the arrangement, as she had to Mitchell Leisen's. She also did her usual homework and visited with a woman who had broken her hip. The woman said that her greatest fear was of falling again and being rendered helpless. Olivia asked her what she would do if she were trapped in her own elevator between floors and the only way out was to jump many feet onto a hard floor. The woman was horrified at the idea and refused to even think of it, but Olivia pressed relentlessly on, and finally the woman, not too surprisingly, said that she would fall on her uninjured side. Olivia rushed back to tell Luther Davis of her findings.

Olivia received ten percent of the profits of *Lady in a Cage*, given her by Davis. (Interestingly, her extraordinary, fierce voluptuousness was visible on the screen this time despite the fact that sexuality was not intended to be an element in the performance.) As it turned out, her ten percent of the picture was ten percent of very little, since the movie was not a great commercial success. The critics attacked it for its extraordinary violence and crudity, and it was banned in Great Britain and Australia. Olivia undertook an extensive promotional tour but became more frustrated because she was unable to save the film. She reiterated often that she had not made the picture to exploit violence but rather to expose violence.

Her romance with Luther Davis burned out in the ashes of the film's failure. Nevertheless, Olivia spoke with her husband and they agreed that he would move across the street. The relationship was in no way strained now; it was based on a convenient arrangement.

Olivia's next picture started under very curious circumstances. *Hush, Hush, Sweet Charlotte* was Bette Davis's vehicle in which she was costarred with Joan Crawford; they had been a great success together in *Whatever Happened to Baby Jane?* During the Louisiana shooting, Crawford claimed she had pneumonia, and had to be hospitalized. A replacement was necessary for the role of Miriam. Bette sent a telegram to Vivien Leigh, cosigned by the director Robert Aldrich, but Vivien was thoroughly bored by the idea and threw the cable in the wastebasket. When a studio contact called her in London, she said that there was no way on earth she would be prepared to face seeing Bette Davis at seven o'clock in the morning. There the matter ended.

Bette now suggested that Olivia enact the role. It seemed a wild example of casting against type—in this extravagant example of southern Grand Guignol, the character Miriam was a total monster, capable of murder—but it was part of Bette's humorous approach to Olivia that she knew and recognized her terrifying strength and resolution.

Olivia received the script in Paris and turned it down flat. She feared that her ladylike performance in real life would perhaps be undermined by having to deliver lines in tones of great rudeness. Aldrich flew to Switzerland where she was vacationing and said to her, "We can fix the problem. But aren't you worried about the ambivalence, the duality of the role of Miriam?"

"That isn't the problem," Olivia said. "It's that the writing *lacks* ambivalence and subtlety. Miriam is all colored in black. *Solid* black, with no relief!"

Aldrich recalled he was astonished. Olivia seemed to have missed the point completely. But then Olivia hit on a very good idea. After reading the script again, she called Aldrich and said she had found the solution: Miriam would be rewritten to be courtly, gracious, and charmingly supercilious (i.e., like Olivia herself). The danger would be greater in the character if it was disguised.

Further discussions took place in Hollywood. And then shooting began.

Olivia told me in 1965 that Bette viewed her as she viewed most actresses: as a challenger she must destroy. There was a scene in which Olivia was to walk up a flight of stairs and pause, a simple action loaded with implications. Bette came on the set when Olivia played the scene, pulled a chair right under the camera, dragged on a cigarette, and fixed a baleful gaze on Olivia. "That was something no actress should do," Olivia said. "Unlike Bette, I'm not a competitive person. If I am attacked, I simply refuse to fight back. I never said a word to Bette. I just did my scene. The next day I was on the set while Bette was working, and I knew she expected me to retaliate. I didn't. I just looked at her, but I'm sure the look said what I didn't verbalize: 'I will not fight you; I will not accept your challenge.' Bette understood."

But it was not quite as simple as that. Later, there was a scene when Miriam slapped Charlotte very hard. Bette was very much afraid of Olivia slapping her. She feared that despite their lifelong friendship, Olivia's old jealousies would emerge and she would slap her to the point of injury. Bette panicked and announced that there was no way she would play the scene, and the furious director had to agree to a stand-in. The stand-in was astonished when Olivia slapped her with terrifying force.

The fact that the "real" Miriam had her mirror image in the real Olivia emerged during the shooting when Olivia's children arrived from Paris as a special vacation treat. According to William Dozier, on one occasion, Olivia went out, locking Benjamin in his room, and was furious to find him missing when she returned. The enterprising boy had climbed down a drainpipe and escaped to take shelter with none other than Dozier and his wife, Ann. Another much-discussed incident occurred during lunch in the famous Twentieth Century-Fox studio commissary in Beverly Hills. Benjamin was very excited by the elaborate murals evoking the world of movies, and gaped—to his mother's consternation—at various stars. Suddenly, jumping up to look at someone, he upset a bottle of catsup on his suit. Olivia was furious. She canceled the vacation for Ben and packed him off to Paris.

Her performance in *Hush, Hush, Sweet Charlotte* was admirable. She played with grim resolution and great intensity and was totally convincing, making a kind of sense of the crazy proceedings. She toured with Bette to promote the picture and they called each other Maxine and LaVerne, a joking reference to the campy Andrews Sisters.

At the New York premiere, a police cordon was formed to hold back the fans the publicity department had whipped up for the occasion. As Olivia entered the lobby, she said to the reporters, "The fans are so young! Their parents could hardly have been born when Bette started out!" After the screening, Olivia said, "Bette gave me good support." And Bette said, with terrifying sweetness, "Olivia, you were wonderful! Even when I was not on the screen, you somehow managed to hold the audience's attention!"

Back in Paris, Olivia began planning a London production of *A Gift of Time*. However, her latest agent, Adza Vincent, was having problems arranging matters in the West End, and Olivia hired a new agent, Roy Moseley. Moseley admired her enormously and was already a very keen movie buff. Though he soon found out that Olivia was far from being the sweet and meaningless creature that she seemed to be to the public, he also found her scrupulously careful in business matters. Moseley says:

> On one occasion I secured an invitation for her to come from Paris to appear on a talk show on television in London. She would have all expenses paid plus $750. She arrived at the Savoy Hotel and checked into her favorite suite above the Grill entrance. But there was a mistake made and the arrangement

was reneged on. I was distraught because I couldn't afford to make up the difference to her. I forced myself to tell her the truth. She replied without flinching, "All right. It doesn't matter. We'll just have to go to the theater and have a good dinner." I never knew such consideration from a star.

Joan's divorce from Collier Young, like her other divorces, was marked by nonpunitive terms: She asked for only modest alimony and a share in the profits of Young's horror-film series on television, "One Step Beyond." Extreme cruelty was charged, but this was simply a convenience and meant nothing.

Olivia, meanwhile, continued to raise her children with loving severity. Even when Benjamin was in his teens, she was constantly reminding him to mind his table manners; to make his bed perfectly, never to leave the cover wrinkled; to shape up in classes and in sports. She was easier on Gisele, who was the apple of her eye. Interestingly, both Benjamin and Gisele inherited Olivia's strength of will, so that Olivia, for all her attempts to bring her children into line, to make them perfect, saw her own rebelliousness against George Fontaine mirrored in them. The difference between the two children was that whereas Ben was very introverted, intense, and scholarly, Gisele was extroverted, as outspoken and prematurely sophisticated as her father, talking ten-to-the-dozen. Olivia told a friend:

> I impose myself on them. Especially on Gisele because she is such a gifted little person, and so I catch myself pushing her. It happened just the other evening. I was discussing her drawings and I began to see a future in art for her and she said, "But, *maman*, I wouldn't like that!" I said, "What do you mean?" And she replied, "Oh, *maman*, I like it just as it is, I like to draw. Just to amuse myself!" And I suddenly realized that I was imposing a dream of my own on her and that was quite wrong. The dream of a happy professional life. I thought, What am I doing? This is not the way to talk to a child. I must find out what her dream for herself is and help her achieve it. And I stopped instantly.

One of Olivia's painful disappointments was that neither of her children had the slightest interest in her film work. When they had visited the set of *Hush, Hush, Sweet Charlotte*, they had become restless and bored within an hour. When they went to see *Gone with the Wind* in Paris, Gisele's only remark was *"Maman*, you had very bad taste. You liked Scarlett, that terrible woman!" Olivia was dismayed. Apart from that, the children were totally bored by Olivia's acting. If she had the slightest idea of them following in her footsteps, she abandoned it very early.

Whenever she traveled to Hollywood, Olivia—like most actresses, a little girl at heart—went through a kind of ritual. She always went to the airport an hour and a half before the flight and stoked up with a few drinks. She always flew on Air France and always on Friday. She always stayed in room 275 at the Beverly Hills Hotel, on the Camden Drive side, with a lemon tree outside the window and a small terrace where she would eat Saturday lunches under the lemon tree.

At home, her life was equally ritualized and rigid. Like many people who procrastinate, who are insecure, she liked to order everything artificially around her, achieving a kind of perfection in a vacuum.

Like Joan's, her professional career drifted into meaninglessness. She made *Noon Wine* for ABC, from the story by Katherine Anne Porter, with Jason Robards, Jr.: she filmed the "Danny Thomas Show" and *The Last Hunters*, about the pursuit of a Nazi war criminal, blissfully unaware of the parallels with Errol Flynn.

In July 1967 she was at the Beverly Hills Hotel being interviewed by the columnist Radie Harris in connection with her proposed trip to Atlanta for the 70-millimeter wide-screen premiere of *Gone with the Wind*, the picture's sixth national release. Ms. Harris was talking about her friendship with Vivien Leigh, and Olivia was saying that now that David O. Selznick was dead and Vivien had had to cancel because she was rehearsing for *A Delicate Balance*, Olivia would be the only one left alive of any importance to attend the screening. In her memoirs, Ms. Harris quotes Olivia making an astonishingly callous statement. "It gets sadder each time around, with everyone popping off like *Ten Little Indians*." Is it possible Olivia could have made such a heartless remark? It certainly goes against the grain of Olivia's public sentiments at the time: her sadness at the loss of Clark Gable, Leslie Howard, and David O. Selznick, to whom she owed everything.

The children's schooling was well advanced by 1967. It was far more disciplined than that to be found in America or England, of an almost nineteenth-century sternness. When Benjamin graduated from the Lycée, he suddenly decided to enlist in the army, but when he went in for the physical he was not feeling very well, and although he had a naturally muscular body, he looked starved. At the physical in Stuttgart, headquarters of the U.S. Army of Occupation, it was found that he was too light to be inducted. Moreover, the army physicians shocked him by telling him that he was actually ill and must immediately return to Paris for some tests.

Olivia was beside herself. She went with Ben to the hospital and suffered the torments of the damned waiting for the test results. They gave evidence of lymphatic illness; this explained the loss of weight. In severe cases, such as the deadly Hodgkin's disease, the sickness could be fatal; in lesser cases, like mononucleosis, from which Joan had suffered, there would be more moderate symptoms. Ben's lymphoma gravely weakened him and left him painfully thin, listless, and unable to perform sports or any other physical activity. Even a rest in Switzerland failed to help.

To give him something to do, Olivia persuaded Benjamin to take up his studies again. But he had to struggle to keep up at the University of Paris's Faculty of Sciences. He had to have chemotherapy, but he was one of the small percentage of people who are allergic to the treatment and he could not eat properly after it. Chemotherapy is an exceptionally devastating treatment for many people, destroying healthy cells along with sick ones. Benjamin's weight went down to one hundred and fourteen pounds, thirty-five pounds below his normal weight for his height of five feet, nine inches.

Olivia, needing all her strength not to go to pieces, worked overtime on Benjamin's diet, trying to make him eat. Professor Jean Bernard, a leading hematologist, took care of Benjamin and his chemotherapy injections. On one occasion, Ben locked himself in the bathroom, clawed the wallpaper in pain, and refused the treatments, wanting to die. Bernard forced his way in and talked him into going on. Benjamin in turn urged Olivia to continue with her acting career when she talked seriously of abandoning it. She forced herself to accept the part of the Mother Superior in the film *Pope Joan*, based on a legend that Pope John VIII, in the ninth century, was a woman. Mother and son grew very close in those days.

During this time, Joan and Martita had a serious falling-out. According to a friend, Joan was having lunch with a reporter and had brought Martita along. The reporter was asking Joan about her investments, and Joan, as usual, enthusiastically detailed her money skills. Suddenly, Martita piped up with "Oh, mother, do you have to talk about money all the time?" From that moment on, the friend says, Martita was doomed.

Martita went to stay with Joan's former secretary, True Boothby, in Maine. Joan tried desperately to have Martita deported back to Peru as an undesirable alien. William Dozier, and others confirm this.* In desperation, Martita called the home of Joan's great friends Abby and Connie Wolf in Bluebell, Pennsylvania. Abby Wolf was a very distinguished attorney in Philadelphia. He was away and Mrs. Wolf said she would take care of the matter. She called one of her husband's partners, and he told her she needed a lawyer who specialized in immigration problems. Fortunately, the man was able to reach the necessary authorities in Maine, Martita's place of residence, who informed him that a child of thirteen or older could choose its own guardian in that state. She chose foster parents—Joan, of course, had never been the adoptive parent because of Peruvian law—and there the matter rested until Joan tried again. Martita and Joan never spoke to each other after that.

However, Martita does not want the door closed forever. She asked Joan to her second wedding, to John Reigeluth, a good-looking young computer specialist, and she was happy when a communication arrived. She remembers the good things Joan did for her—teaching her to garden, a talent she treasures; opening her eyes to the world and gaining a large perspective. It is clear that Martita has risen above the bitterness of the past.

One has to see the entire episode of Martita and Joan in perspective. It was not really Joan's fault that the "adoption" was a disaster; that Martita could not become what Joan dreamed. Nor was it Martita's fault that the experiment with a young life backfired.

---

*According to Joan's memoirs, she simply wanted Martita to revisit her parents. This is flatly denied by all concerned.

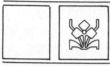

# Twelve

During the mid-1960s, Joan became involved with Alfred Wright, Jr., the charming and intelligent golf editor of *Sports Illustrated* and son of a famous lawyer at Twentieth Century-Fox. In the mid-1940s, he had interviewed both Joan and Olivia for *Life* magazine. Joan had been furious about the piece, which was entitled "Sister Act." But when they met again she liked him. He was warm and attractive; and during one of Joan's recurring illnesses, he proved to be a good friend. They also had golf in common: Joan's greatest boast was that she had once managed a hole in one.

Wright was strongly attracted to Joan and she to him, but she seems never to have learned her lessons and she plunged into the relationship. He represented old money, settled ways, and distinguished friends and family. He knew many of the leading golfers. The chief drawbacks in their romance were Joan's constant ill health, and that he himself became ill with some obscure malady.

Joan married Wright much too precipitately in February 1964, in a courthouse basement in Elkton, Maryland. John O'Hara, the well-known author of *Appointment in Samara*, gave the bride away. As always, Lilian was absent from the wedding—nor did she send a wedding gift. The bride and groom and the members of the wedding party drove to a nearby roadhouse for the wedding breakfast of omelets and champagne. "Now, Al," O'Hara said, referring to Wright's previous wedding nineteen years earlier, "this is it. I'm not giving any other brides away." Joan said, "John's is a success story. He worked his way up from usher to father of the bride in nineteen easy years."

Joan married Wright while still in the grip of illness. No sooner had she done so than she was telling the press, "Marriage, as an institution, is as dead as the dodo bird." She adored Alfred, but married him as much for therapy; she went to Spain with him when he reported a golf tournament, but he worked each night till 10:00 P.M. writing his report, and Joan grumbled and growled, bored to tears by the various golf widows and very upset because she had to turn down film contracts to be with him. On one occasion, when she promised to spend Christmas with him, she again had to turn down a part and she was in a temper all through the holidays because of it.

Once again, Joan regretted that she had tied herself to domesticity. She hated the feeling of responsibility and was unable to cope with the lack of attention inevitable when a woman married a writer. She enjoyed entertaining, cooking, using her own electric drill and soldering iron, and even changing a tire, but she felt that Wright resented that, and she made the fatal mistake of not praising her husband constantly. She was too honest, too direct, she told a reporter for the *London Daily Express*, "not enough of a hypocrite to make the man feel he is not only Adonis but Hercules as well." She went on to say:

> I've been at fault rather than my husband. I am too highly geared. And I am just not going to pretend. If my husband feels that his masculinity has been dented by this, I am sorry. I think I can make a man's life pretty pleasant but soon he seems to resent all the perfection. One husband said to me, "Damn it, if only you wouldn't always think you're right—and you *are. . . .*"
>
> What a marvelous life of travel, theatre, opera, and music a husband has had through me! That is if he has been sufficiently secure to enjoy it. But life with me is eighteen hours of activity a day and a man doesn't want that. He just wants maybe two hours of excitement with me a day and I don't find that enough. I haven't learned to be selfish [!] and sit back and say: "Right, you do it. You bring home the caviar, invite the interesting guests, plan the next trip."
>
> It is so hard on the children having a highly-geared mother. I

utilize every minute. If I am walking in the woods I am studying the birds and seeing which way the wind blows and looking at the moss on the trees to see which is north or collecting wood for a fire. I can't just daydream. But I am still highly romantic as long as it doesn't mean being leisurely.

I've always tried to be the ideal wife. But evidently I haven't succeeded. You should make the husband feel terribly comfortable, take care of all his tastes from liver to bacon to what have you. But somehow I make a man feel too much like a guest king. The only way I could have gotten round that is by being dishonest, by pretending. I just can't do that. I just can't gush and say, "That last thing you just said should be knitted into a sampler."

She really put the nail in Alfred Wright's coffin when she said, finally, "Obviously a wife has to do a lot of pretending to be success- ful; to make a difficult, selfish husband of hers feel that he is the greatest man alive even when she knows damned well that he isn't."

Reading this can have scarcely been encouraging to Wright. Cer- tainly, it's easy to see that Joan was totally incapable of the shifts of ground, the self-sacrifices, adjustments, and considerations necessary in any marriage. Like Olivia, she was far too strong to be married; her will completely squashed all in her path and eliminated any chance she might have had for personal happiness. It was as though she could not help sending in the barbs, seeking out the weaknesses of her mates, the faults she called jocularly "Achilles heels."

Her enemies were delighted to learn that she bought the rights to the book entitled *The Devil's Own*, assuming she would play the title role, but were surprised to discover that she cast herself in the part of a shy and retiring woman, the antithesis of her nature in every way, caught up in a witchcraft cult in Cornwall.

She arrived in London in the summer of 1966, still not feeling well, and embarked on the picture with Cyril Frankel directing. She rose at 5:30 A.M. every morning and was driven to the studio by a chauffeur while she lay down in the back, her hair in rollers. Sometimes while the car was halted at intersections, men would peep through and see her lying on her back with her feet up, reading the paper. She grum- bled about the cramped facilities at the tiny Bray Studios, home of the Hammer horror films, and would slope off with her odd stooped stride to her humble hardboard-and-timber dressing room to lie down between takes.

Nobody ever forgot she was a star, even in this modest effort. She tried to keep calm when a fan came up to her unexpectedly and told her she had seen *Wuthering Heights* five times and admired Joan to distraction in it. She told a correspondent for the *Hollywood Reporter* in London, "All I want now is to grow up and become an imperious, demanding old bag." When the author mentioned this to Hollywood press agent Helen Ferguson, Miss Ferguson said, "She's already made it."

Not content with her previous stabs at Alfred Wright, Joan said to Earl Wilson for his column:

> Alfred's first and only love is writing sports and everybody and everything is secondary to that. I can't trudge all over the world of golf clubs following him, he wouldn't want me to if I could. He doesn't need a home, he just needs a place to pick up his laundry. He has his homes in all the golf clubs of the country. That's the life he loves and I can't expect him to give it up for me. And I can't give up my acting life for him. We made a pact that we would see each other every five days but we can't do it. I will have my own apartment and we will be friends, but he will pick up his laundry somewhere else.

During her stay in London, Joan put up at Vivien Leigh's handsome, antique-filled apartment in fashionable Eaton Square while Vivien, who was starring on Broadway in *Ivanov*, stayed in Joan's apartment. Joan told reporters they had been friendly at the Selznick studio when Joan had been making *Rebecca* and Vivien *Gone with the Wind*, but in fact there had been tension when she won the part in *Rebecca* from Vivien, and Vivien and she were not working at the studio at the same time.

Vivien entrusted her adored Siamese cat, Poo Jones, to Joan—an act of attempted friendship. Unfortunately, Joan claimed that the moment she arrived with Lilian, who had come along to London, they were bowled over by the powerful stench of Kittylitter and the peculiar musky scent emitted by felines in heat. The smell was so pervasive, Joan told friends, that she woke up each morning feeling nauseous. Lilian also suffered from the smell, and nothing they could do seemed to get rid of it. Joan also claimed that Vivien refused to allow her to use her garage to park her car. Eventually, the infuriated Joan checked out—Lilian had left earlier after a quarrel with Joan.

Vivien angrily denied Joan's charges, saying that she was scrupulously clean and that the cat odor was a figment of Joan's imagination. She also stated that she needed the garage for her own automobile.

The columnist Radie Harris wrote: "When Joan went to London, I warned Vivien not to make the exchange of apartments because I knew there would be trouble ahead, and my psychic waves proved right." She added that what really happened was that Joan had a violent quarrel with Lilian, who left in a temper, followed by Vivien's beloved housekeeper, Mrs. Mack, and that Vivien was beside herself when she learned of this. Referring to Joan's charges about the cat litter, Radie Harris said, "Not only me [sic], but all of Vivien's close friends know how outrageous these accusations are . . ."

Walter de Havilland died in 1968. He was ninety-six years old. His widow contacted Joan and Olivia and told them that he had wanted his ashes scattered in Guernsey; she retained a third in Vancouver. According to the wine authority Robert Balzer, a friend of the family, Joan and Lilian and Olivia went to Guernsey, with the two thirds, Lilian carrying the urn. Olivia, as usual, was late—delayed on the boat from Britain. At dusk, the three women stood on a cliff near St. Peter Port, where Walter had walked so often through the gusty winds in his boyhood. Lilian took the urn and opened it. As she tossed the ashes out, a strong wind blew them into her face. It was Walter de Havilland's last gesture toward his hated wife.

Joan split from Wright and embarked in the late 1960s on a world golfing trip with the well-known New York society physician Ben Kean, with whom she was involved. It was ironic that after complaining miserably about Wright's golfing mania and the fact that she had had to follow him everywhere to tournaments, her new lover was a golfing enthusiast who spent more time on the fairways than in his clinic. Since he was protective of his privacy, she managed to persuade reporters everywhere never to disclose his name.

Olivia and Joan met in Paris in 1969. Olivia had summoned Joan there in sheer desperation. She had run short of money; the costs of Benjamin's treatments were enormous, and Gisele's expensive education was also a heavy burden. Galante's salary was insufficient to meet Olivia's standards of living, and now that she was working much less frequently, the money simply wasn't coming in. It was agonizing for her to have to let her servants go and struggle with the housekeeping herself. Given her fanatical tidiness, she worked on every speck of dust or fleck in a mirror, and made herself be less severe with her ailing, exhausted son, but the effort inevitably wore her down. Quite desperate by now, Olivia asked Joan for money. It was a supreme irony that Joan, the younger sister who had been first in everything— marrying, obtaining an Oscar, achieving independence in her career—should now be more than a millionairess due to the windfall of the Bel Air fire insurance and her clever investments while Olivia was in financial trouble.

The sisters' meeting at the rue de Benouville was very strained and awkward. Olivia put all of her cards on the table, and Joan wrote a check. She advised her sister to start lecturing for a living. At the time, fading stars were able to net decent profits by touring America and addressing women's clubs, telling anecdotes about their careers and about other stars they had worked with. Joan also mentioned the possibilities offered by dinner theaters, which were just emerging at the time: The great performers of yesteryear could act while those who remembered them, isolated from their children's world of rock 'n' roll and fast sex, could indulge in an orgy of nostalgia.

Olivia embarked on lecture tours twice a year in the 1970s. The tours were booked a year in advance but took only six weeks. Although most people would have been exhausted by the schedules— which involved flying from one city to another virtually every day, and many changes of time zone, climate, and conditions—Olivia, like her fellow star lecturers, was buoyed up by her ego, her irrepressible passion for talking about herself, and the adulation of her audiences, who were thrilled to see a legend in person.

It was difficult wrenching herself away from Benjamin even for a few years, but he pressed ahead with his studies with courage and determination, and his expensive doctors managed to arrest his condition at least for the time being. He majored at the university in the field of statistics and in the burgeoning field of computers. He inherited some of this interest from his mother, who, as she started earning again, actually did her own income-tax returns. She and Ben used to cheer each other up by joking about bizarre aspects of geometry; Olivia had been exceptionally bad at this at first, but now was an expert in it.

Gisele was as scholarly: She wanted to go into journalism; she wrote books for children and wanted to design children's books. She spoke German and Spanish fluently. Benjamin also spoke German quite well. Ben graduated in mathematics and decided to return to the United States; he had always been fond of his father, Marcus Goodrich, and he joined him in Austin, Texas, where he entered a student commune and then worked as a statistician. Gisele developed a flair for law studies and obtained her Paris law baccalaureate with honors. Olivia planned to move to the United States also, to Savannah, where she dreamed of restoring an old Civil War house near the Savannah River, or to Georgetown in Washington, D.C., where she could preside over the political and diplomatic social set. It was typical of her that she never acted on these ambitions, talking about them incessantly but remaining a firm fixture in Paris.

In 1971, Olivia was back in the headlines. She resumed her earlier friendship with Edward Heath, who was now British prime minister, and a sensation was created when Heath invited her to dinner at his residence, Chequers. Olivia was excited by the invitation, and the press was in a hubbub over the prospective romance. But Heath had never been known to have an affair with a woman; he was believed to be a lifelong celibate, too focused on his own career to have any romantic interests. Olivia went to extraordinary lengths to dress for the occasion. Christian Dior designed a loose, rainbow-colored chiffon shift dress over a body garment designed to hide Olivia's increasing girth, inherited from her mother. A special Rolls-Royce with chauffeur took her from the Dorchester Hotel to Chequers and a knot of fans gathered outside the hotel as the top-hatted doorman ushered her into the car.

For once in her life, Olivia was on time. She lied to the press, "I love to be on time—it was part of my training at the Hollywood studios in the Forties." A legion of studio managers must have laughed when they read that.

In fact, so punctual was Olivia that she arrived a little ahead of schedule and asked the chauffeur to pull up outside the gate. When she finally rolled up the drive, Heath, without a bodyguard (this was England), was standing on the lawn in a white dinner jacket. He said, "I was beckoning to you to come on. I spotted your car. But you obviously didn't see me." They strolled in the garden in the English twilight and talked about their meeting on the S.S. *Queen Elizabeth* in the storm. They had a dinner of roast duck—Olivia's favorite and very fattening dish—with Robert Allan, of the publishers Allan and Unwin, and six others. Heath talked warmly of Paris, telling of his passion for the city and saying that it must be "adorable" to live there.

After dinner, he showed her the treasures of Chequers, Cromwell family portraits among them, and Olivia told him of her Roundhead de Havilland ancestors. When he showed her a ruby ring that belonged to Elizabeth of England, she mentioned *The Private Lives of Elizabeth and Essex*—but without the details of the misery of making it. She was impressed with Heath's knowledge of music, and her only disappointment that evening was that he didn't play the piano for the guests. As she left him at midnight, she promised to light a candle for him at Notre Dame.

Olivia traveled to Hollywood to make ABC-TV's *Screaming Woman* for her friend, the producer William Frye. Like *Hush, Hush, Sweet Charlotte*, it was scarcely a distinguished contribution to drama, but it was an opportunity for an unbridled display of histrionics, and Olivia seized that opportunity with both hands.

During the shooting, she was doodling with her memoirs, determined to be ahead of Joan in telling her life story, and stimulated by the lecture tours into believing that audiences would make the book a best seller. Ross Claiborne, chief editor of Delacorte Press, a most charming and civilized man and a keen movie buff, had had a wonderful experience working with Mary Astor on her own life story and was firmly convinced that Olivia's could be as interesting. He made a substantial deal with her for the hard- and softcover rights and recalls that he would lunch with her at his favorite New York restaurant, Le Madrigal, discussing her work in progress. But soon he began to realize that Olivia was not really committed to the project; by the late 1970s, she had delivered nothing, and she returned the advance money. "It was a very frustrating experience," he says.

Joan more seriously embarked on her own book, for William Morrow, and also went off on tour with *Dial M for Murder*, in the part that Grace Kelly had played on the screen. The South African tour was a disaster—there was talk of fights with the producers. She was miserable throughout the trip and in fact had a recurrence of an old throat problem. At the end of the tour in Durban, Joan launched an attack on the tour manager, Pieter Toerien, charging that he had failed to supply promised transportation, meals between performances, and a personal maid. She also claimed payment for a performance missed because of her laryngitis.

Toerien stated in an interview with *Variety*'s Johannesburg correspondent that he would sue Joan for $70,000 in damages for defamation of reputation and character. He said that all clauses in her agreement were honored and that a car and driver were at her beck and call at all times except for a few days in Natal when friends lent her a car. He said she had chosen not to live in the hotels in which she had been booked but had stayed in apartments, collecting the balance of her living expenses. He also said that the tour had had poor reviews and that her name had not proved to be a sufficient draw to ensure financial success. The remaining cast, including the actor John Gregson, supported Toerien in his charges. Simultaneously, Julia Films of Italy sued Joan for having walked out of a picture there.

Both cases were settled out of court, but the effect was damaging and Joan retained a reputation for being difficult, which was not to leave her. When Toerien was asked by reporters if he would bring Olivia to South Africa, he groaned and said, "One of those sisters is quite enough!"

The one consolation for Joan on her return to Hollywood was that for the first time in her life she found brief friendship with Olivia. It was as though now that their careers had disintegrated, now that they were both working on their memoirs, now that one was reduced to lecture tours and the other to South African excursions, they no longer were in competition; they were meeting at last on common ground.

When Joan's Best Friend, Dr. Ben Kean, finally broke up with her in 1974, Joan had a form of breakdown, taking to her bed with a severe fever at a friend's house in Quogue, Long Island. Olivia, who was lecturing nearby, took care of her and—in a scene that none of their scriptwriters would have dared to create—sang her to sleep with a Japanese lullaby.

## Thirteen

During 1974, Lilian Fontaine began to suffer from symptoms of cancer. Frequently bedridden and in great pain, she was greatly helped by Olivia's loving care. But it was not until January 1975 that Joan, who was rehearsing a play for a dinner theater on Rhode Island, received word that Lilian was dying. The producer of the show, she says, pointed out that there could be no understudy for Joan and therefore she could not be released from her contract. In considerable anguish, Joan, who in spite of everything still loved her mother, had to advise Lilian's doctors that she would be unable to go out to California.

It was a great blow to Lilian, despite the fact that she was not at the time friendly with Joan. She very much blamed her for the decision—and indeed, while in pain and with only a few days left to live, summoned her friend, The wine authority Robert Balzer to her bedside and said to him, "Make sure Joan doesn't get that!" She was pointing at one of her favorite possessions: a T'ang horse.

Olivia called Joan to tell her that she felt the diagnosis of cancer was wrong and that Lilian should have exploratory surgery. Joan was furious. She wrote in her memoirs that many times in the last two months she had held long telephone conversations with her mother as they prepared each other for the inevitable.

And now Olivia was suggesting that mother go through pain and indignity, possibly to die on the operating table . . . Olivia, who had not been in touch with mother for many, many months and knew nothing of the stages of her worsening condition, was now taking charge of the life and death of our eighty-eight-year-old mother.

Joan continued the tour under great strain while William Dozier and Debbie were at Lilian's bedside with Olivia. At last, in February 1975, Lilian died. By her own wish, she was cremated, and Joan was told that the memorial service would be held at Montalvo, California, after two weeks, when Joan would still not be able to go. She was not invited. She demanded that she go—and that the service be delayed until her Easter vacation—when she could obtain her share of the ashes—or would make a tremendous fuss in the papers. The executors yielded to this pressure.

Joan was enraged with Olivia for having with alleged high-handedness taken over everything, but it is hard to know what else Olivia could have done, since Joan was not present and Olivia was the next of kin. To have called Joan at her various locations across the country for consultation on every aspect of the illness, method of destruction of the body, and disposition of the property would have been impossibly exhausting and difficult in the circumstances.

When Joan finally arrived at Easter, her meeting with Dozier and her daughter, whom she had not seen much since the age of thirteen, was very strained, and she could not bring herself to even speak to Olivia. After the memorial service, Dozier recalls, "We went up a hillside near the place where Lilian taught drama to the local young people. Olivia and Joan and Balzer scattered Lilian's ashes in three instalments. Olivia gave a very dramatic, theatrical, deep-chested sigh as she threw the ashes. Joan, very characteristically, just tossed them away!"

Lilian's death snapped the thread between Olivia and Joan forever. They never forgave each other for what each took to be the other's intolerable behavior at the time. Joan would seldom comment on her sister, and wrote of her contemptuously in her memoirs, which were published in 1978 and entitled *No Bed of Roses*, an odd reference back to *Born to Be Bad* and to William Dozier's gift to her of roses at the time. His only comment on the book was "It should have been called *No Shred of Truth*."

Joan ceased making motion pictures in the 1970s and devoted much of her energy to her social life in Manhattan, rushing from party to party, enjoying a luxurious semi-retirement. In 1979 she appeared with great success in *A Lion in Winter* at the English Theatre in Vienna, playing with a startling intensity and attack that were quite unprecedented in her career. She was amusing as a partymaker and society broker in *The Users* on television.

On September 18, 1979, her daughter, Debbie, was married to the Santa Fe attorney Earl Potter in a Buddhist ceremony at Etiwanda. Potter was the son of the director H. C. Potter, who had directed Joan in *You Gotta Stay Happy*, for William Dozier. Dozier and his wife, Ann Rutherford, gave the wedding reception at the Beverly Hills hotel. Joan, in Vienna, did not even send a wedding present. Later, when Debbie was in New York, Debbie says she would sometimes call Joan and get her answering service, leaving the number where she could be reached. Joan never returned her calls.

Both Olivia and Joan were constantly busy in the late 1970s. Joan continued to love New York, leaving the city only in the summer to stay in a leased house in Pebble Beach, a fashionable resort near Carmel in northern California. She never missed a Christmas in Manhattan, where she always cooked a traditional dinner for about seventy-five people, all of whom had to be unmarried; she called them her "waifs and strays." She was very happy in her apartment, which she had lived in since 1963; it had paneled walls, four fireplaces, and six bathrooms, and friends would come in from Long Island during her absences, stay overnight to see the latest opera or show, take care of her mail, and water her plants. Her favorite restaurants remained Chantilly, Le Cirque, and La Grenouille. In an interview with George Christy of the *Hollywood Reporter* on October 12, 1978, she said, "I married first, won the Oscar before Olivia did, and if I die first, she'll undoubtedly be livid because I beat her to it!" She added, "I hope I'll die on stage at the age of 105, playing Peter Pan." Joan remained an expert cook, cleaner, and handyman in her own apartment, able to repair light switches and plumbing as ably as a man.

Olivia worked busily in pictures for her friend William Frye. She appeared in *Airport 1977* as a passenger on a plane owned by James Stewart, her old flame of the 1940s, which is hijacked and crashes into the shark-infested waters of the Bermuda triangle. Olivia enjoyed the experience of riding in the jet, which was mounted on cantilevers at Universal Studios and rocked alarmingly, and she gamely allowed herself to be immersed in water, like Shelley Winters in *The Poseidon Adventure* and Ava Gardner in *Earthquake*.

Olivia also appeared in *The Swarm*, which took her back to Warner Brothers, an experience that filled her with equal amounts of pain and nostalgia. The story concerned an invasion of Brazilian killer bees, and in one scene Olivia is attacked by the insects, which crawl all over her for fifteen minutes. Despite the fact that her friend Bette Davis had been stung by a bee in Scotland and had had a violent allergic reaction that almost killed her, Olivia faced her ordeal quite intrepidly. The bees had allegedly been deprived of their stings, but one of them unfortunately had not, and stung her hard on the right hand. "Joan must have sent it," somebody quipped.

She also attended yet another revival of *Gone with the Wind*, a gala fortieth-anniversary celebration commemorating the Hollywood premiere of the film. The event was held at the Los Angeles County Museum on December 28, 1979. A live band played music from the Civil War era, and a southern-style buffet dinner was served. Once more Olivia watched the movie unfold. Seated close to her was Ann Rutherford Dozier; Olivia and Dozier were close friends—indeed, by 1981 Olivia had become a kind of surrogate mother to Debbie, and had also become friendly with Martita.

It is scarcely surprising in the circumstances that Joan preferred to escape into the pleasures of her social life. She told Paul Rosenfeld of the *Los Angeles Times*, "My life now? I run my own show and I dare anyone else to try. I was up at five-thirty doing my ironing. In the old days in my apartment, there was 24-hour valet service. Now I'm my own maid, secretary, everything." She talked about marriage, saying, "The price is too high. You're a big star and you've been working all day. You come home, when the husband says, 'Where are my slippers?' Well what about *my* slippers? I'd adore a man who's a backup. Helpful when help is needed! But if he's Mr. Fontaine, he'll find ways to get back at you."

Joan remained more and more isolated from everyone, while Olivia, very close to Gisele and Ben, remained very friendly with Joan's children. Radie Harris was first in line to tear Joan to pieces when her book came out. She wrote, "According to the fantasy world in which Joan lives, isn't it awful that she is the innocent victim of all these ungrateful people?"

Early in 1981, Olivia appeared on television with Joseph Cotten in an episode of "The Love Boat." She played a very rich woman, and told Betty Goodwin of the *Los Angeles Herald Examiner* that the reason the part attracted her so much was that "I have a glorious fantasy life." She also talked to Goodwin of her life in Paris, only two doors away from the then president of France, Valéry Giscard d'Estaing, whose red spaniel made its way past her house every day. One day the president dropped by to see her chestnut tree, which hung over the fence and into the yard of a neighboring house, which he also owned. Olivia had tea with Madame Giscard d'Estaing and they agreed the tree should not be touched. In this same interview, Olivia expressed great pride in Gisele, who was now planning to work as a lawyer.

Olivia went on working in 1982. Following *Roots*, and *Murder Is Easy* for television in London, she starred in *A Royal Romance*, based on the story of Princess Diana and Prince Charles, in which she achieved an apotheosis of a kind, firmly cast to type as the Queen Mother. She gained ten pounds for the role and then had to starve and exercise them off in a grueling regime at the Sonoma Mission Inn Spa near San Francisco. But she remained very plump, and Joan, too, in her sixties was heavy.

Perhaps the most remarkable metamorphosis achieved by Olivia was that she became a spokeswoman and visiting speaker for the Episcopal church's celebrated Venture in Mission fund-raising drive. She raised a large sum in speaking engagements in the United States. She was one of the first women in the world to be allowed to read the Epistles and Lessons at services, and historically appeared at the American Cathedral in Paris in that category. She had always been somewhat religious, and when Benjamin was so ill she had prayed for him constantly, along with the very Reverend Sturgis Riddle, dean emeritus of the Episcopal Cathedral in Paris. When Ben recovered, she gave much to the church.

It is unlikely that Joan and Olivia will ever talk to each other again; when both turned up at the fiftieth anniversary of the Academy Awards in 1979, they had to be placed at opposite ends of the stage; and when they ran into each other in the corridor of the Beverly Hills Hotel, they marched past each other without a word.

But although the ultimate break in their relationship is sad, each, finally, has achieved her goals. Olivia, warm and motherly now, yet still quite regal, has become Queen Mother to her special circle and she still has the total and unqualified devotion of her son, Benjamin, her daughter, Gisele, and the Dozier family.

By contrast, Joan obviously enjoys being free of people. Her pleasure in society, in social life, in the razzle-dazzle, the whirl of parties and first nights, of attendance at meetings of various opera or ballet boards, in her own enjoyable soirées, is probably more fulfilling than any romance or marriage or experience of parenthood she has known. Olivia has always wanted to be surrounded by love and attention; to command; to be the focus. Joan has always wanted to be totally free. So the sisters have achieved, each in her way, a purpose in their extraordinary lives—at last.

## Acknowledgments

 David Chierichetti's book *Hollywood Director* and Joan Fontaine's memoirs *No Bed of Roses* have been useful sources. The writer Henry Gris gave me access to his indispensable files on Olivia de Havilland. The University of Southern California's Special Collections Division and Dr. Robert Knutson helpfully supplied Warner Brothers files, and John Hall and RKO–Radio Pictures supplied the RKO records. Others who talked to me include Dame Judith Anderson; Max Arnow; Lew Ayres; Robert Balzer; Hazel Bargas; Rudy Behlmer; Charles Bennett; the late Phil Berg; Anna Maria Bernhardt; the late Curtis Bernhardt; the late Mel Berns; the late Henry Blanke; the late George Brent; Lenore Coffee; the late George Cukor; Gabriel Curtiz; the late William Dieterle; Debbie Dozier; William Dozier; Donnfeld; Duo Agency; William Frye; James Hall of the FBI; Ron Haver; the late Howard Hawks; the late Alfred Hitchcock; John Houseman; Marsha Hunt; David Ladd; Mervyn LeRoy; David Lewis; the late Margaret Lindsay; Dudley Field Malone; Mrs. Fredric March; the late Jessie Matthews; Anne Robinson McWilliams; the late Johnny Meyer; Lord Herman Michelham; Roy Moseley; Jean Muir; Gerry Perreau; Gottfried Reinhardt; Donald Richie; Phyllis Seaton; Gloria Stuart;

Hal Wallis; Minna Wallis; Abby and Connie Wolf; the late William Wyler; Mrs. Collier Young; Terence Young; the staff of the American School, Tokyo; and the staffs of Los Gatos High School and of Saratoga School. And my appreciation is also extended to Howard Davis, who admirably handled the research, and to Joan Sanger, who masterfully edited the manuscript.

# *Index*

Rooney, Mickey, 37, 43–45, 47
Roosevelt, Franklin D., 147, 163
Roosevelt, James, 163
Rosay, Françoise, 178
Rosenfeld, Paul, 242
Rouveral, Jean, 37, 38
Rubin, Henry J., 215
Ruse, Lilian Augusta, *see* De Havil-
    land, Lilian Augusta Ruse
Russell, Rosalind, 69, 88
Rutherford, Ann, 186, 224, 241–43

Sagan, Françoise, 213
Sakall, S. Z., 110–11
Sanders, George, 109
Sassoon, Siegfried, 203
Schary, Dore, 174
Schulberg, Budd, 210
Scofield, Paul, 200, 201
Scott, Sir Walter, 189
Seaton, George, 161
Seaton, Phyllis (Phyllis Laughton),
    123, 154, 158, 159, 161,
    162, 197
Selznick, David O.
  and *Gone with the Wind*, 78–87,
    92–94, 97–99, 106, 107
  and Joan, 89, 91, 94–96, 103, 104,
    109–14, 132–33, 142–43,
    145, 219, 226
Selznick, Irene, 80, 161, 162
Selznick, Myron, 112, 125, 133, 145,
    163
Shakespeare, William, 35, 36, 39,
    44, 183, 188
Shaw, Artie, 188
Shaw, George Bernard, 188
Shearer, Norma, 39, 47, 88
Sheridan, Ann, 117
Shirley, Anne, 80, 108
Sibley, Catherine, 36, 37
Sieber, Maria (daughter of Marlene
    Dietrich), 96
Siodmak, Robert, 157
Sleeth, Caroline, 158
Smith, C. Aubrey, 109
Smith, Gerald L. K., 208
Sothern, Ann, 221
Sparks, Robert, 62
Spitz, Leo, 73
Stacey, Eric, 137, 138, 141
Stanwyck, Barbara, 136, 138
Steiner, Max, 105, 107

Sternberg, Josef von, 174
Stevens, George, 59, 63, 64, 71, 74,
    103
Stevens, Mark, 166
Stevenson, Adlai, 220
Stevenson, Robert, 142
Stewart, James, 82
  and Olivia, 99, 109, 111, 112, 121,
    159, 241
  end of affair, 115, 116, 125, 127
  Huston compared, 128, 129
Stradling, Harry, 124
Stravinsky, Igor, 210
Stuart, Gloria, 37, 38
Sullavan, Margaret, 95
Swanson, Gloria, 180

Tandy, Jessica, 175
Tavenner, Frank, 208
Thalberg, Irving, 47
Thompson, Morton, 198
Tibbett, Lawrence, 176
Toerien, Pieter, 236–37
Tone, Franchot, 51
Toulouse Lautrec, Henri de, 196
Tover, Leo, 172
Townsend, Jimmy, 96, 125, 126,
    132, 133, 143, 163, 164
Tree, Sir Herbert Beerbohm, 22
Trilling, Steve, 108–9, 133
Tufts, Sonny, 141–43, 149

Umberto (King of Spain), 192
Ustinov, Peter, 177

Valentino, Rudolph, 121
Vidor, King, 86
Viertel, Berthold, 210
Viertel, Christine, 211
Viertel, Peter, 210–16
Viertel, Salka, 210, 211, 213
Viertel, Virginia (Gige), 210–14, 216
Vincent, Ann, 224
Vruwink, John, 110

Wallis, Hal, 52–54, 108
  Joan and, 174, 176–80
  Olivia and, 40, 44, 45, 53, 55–56,
    65–69, 75, 91, 92, 117,
    126, 130–34, 144–49
Wallis, Louise (Louise Fazenda), 40
Walpole, Hugh, 49
Walsh, Raoul, 124, 125, 131